THE
STRANGE
ALLIES

THE

THE UNITED STATES

STRANGE

AND POLAND, 1941-1945

ALLIES

RICHARD C. LUKAS

THE UNIVERSITY OF TENNESSEE PRESS
KNOXVILLE

Library of Congress Cataloging in Publication Data

Lukas, Richard C   1937–
  The strange allies, the United States and Poland, 1941–1945.

  Bibliography: p.
  Includes index.
  1. World War, 1939—1945—Diplomatic history.
2. United States—Foreign relations—Poland.
3. Poland Foreign relations—United States.
4. Crimea Conference, Yalta, 1945. I. Title.
D753.L85   940.53'22'73   77-8585
ISBN 0-87049-229-2

To Marita, Jennifer, and Renée

PREFACE

In a day when there is so much interest in the history of World War II
and the cold war, it is ironic that no American historian has written
a scholarly up-to-date account of United States policy toward Poland
during the Second World War. After all, the Polish problem was a
major issue in the diplomacy of World War II and in the origins of
the cold war. Therefore, my purpose in writing this book is to present an authoritative account which goes deeper into the subject
than the present literature allows.

No one can write a book without the help of others. I am privileged
to have friends and colleagues who freely gave their assistance to me.
I am indebted to B.F. Jones, chairman of the Department of History,
Richard Fraser, dean of the College of Arts and Sciences, and Wallace
Prescott, provost and vice-president for Academic Affairs—all at
Tennessee Technological University—who helped in countless ways,
including providing me with funds to travel to the libraries and archives where most of the research material for this book is located.
I am grateful to Wacław Jedrzejewicz, who not only assisted me in
my search for materials at the Józef Piłsudski Institute of America
but also shared much of his knowledge and experience with me in
several enjoyable conversations. The courteous and efficient aid of
Mattie Sue Cooper and Linda Ogletree, two dedicated librarians at
the Jere Whitson Memorial Library on the campus of Tennessee
Technological University, was crucial in acquiring historical materials
through interlibrary loan services. I also appreciate the help of the
Reverend Donald Bilinski, curator of the Polish Roman Catholic
Union of America Archives and Museum, in sending me several of
the Polish American newspapers used in this volume. I owe a special
debt to Ludwig Krzyżanowski, editor of *The Polish Review,* and
Robert Divine, professor of History at the University of Texas, for
reading and commenting upon parts of the manuscript. Without the
research assistance of Andrew Sorokowski and John W. Allen, the

excellent maps of Harry Lane, and the typing of Patsy Kemp, this book would have been the poorer.

The help of many fine organizations, including the staffs of many libraries and archives, helped to make this book a reality. My thanks go to the Kosciuszko Foundation, Eleanor Roosevelt Institute, and the American Philosophical Society for providing me with funds to research various aspects of this project. The Faculty Research Committee of Tennessee Technological University generously gave me a reduction in my teaching load for several years to complete the manuscript. I also owe a debt to the staffs of the Hoover Institution of War, Revolution and Peace Archives, Library of Congress, National Archives, Józef Piłsudski Institute of America, Franklin D. Roosevelt Library, Harry S Truman Library, University of Virginia Library, and Yale University Library.

No list of acknowledgments would be complete without mentioning Arliss Roaden, president of Tennessee Technological University, whose encouragement and support have meant more to me than he realizes. Above all, my sincere gratitude goes to my wife, Marita, who gave me what every author needs in large measure—encouragement and understanding.

RICHARD C. LUKAS

Cookeville, Tennessee
April, 1977

CONTENTS

I

THE ROAD TO RAPPROCHEMENT

The course of United States-Polish relations during World War II resembled that of many friendships. The relationship was close, even warm, at first but grew more distant when the Soviet Union replaced Poland as the principal beneficiary of American wartime support. Before June 1941, when Hitler invaded the Soviet Union, Americans looked with sympathy upon Poland and with hostility toward the Soviet Union. After all, Poland was the first victim of a war that the Soviets had hastened by the German-Soviet Nonaggression Pact of August 1939. Moreover, the American image of the Soviet Union had been fashioned by Stalin's purges, collectivization campaign, Comintern, and perhaps most of all, persecution of the church. To most Americans, Stalin was a tyrant and the Soviet Union was a dreadful place to live.[1]

While the Soviet Union confirmed its negative image among Americans when it went to war with Finland in the winter of 1939–1940, Roosevelt offered the former president of Poland asylum in the United States. During the months of the German-Soviet rapprochement, Americans responded to Poland's plight with aid, offered help in equipping a Polish army in Canada with lend-lease, and warmly received the Polish premier on his visit to Washington in April 1941.

But in June 1941, when Hitler betrayed Stalin and invaded Russia, a new and major dimension to the emerging Allied alliance came to the fore. Soon the Soviet Union—large, powerful, and winning battles—became the decisive military and political fact with which the United States and Poland had to reckon. It became apparent to the United States that the Soviet Union was needed not only to win the war but also to plan and preserve the postwar peace. That meant the Polish expectancies concerning the restoration of their pre-1939 boundary and of their government, then in exile in London, were tied more to the aims of the Soviet Union in eastern Europe than to

the desires of the United States. The exigencies of the war, then,
were responsible for stamping United States relations with Poland
with the aspect of a friend who is sympathetic with another but is unable or unwilling to support him. It is therefore no exaggeration to
describe the United States and Poland as strange wartime allies.

When World War II broke out, Americans saw the Poles as a courageous
people who single-handedly tried to resist the aggression of the Germans
from the West and the occupation of the eastern part of their country by
rapacious Soviets.[2] The September campaign and the flight of the Polish
government and embassies from Warsaw to Romania were sympathetically
chronicled by the American ambassador to Poland, Anthony J. Drexel
Biddle, Jr., who remained accredited to the Polish government-in-exile
in France and after June 1940 in England. On his part, President Roosevelt appealed to the Germans and other belligerents not to resort to air
bombardment of civilians and unfortified cities. If the Germans had accepted the appeal, Poland would have been the major beneficiary. Roosevelt showed a touching concern for the fate of the former president of
Poland, Ignacy Mościcki, who was interned in Romania. Roosevelt
wanted the Romanians to know that the United States would gladly receive the Polish leader. He told his secretary of state, Cordell Hull, "I
think the moral effect of such action on our part would be good throughout the world." When Roosevelt learned that Romania intended to keep
Mościcki because it feared his release would give the Germans a pretext
for intervention, he told Hull that he wanted to make "some further
move in behalf of the poor old ex-President of Poland" and insisted that
the American minister to Romania, Franklin Mott Gunther, inform
King Carol of the American invitation to Mościcki to come to the United
States. As it turned out, Mościcki was ill and preferred to go to Swit-
zerland, where he had held citizenship since his youth.[3]
    A short time later, there was serious discussion in Washington about
offering asylum to the former foreign minister of Poland, Józef Beck,
but nothing came of it. Roosevelt did succeed in intervening on behalf of one of Poland's heroes and the president's friend, Ignacy
Paderewski, who had been detained by the war abroad, and secured
his passage to the United States. Several months later the Polish pia-
nist and statesman died. Again Roosevelt interceded and made special
arrangements for Paderewski's burial in Arlington Cemetery.[4]
    These gestures deeply impressed Americans, especially those of
Polish extraction. When Ambassador Biddle told an enthusiastic crowd
of ten thousand Polish Americans celebrating Pulaski Day at Wilkes-
Barre, Pennsylvania, that Roosevelt had instructed him to continue at
his post to the new Polish government formed temporarily in France,

Biddle "thought the house would come down." Biddle, who helped Roosevelt's reelection campaign in 1940, visited forty-five cities in fifteen states. Impressed by Polish American support for Roosevelt, Biddle wrote after the election: "What is more I am happy to tell you that the great Polish-American community voted for you practically as a solid block. They love you, respect and admire, and are deeply grateful for your continued recognition of the Polish Government, thus bearing out your refusal to recognize territorial gains by force."[5]

Polish Americans were staunch supporters of Roosevelt's foreign policy, first supporting the modifications of the neutrality laws in 1939 and later the passage of the Lend-Lease Bill in 1941. So strong was the support for lend-lease that when Congressman R.G. Tennerowicz voted against it one Polish American organization declared "he has disgraced the Americans of Polish extraction" and demanded his resignation.[6]

The most pressing need of the Polish government was to raise money and supplies for refugees in Poland and those scattered in other European countries, especially the 1.5 million Poles in the Soviet Union. The American Red Cross and the Polish American Council, or *Rada* as it was known in Polish American circles, were the key agencies behind relief activities for the Poles during the war. The Polish American Council federated all national church and press organizations of Americans of Polish descent in order to unify and centralize humanitarian efforts on behalf of Polish war victims.[7]

The Polish government sent Ludwik Rajchman, a gray eminence who enjoyed the confidence of Polish premier Władysław Sikorski, to the United States early in 1940 to coordinate the various relief activities for Poland. Rajchman tried but failed to get official American participation in a relief program jointly funded by Britain, France, and Poland. The State Department opposed the scheme on the grounds that it might draw the United States into the conflict with Germany. Secretary Hull was particularly irked at the way the Polish government sent agents like Rajchman to the United States on special missions instead of concentrating all activities, including relief, in diplomatic channels. No doubt the major explanation was that Sikorski did not have confidence in the Polish ambassador to the United States, Jerzy Potocki. Sikorski replaced Potocki with Jan Ciechanowski who, unlike his predecessor, was not identified with the regime of Marshal Józef Piłsudski, who ruled Poland in the 1920s and 1930s, and was better suited for the position because of his wide familiarity with the country and its leaders.[8]

It was easier to raise funds and supplies for Polish refugees in the United States in 1940 and 1941 than it was to get the aid to them. By

February 1940 the American Red Cross raised $400,000 and Rajch-
man's Commission for Polish Relief, a clearing house for Polish American relief groups, acquired $200,000. The Germans had agreed to
allow the Red Cross to send relief supplies from the United States to
Poland, but the British refused to make any exceptions to contraband
regulations through British-controlled communications. The consequence was that relief from the United States to Polish war victims in
occupied Poland had to go through the Mediterranean until Italy became a belligerent in June 1940, when American ships had to cease
activities by the terms of the neutrality laws. But some relief did
reach the Poles through American contributions to the League of Red
Cross Societies at Geneva.[9]

Polish war victims who lived under Soviet control were declared
citizens of the Soviet Union in November 1939 and were conscripted
into the Red Army.[10] When Polish officials tried to get the United
States to intervene and make inquiries concerning the treatment of
the refugees, the Kremlin refused to discuss anything with the United
States Embassy not relating to American citizens. And the Soviets
even refused American requests to allow Red Cross workers to enter
Siberia in order to get into eastern Poland to distribute supplies. Despite numerous impassioned appeals by Polish American organizations
for Washington to do something to help their kinsmen in the Soviet
Union, the United States was powerless.[11]

In desperation Sikorski urged American relief organizations to send
money to Polish refugees to enable them to buy food and clothing
in the Soviet Union. But one State Department official argued that,
given artificial rates of exchange, seventy-five cents out of every dollar
would end up in Soviet coffers. Polish American relief agencies concurred with the State Department's analysis of the situation, adding
their belief that the Soviets would never allow the Poles to use any of
the funds sent to them.[12] Neither the Polish nor the American government could do anything to help the Poles in the Soviet Union until
"Barbarossa" made the Soviet Union an ally of the West and diplomatic relations between the two Slavic states were resumed.

The passage of the Lend-Lease Act in March 1941 caused great ex-
citement within the Polish government. It opened the prospect of
tapping the large manpower pool in the United States for the organization of a Polish army in North America. The English and the Canadians encouraged the Poles with the idea of organizing an army in
Canada but became somewhat alarmed by the scale and tempo of
Polish plans. Sikorski, en route to the United States in April 1941,
reassured the Canadians and signed an agreement providing for the
training of a Polish army for later service with the British forces

overseas.[13] When the Polish premier arrived in the United States, he
asked for lend-lease aid and for help in getting volunteers for the Polish
army in Canada. American officials were responsive to giving the Poles
equipment and supplies for the army in Canada, and within two
months of the premier's visit Roosevelt included Poland under lend-
lease, though it was not formally announced until September 1941.
But American deliveries of equipment to the Polish Training Center
at Owen Sound, Canada, were pitifully slow,[14] a product of scarcity
of equipment and the growing number of claimants upon the meager
sources of supplies in the United States at the time.

   Washington also assisted the Polish government by facilitating travel
of volunteers from the United States to the point of enlistment in
Canada and informing Americans who volunteered to serve in the
Polish army that they would receive the same status and privileges as
Americans who joined the British army. That meant, in effect, that
the men were deferred from military service in the United States and
were classified in work considered vital to the defense of the country.
Despite the fervent appeals of Polish officials and the exhortations of
Polish American organizations, enlistments in the Polish armed forces
in Canada were fewer than anticipated. *Naród Polski (Polish Nation)*,
a Polish American weekly published by the Polish Roman Catholic
Union of America (PRCU), gave prominent attention to the recruiting effort in its issues, mixing patriotic appeals to Polish American
youth with reprimands to Polonia that so few men volunteered. In a
front page appeal on March 26, 1942, *Naród Polski* emotionally appealed to Polish youth in America: "The Nazi enemy murders the
Polish nation. The Nazi enemy destroys Polish culture. The Nazi
enemy strikes the body and soul of Poland." But enlistments were
too few to justify continuation of the project, forcing the Polish
government to end operations in Canada in the spring of 1942 and
to concentrate all training in England.[15]

   The need for recruits for the Polish armed forces fighting with the
British persisted. After all, the Poles fought and lost men on several
fronts. The Polish government tried to work out an arrangement with
the United States whereby all Polish citizens—whether they declared
to be American citizens or not—were to be drafted into the Polish
army. The Sikorski government was well aware of the implications
of its proposal. In effect, Ciechanowski told Hull, it "would be equiva-
lent to the grant of exceptional treatment in the case of Poland on
the part of the U.S. Government." Poland's war effort, the Polish
ambassador added, "is an exceptional one and its continuation depends
on the further indispensable replenishment of Polish fighting forces."
But the United States was unable to go as far as the Poles wanted: as

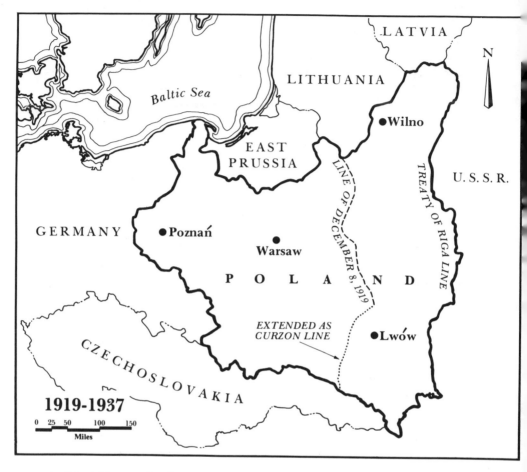

in World War I, it allowed only Polish nationals who had not declared their intention to become Americans the right to elect to serve in the Polish army instead of the United States Army. The Sikorski government hoped to make it a matter of compulsion rather than choice because it feared, and correctly as it turned out, that enlistments would not be large.[16] In retrospect, the hopes and plans of the Polish government to recruit large numbers of men in the United States were based upon assumptions about Polish Americans and Polish nationals resident in the United States that proved to be incorrect. Most Polish Americans and Polish nationals who had declared to be American citizens preferred to serve in the United States Army rather than in the Polish army.

Two months after Sikorski's visit to Washington, the Germans launched their invasion of Russia. The United States responded almost immediately by declaring Soviet resistance vital to American defense and security. Churchill welcomed the Soviet Union as an ally and offered to help. Washington went on to free Soviet assets in the United States and made it clear that it would aid the Kremlin too if it made known its needs. By the end of June 1941 the Soviet ambassador to Washington, Constantine Oumansky, presented a nine-point list of Soviet requests which included massive quantities of military and industrial aid. The United States government initiated a stopgap program of aid to the Soviet Union during the summer, and by the fall it dispatched, along with the British, a joint Anglo-American mission, headed by Lord William Beaverbrook and Averell Harriman, which inaugurated a long-range program of assistance by the first supply protocol signed in Moscow on October 1, 1941.[17]

While England became an ally and the United States a quasi ally of the Soviet Union during the summer of 1941, Poland had no choice but to follow suit. It was not an easy task for the Polish government to do so, and when Premier Sikorski finally signed the Polish-Soviet Treaty, which formally established diplomatic relations between the two governments, it precipitated a major cabinet crisis that seriously tested confidence in Sikorski's leadership.

The day after the German invasion of the Soviet Union, Sikorski spoke on the BBC and offered to improve relations with the Soviet Union, provided the Kremlin recognized the prewar boundary, the Riga Line, which, he conspicuously pointed out, had been recognized not only by the Conference of Ambassadors but also by the United States. The pointed reference to the United States was deliberate and had special significance at a time when the Soviets sought military aid from Washington. In his radio address, Sikorski also asked for the release of 300,000 Polish soldiers who were in Soviet prison camps.[18] For almost two weeks there was no response to Sikorski's initiative. Then on July 4, 1941, the Soviet ambassador to England, Ivan Maisky, asked Foreign Minister Anthony Eden to act as an intermediary in Polish-Soviet negotiations. Since his government was eager to see a Polish-Soviet agreement, Eden readily obliged.[19]

The initial Soviet proposal to normalize relations with the Poles showed no inclination to reestablish the Riga Line or, for that matter, even to recognize the Polish government-in-exile. The Soviets declared they favored only an ethnographic Poland and wanted to establish a national committee to which Polish prisoners of war would be released and form a Polish army, equipped and supplied by the Soviets, to fight on the eastern front.[20]

Sikorski, unimpressed with the Soviet offer, responded with

proposals of his own. He wanted Moscow to recognize the London Poles as the government of Poland, to dissociate itself from the 1939 agreements with Germany, and to release all military and civilian prisoners in Soviet camps. The Polish premier, on his part, offered to establish a Polish army under Soviet operational control. Polish officials hoped to get American support for an agreement with the Soviet Union along the lines suggested by Sikorski, but Washington, unlike London, did not want to take an active role in the discussions. Under secretary of state Sumner Welles told Ciechanowski that the United States would confine itself "to an expression in general terms."[21]

The Kremlin came close to Sikorski's position, but it preferred not to make the matter of Polish prisoners in the Soviet Union an integral part of a political agreement between the two governments. Moreover, while the Poles contended there were 180,000 military prisoners of war in the Soviet Union, a figure Polish authorities had taken earlier from the Soviet press, the Soviets now claimed that there were only 20,000 Poles in their camps. As for political prisoners, the Kremlin claimed that most of them were not Poles anyway and refused to release them.[22] The question of the release of military and civilian prisoners was a crucial one for Sikorski's government. Had he failed to extract some concession from the Soviets on this point, Sikorski probably would have been unable to hold power.

The most controversial point in the Polish-Soviet negotiations was the question of Poland's frontier with the Soviet Union. The Poles wanted the Soviets to recognize unequivocally the restoration of the Riga Line, violated by the Soviet pact with Germany in 1939. The Soviets, on the other hand, would admit only that the agreements with Germany in 1939 affecting Poland's boundary with the Soviet Union were invalid without commiting themselves to a restoration of the pre-1939 line.[23]

The British, anxious to forge a strong coalition with the Soviet Union, were eager for a Polish-Soviet agreement. Eden bluntly told Sikorski, "Whether you wish it or not, the treaty must be signed."[24] In order to make it easier for the Poles to accept a treaty without the Soviets specifically recognizing the Riga Line, Eden assured Polish leaders that Poland's point of view was legally safeguarded by Soviet annulment of the 1939 pact with Hitler. To give more substance to the British position, Eden in a note to August Zaleski, the Polish foreign minister, stated that Britain would not recognize territorial changes during the war without the consent of the parties concerned. The Poles hoped to get a specific American endorsement of the Riga Line but found that Washington took the same position as the British.[25]

The Polish cabinet was divided. Zaleski, the most articulate conservative on the issue, argued against signing any treaty that did not
specifically spell out the Riga Line as Poland's boundary and the release of all Poles detained in Soviet camps. Fearing military expediency
would transcend moral and legal considerations involving Poland,
Zaleski admonished: "The present state of military collaboration between the Allies and America on the one hand and Soviet Russia on
the other should not divert the Allies' attention from the actual situation in Eastern Europe."[26]

Sikorski realized that the climate for the current Polish-Soviet negotiations was unfavorable for Poland. Britain was eager to solidify
an alliance with the Soviet Union. The United States, by sending aid
to the Soviets, had become at least a quasi ally of the Soviet Union.
Even public opinion in England and the United States began to move
away from the hostility with which it viewed the Soviet Union before
June 1941. Eden went so far as to tell Sikorski that if he did not
quickly sign a treaty with the Soviets, he would jeopardize Poland's
standing with the British and the Americans. Sikorski told his cabinet
that the Poles simply could not get the kind of treaty Zaleski and the
other conservatives wanted. He warned his ministers that if the Polish
government did not sign a treaty soon, it ran the serious risk of giving
the Soviets a free hand to do what they pleased with the thousands of
Polish refugees in the Soviet Union.[27] If nothing else, the agreement
with the Soviet Union would allow Poland, along with England and
the United States, to provide relief to the Polish deportees in the
Soviet Union. Revealing how important these refugees were to him,
Sikorski, immediately after he concluded the treaty with the Kremlin,
appealed to Polish Americans to aid the refugees in the Soviet Union.[28]

On the night of July 27 the Polish cabinet approved the Polish-
Soviet treaty that Sikorski and Maisky signed in a simple ceremony
on July 30, 1941. The treaty was a compromise: it went farther
than the Soviets preferred, yet it did not go far enough to satisfy the
Poles. It provided for a restoration of diplomatic relations, annulled
the German-Soviet Pact of 1939 without recognizing the Riga Line,
provided for the formation of a Polish army in the Soviet Union under a Polish commander appointed by and in agreement with the
Kremlin, provided for mutual support against Germany, and attached
a protocol which promised amnesty to Poles detained in the Soviet
Union after the restoration of Polish-Soviet diplomatic relations. The
last point was extracted from a reluctant Stalin by the British ambassador to the Soviet Union, Sir Stafford Cripps, who urged him:
"Make a gesture. Show the world you sincerely desire an agreement."
Stalin relented.[29]

Neither side had any illusions about the agreement. It settled none of the thorny issues between the two countries but it did provide the mechanics to do so. For example, immediately after the treaty had been signed, Sikorski declared that the treaty with the Soviet Union "does not permit even of the suggestion that the 1939 frontier of the Polish State could ever be in question." The Soviet Union immediately took issue with his remarks.[30] Furthermore, the release of Polish prisoners had political and legal aspects which were not even touched upon in the agreement. And the details concerning the formation of the Polish army, a source of much trouble later, were left to be worked out by Soviet and Polish military authorities. From the standpoint of the emerging Allied alliance, the most important aspect of the agreement was that it announced to the world that the Soviet Union and Poland would fight the Nazis and not each other.

No sooner had the treaty been signed than three ministers of Sikorski's cabinet resigned in protest—Marian Seyda, minister of justice; General Kazimierz Sosnkowski, deputy prime minister; and August Zaleski. The opposition of these men to the Polish-Soviet Treaty had been strengthened by reports from Ambassador Ciechanowski who either had misinterpreted or had misrepresented Washington's attitude toward the proposed agreement. Ciechanowski claimed that the United States opposed the signing of the Polish-Soviet Treaty as drafted, but that was not true. Hull said later that the United States could not oppose a treaty about which it knew almost nothing. Regarding territorial matters, Hull affirmed the American position, which had been repeated several times to the Polish ambassador, that it did not recognize the acquisition of territory taken by conquest. Like England, the United States would not give Poland guarantees for its prewar frontiers. Hull stated: "This Government is also adhering to its policy of taking upon itself no obligations with regard to what the boundaries of continental Europe are to be following the conclusion of the present war and sincerely hopes that the British Government will follow a like policy."[31]

In retrospect, Ciechanowski appears to have shared the doubts about the treaty that Zaleski, Seyda, and Sosnkowski had. He claimed in his memoirs of the war years that Sikorski, unlike Zaleski who came from former Soviet-controlled Poland, did not understand the Soviets and naïvely believed that once the Molotov-Ribbentrop Pact was rescinded, the Riga Line automatically came into force. British refusal to guarantee the Riga frontier was to Ciechanowski "the first swallow on the rising dawn of a new British policy of appeasement."[32]

But not all Polish officials shared the gloom of Poland's Russophobes about the treaty. Count Edward Raczyński, the Polish ambassador to

LATVIA

LITHUANIA

Baltic Sea

●Wilno

EAST
PRUSSIA

U.S.S.R.

●Poznań

●Warsaw

MOLOTOV-RIBBENTROP LINE

P O L A   N   D

GERMANY

●Lwów

1939

0 25 50   100   150
Miles

HUNGARY

ROMANIA

England and successor to Zaleski after he resigned as foreign minister, believed the treaty was a moot question because he, like countless other Western observers, believed that the Soviet Union would soon be defeated by the Germans. Thus, as Raczyński saw it, Poland's frontiers "will eventually be determined by the victorious States and presumably in the first instance by Britain and the USA." Others like Joseph Retinger, Sikorski's adviser and friend, shared the desire of the Polish premier to "make a final, historical settlement with the Soviets."[33] Whatever Sikorski's true feelings were at the time of the signing of the Polish-Soviet Treaty, he later developed a realistic, if not fatalistic, sense that it would be difficult, probably impossible, for Poland to restore the Riga Line with the Soviet Union.[34] Had he given expression to these sentiments, Sikorski probably would have been thrown out of office.

II

FROM AGREEMENT TO DISAGREEMENT

The Polish-Soviet Treaty of July 1941 inaugurated a brief era of good feelings between the Soviet Union and Poland. The Soviet Union's survival was at stake, and the Kremlin could not afford to alienate its Western allies over Polish issues during the early months of the German-Soviet conflict. But as Soviet military fortunes improved, defying all the grim predictions of imminent collapse, the Kremlin established a position of military strength in 1942 substantial enough to enable it to deal more independently, even arbitrarily, with the Poles in settling the outstanding issues between the Soviet and Polish governments, left unresolved by the Polish-Soviet Treaty. Increasingly, the Polish government looked to the United States to intervene in its behalf with the Kremlin on the supply and recruitment of the Polish army in the Soviet Union, the relief and evacuation of Polish refugees, and most importantly, the controversial boundary dispute.

THE POLISH ARMY

The United States showed greater willingness to take diplomatic initiatives with the Kremlin on the relief of Polish deportees than it did on the army and citizenship questions because in the case of the former the intervention could be easily justified on humanitarian grounds. But, for fear of jeopardizing the wartime alliance with Moscow, Washington was most restrained when asked by the Sikorski government to intervene on issues in Polish-Soviet relations that carried political overtones.

One of the major issues in Polish-Soviet relations in 1941–1942 concerned the formation and supply of the Polish army in the Soviet Union. The Poles sent a military mission to the Soviet Union, headed by General Bohusz-Szysko, which negotiated a military agreement with the Soviets on August 14, 1941. The agreement and subsequent protocols arranged between General Władysław Anders, appointed by Sikorski to head the army, and General Panfilov provided for the creation of two infantry divisions consisting of 10,000 men and a reserve regiment of 5,000 men. Poles who had been conscripted into the Red Army could now transfer into the Polish army based at Tock and Tatischev. Polish headquarters was located at Buzuluk, a primitive town, where "even obtaining a board or nail was nearly impossible," Anders said. In response to a Polish request, the Soviets provided a surprisingly small list of names of Polish army officers— 1,658—who had been detained in Soviet camps since 1939. This sharply contradicted figures published in 1940 in *Red Star,* a Soviet periodical, which revealed that 10 generals, 52 colonels, 72 lieutenant colonels, 5,131 regular army officers, and 4,096 army reserve officers were in Soviet detention centers. When Stanisław Kot, the Polish ambassador to the Soviet Union, tried to find out from Stalin what had happened to the missing men, Stalin dramatically telephoned the NKVD in the Pole's presence in order to find out. But after his conversation with the NKVD, Stalin said nothing about the matter to Kot. When Sikorski later inquired about the men with Stalin, the Soviet chief, apparently straight-faced, was bold enough to claim that the Polish officers had escaped to Manchuria![1] Despite the persistent efforts of Polish diplomatic and military officials to determine the whereabouts of the Polish officers, the Soviets were evasive and uncooperative until the Germans told the world in April 1943 what had happened to the missing men.

The weeks following the signing of the Polish-Soviet Treaty witnessed cordiality and cooperativeness between Polish and Soviet officials. By the end of August 1941 Anders succeeded in organizing two divisions, though they were not fully equipped yet. Anders was so optimistic about the number of Polish soldiers released from Soviet camps who reported for duty that he expected to organize two more, and ultimately six, divisions. Sikorski estimated there were 100,000 Poles of military age who were eligible to serve in the Polish army.[2]

The problem was not getting men to join the Polish army in the Soviet Union—the Soviets had released thousands of them from confinement—but properly equipping and supplying the units that Anders commanded. The Soviets faced understandable equipment and supply problems of their own. "Barbarossa" had surprised Stalin and taken a grim toll of manpower and material. The Soviet air force had been virtually wiped out on the first day of the German-Soviet conflict. The Soviets therefore told the Poles they could supply only one division. Beyond that, Premier Sikorski had to get British and American help to supply the remaining Polish units. In order to assure the Poles in the Soviet Union a steady flow of equipment and supplies, Sikorski wanted Anders and Ambassador Kot to participate with British and American representatives in the Anglo-American supply conference scheduled to meet in Moscow at the end of September 1941. No doubt Sikorski had some political aims too—namely, a Polish place at the meeting would underscore the strong ties the London Poles had with the United States and Great Britain. Roosevelt agreed to help supply the Polish army in the Soviet Union but vetoed any role for Poland in the forthcoming Moscow Conference, which was to be a joint Anglo-American affair intended to assess only Soviet military needs and to make a Western commitment to meet them. On the other hand, Roosevelt wanted the Poles to make known their needs to Harriman and deal directly with him, and not the Soviets, for American aid. The president revealed that he was not insensitive to the political aspects of the problem when he told Harriman: "It is believed that it would be in conformity with our policy of maintaining so far as possible Polish prestige and influence in Eastern Europe for us to deal direct with the Poles with regard to the supplying of the Polish forces in Russia since such direct negotiations would be likely to enhance the prestige and stress the individuality of those forces now as well as in the future."[3]

Contrary to Roosevelt's wishes, however, the Anglo-American supply mission, led by Lord Beaverbrook with Harriman playing a lesser role, did not insist on specifically earmarking for the Poles Western aid sent to the Soviet Union. Harriman later explained to a disappointed Ciechanowski that the Anglo-American mission went to Moscow to encourage the Soviets to resist the Germans and therefore could not give the impression there were strings attached to American and British aid. Ambassador Kot, furious with Beaverbrook for letting the Poles down, observed bitterly: "Beaverbrook dominated everything." Sikorski was so upset with the way the Beaverbrook-Harriman mission left Polish supply needs up to the Soviets that he was pessimistic about the future of the Polish army in the Soviet Union.[4]

Neither the British nor the Americans were particularly enthusiastic about the maintenance and supply of a Polish army in the Soviet Union when they had their hands full meeting and delivering the commitments promised the Soviets in the Moscow Protocol. Moreover, leaving Polish troops in the Soviet Union at a time when the Soviet Union's military future still looked grim and the British desperately needed seasoned soldiers in the Middle East seemed militarily foolish. Sikorski agreed with Churchill that it would be better to base the Polish army in the Caucasus where at least it would be closer to British forces in the Middle East. That way Britain and the United States would be in a better position to supply the Poles through Iran and, in the event of a Soviet collapse, to evacuate the Polish army to the Middle East or to India. Ideally, Churchill wanted the Soviets to withdraw their five divisions from Iran for use against the Germans along the Volga, but he doubted that Stalin would do it. Churchill believed Stalin would rather lose Moscow than leave Persia. To Sikorski, deploying the army in the Caucasus would also enable the Poles to operate in an important area and to "have the opportunity of stretching a hand to our British Allies and of fighting side by side with them as well as with the Russian Ally." There was no thought of the Poles abandoning the Soviets. Sikorski told Anders: "We wish to co-operate closely and loyally with the USSR, during this war and after it."[5]

Meanwhile, Sikorski, needing replacements to strengthen Polish armed forces based in Britain and the Middle East, asked Anders to evacuate 10,000 men—later inflated to 15,000–25,000—from the Soviet Union. The timing of Sikorski's request could not have been worse: the Germans drove relentlessly eastward, gobbling up the Ukraine and coming perilously close to Leningrad, Moscow, and the Caucasus by the fall of 1941. The Soviets naturally regarded with suspicion Polish requests for even a partial evacuation of Polish troops, let alone a deployment of all of them to the southern part of the Soviet Union.[6]

The supply situation for the Poles reached critical proportions by October 1941 when the Soviets cut the food rations for Polish soldiers to 44,000, which meant that further recruiting and organizing of additional military units had to stop unless the British and the Americans could relieve the situation. Moreover, the Soviets now transported the Polish war prisoners they had released from detention camps to cotton plantations in Tashkent and construction projects in Uzbekistan. The gravity of the food situation in the Soviet Union made it essential to withdraw the Polish army either to Iran or to the Caucasus. Both Britain and the United States supported the proposal, but while Polish authorities planned to return the troops to the Soviet front when they were combat ready, the British talked as though they did not want the Poles to return. By early November the Soviets told Anders to reduce his troops even more—this time to 30,000 men. Apparently irked by Polish efforts to get Anglo-American help in the supply matter, General Panfilov bluntly told Anders: "In [the] future the organization of Polish units as well as supplying them with food and equipment will be carried out solely through me."[7]

Like Churchill, Roosevelt preferred to see Polish troops taken out of the Soviet Union. He told Ciechanowski "to use splendid fighting men as workmen in camps, rather than soldiers, would be contrary to allied interests; it would be squandering very valuable fighting material." General James H. Burns, head of the Munitions Assignments Board, strongly endorsed the idea of a Polish evacuation, claiming that one Pole was worth six soldiers from any other nation. The president directed Harriman to intervene and ask Stalin to allow the Polish army to leave for Persia. Harriman made the request in a note of November 7, 1941, which did not reach Stalin for several days. Stalin promised to consider it. Until the Kremlin reacted to the idea, American officials promised Ciechanowski to coordinate efforts with the British to work out a priority on supplies sent through Iran for the Poles. But any priority to supply the Poles would further cut into the small quantity of supplies getting through Iran for the Soviets[8] who, in the final analysis, were holding down the bulk of the German war machine. Britain and the United States simply could not get enough supplies under lend-lease to the Soviets let alone the Poles, over existing communications. The bitter truth was that Britain and the United States simply could not adequately supply the Polish troops any more than the Soviets could.

One problem that disturbed Polish relations with the Soviets was the refusal of the Soviets after November 1941 to allow Polish Jews to enlist in the Polish army. After that date the Kremlin recognized only ethnic Poles as Polish citizens, thus excluding Jews, White Russians, and Ukrainians. However, until the new Soviet policy was announced, large numbers of Jews had enrolled in the Polish army. Some detachments consisted of as many as 30 percent Jews. Anders and Kot, in agreement with leaders of the Jewish refugees in the Soviet Union, believed that Polish Jews should serve in units with ethnic Poles. To be sure, some anti-Semites and Jewish nationalists wanted separate units, but they did not get them.[9]

Sikorski had planned for some time to go to Moscow and work out the supply problem for the Polish army and other Polish-Soviet issues with Stalin, but Kot urged him to postpone his visit. On October 24, 1941, Kot telegraphed Sikorski that most of the Soviet government, evacuated to Kuibyshev to get out of range of the advancing Germans, was not functioning yet. Most Soviet functionaries there, Kot explained, were "wandering around unpacked." The Polish ambassador wanted to use the postponement of the Sikorski visit as leverage to extract concessions from the Soviets not only on supplying and forming additional Polish military units but also on releasing and aiding Polish civilian refugees in various parts of the Soviet Union. Sikorski's name, revered among the Poles in the Soviet Union to the point that it almost acquired the aspect of a religious cult, tremendously bolstered Polish morale, a fact not lost on the Soviets. On November 8,

Kot cabled from the Soviet Union: "We are trying to exploit the announcement of General Sikorski's visit in order to obtain the release of those still detained, and agreement to further formations of Polish forces."[10]

The threat that Sikorski might cancel his visit and the intervention of the United States marked the beginning of a change in Soviet policy. In an effort to offset the combined pressures of the United States, Britain, and Poland to evacuate Polish troops from the Soviet Union at a time when Soviet fortunes still appeared grim, Stalin cordially received Ambassador Kot on November 14 and told him that he had no objections to the Poles' organizing as many as seven divisions, provided they found arms and equipment for them from the West. He also made concessions on two other issues that had greatly disturbed the London Poles—namely, accelerating the release of Poles still in confinement and allowing the Polish Embassy to establish offices in districts where there were large concentrations of Polish refugees. "After all, we are allies," Stalin told Kot. "Who wishes to have a weak ally? We shall do all we can." Two days later, Kot reversed himself, and now advised that it was time for Sikorski to come to the Soviet Union. Lest Stalin do something drastic, Kot preferred not even to mention Sikorski's proposal of temporarily evacuating Polish troops from the Soviet Union.[11]

Sikorski went to Moscow in December 1941 in order to resolve, among other things, the problem of the Polish army in Russia. During his two-and-one-half-hour conversation with Stalin on December 3, Sikorski spent most of the time detailing the inadequate conditions in which Polish soldiers had to live and train. He told Stalin that the Poles lived in summer quarters during the winter, ate inadequate rations, and trained when 60 percent of the men still had no shoes. As a consequence, Sikorski proposed the withdrawal of Polish troops to Iran for supply and training until they were combat ready to take over an assigned sector on the Soviet front.

Stalin was displeased with what he heard. "I am a person of experience and of age," he told Sikorski. "I know that if you go to Persia you will never return here. I see that England has much to do and needs Polish soldiers." When Anders, who was also present at the meeting, tried to explain how impossible the situation was for Polish troops in the Soviet Union, Stalin excitedly exclaimed: "If the Poles do not want to fight then let them go. We cannot hold back the Poles. If they want to they may go away." By that time, Sikorski's temper began to flair and he asked Stalin to offer a better solution to the problem. Stalin, however, preferred to impugn the motives of the Poles. "I am rough and I want to know clearly whether you want to fight or not?" Stalin asked. Sikorski retorted emphatically: "That we want to is proven not by words but by facts." And the dialogue got even sharper:

> Stalin: That means that we are savages, and that we cannot improve anything. It amounts to this, that a Russian can only oppress a Pole, but is unable to do anything good for him. However, we can do without you. We can give back all of them. We will manage ourselves. We will conquer Poland and then we will give her back to you. But what will people say to this? They will ridicule us all over the world that we are not able to achieve anything here.
>
> Sikorski: I did not receive a reply as to where I am to establish an army so that it could participate in the war but not perish from the horrible climatic conditions. I ask for concrete counterpropositions. I categorically confirm once again that we want to fight for Poland at your side.
>
> Stalin: When you go to Iran then perhaps you will have to fight in Turkey against the Germans. Tomorrow Japan will enter the war, then against Japan. So as the English will order. Perhaps in Singapore.
>
> Anders: It is on the continent that we want to fight the Germans for Poland. Our people have not seen their country for a long time, and no one loves his country as much as the Poles do. From here it is closest to Poland.

It is impossible to determine whether Stalin really meant what he told Sikorski, or whether he deliberately assumed a pose of aggrieved sensibility. Either way it worked. Sikorski, obliged to prove the good faith of the Poles which Stalin had questioned, offered to keep his entire army in the Soviet Union if the Kremlin supplied and equipped it properly. As if to prove his own good faith, Stalin went out of his way to vent his anger on General Panfilov for having failed to obey his earlier orders to restore Polish rations from 30,000 to 44,000.[12]

Sikorski never really intended to evacuate permanently the Polish troops from the Soviet Union for several reasons: As long as a Polish army remained in the Soviet Union, the Polish government was in a position to recruit replacements for its troops in the West, a vital life line for the continued viability of Poland's armed forces abroad, and to look after the thousands of Polish civilian refugees in the Soviet Union. Moreover, Sikorski was enough of an idealist to hope that genuine reconciliation between the Poles and the Soviets had a better chance of developing in a relationship of comrades-in-arms.[13]

After the tense conversation of December 3, the atmosphere the next day changed dramatically to cordiality and even warmth. At a dinner in the Kremlin given in honor of the Polish premier, Stalin and Sikorski signed a "Declaration of Friendship and Mutual Assistance," which was an important document not so much because of its content as the fact that both countries dealt with each other as equals, not as victor and vanquished. Stalin, after the usual orgy of Soviet toasts, was so ebullient that he ordered the declaration and Sikorski's radio speech that day translated into twenty-seven languages and distributed among Soviet and even German troops.[14]

Now the British were unhappy with Sikorski. Leaving the Polish army in the Soviet Union did not solve the supply problem for it. All Sikorski got was a promise from Stalin that he had been unable to keep before. Moreover, the British erroneously believed that all Polish troops would remain in the Soviet Union, but that was not true. Sikorski had emphasized to Stalin the need for reinforcements for Polish units training with the British in Scotland and fighting with them in the Middle East. The need was sharpened by the unsuccessful efforts of the Polish government to recruit large numbers of Polish Americans for the Polish force at Owen Sound, Canada. Sikorski told Stalin he wanted to evacuate 25,000 replacement troops for service elsewhere, and the Soviet leader offered no objections. Also, in order to ease the supply problem for Polish soldiers who were to remain in the Soviet Union, the army and a majority of civilians were to be transferred to Soviet Central Asia, near the Persian and Afghani frontiers.[15]

The Polish premier's visit to the Soviet Union marked the high-water mark of good will between the two governments during World War II. Both sides were pleased with it. Shortly after Sikorski returned to England, the Soviets approved a 100 million ruble loan for Polish civilians and a 300 million ruble loan for Anders' army. The Kremlin allowed Kot to speak a few minutes several times a week on the Soviet radio. The Polish army could now publish its own newspaper, *Orzeł Biały (White Eagle)*. And in a rare gesture of recognition of Polish religious feelings, the Kremlin even allowed Poles not to report for work on Christmas Eve and Christmas Day.[16] Sikorski was euphoric about the impact of his trip. Despite the fact that there were numerous serious problems in Polish-Soviet relations that had to be resolved yet, Sikorski excitedly told Churchill: "I feel my visit to Russia resulted in a solution of nearly all the outstanding Polish-Soviet problems and also resulted in some benefit to the Allied cause."[17]

One of the features of Polish relations with the Soviets was the lack of harmony and unity of purpose among Polish officials themselves. Anders did not get along well with Kot, and there was serious tension between Sikorski and Anders at times.[18] The basis of the conflict was the conviction, shared by Sikorski and his friend Kot, that it was essential for Poland to leave some military force in the Soviet Union for political, military, and humanitarian reasons. Anders, understandably disturbed by the lack of food, the poor conditions, and the inadequate equipment for his troops, which did not improve, saw Polish interests through a narrow prism. He thought in terms of the hardships of

Polish soldiers and civilians whose sufferings confronted him daily.
Extremely popular with his men, Anders later violated the explicit
instructions of his commander-in-chief, Sikorski, and the will of the
Polish cabinet and asked Stalin for the complete evacuation of Polish
troops from the Soviet Union.

By early 1942 the Soviets approved the deployment of Polish troops
to the south near Tashkent but they either could not or would not
supply them adequately. The Kremlin wanted to send the only Polish
division close to combat readiness, the Fifth, to the front. Anders opposed the idea, and Sikorski backed him up because neither man
wanted to see the Poles swallowed up along the limitless Soviet front.
They preferred to have a minimum of four divisions acting as a single
force in combat in order to derive the maximum military and political
benefits from the participation of the Polish army on the eastern
front.[19]

The supply problem became so bad that Anders went directly to
Stalin about it on March 18, 1942. Stalin told him there were not
enough rations for more than 44,000 men, and he blamed the United
States for not delivering adequate supplies of grain. What the Soviet
Union had received under lend-lease, Stalin complained, amounted to
"the tears of a cat." When he heard of it, Harriman with justification
took issue with the claim, pointing out that the United States had
promised to make deliveries only to American ports where the Soviets
were to work out transport arrangements. When Anders replied that
he wanted to keep the entire army in the Soviet Union, which numbered 75,000–78,000 men with recruits arriving daily, and urged
Stalin to provide for all of them until the British could expedite food
supplies to the Poles, the Soviet chief repeated that he could feed
only 44,000. That is when Anders suggested that the rest of the troops
be evacuated to Iran. Stalin immediately agreed and promised to expedite the evacuation.[20]

By mid-April 1942 over 40,000 evacuees, including women and
children, had reached Iran.[21] Once the Poles got out, Sikorski wanted
the bulk of the force to go to Britain to complete his armored division and paratroop brigade. The British did not like the idea, claiming
inadequate transport, and told Sikorski that most of the Poles should
stay in the Middle East. To make matters worse, the Soviets discon-
tinued further recruitment of Poles in the Soviet Union, which effectively dried up the major source of replacement manpower for the
Polish armed forces in the Soviet Union and in the West, and ordered
all able-bodied Poles into labor battalions. According to Polish military authorities, there were as many as 120,000 men deprived of
joining the Polish armed forces. Molotov told Kot the Soviet Union

saw no "purpose" to continue recruitment of Poles in the USSR.[22]

The London Poles asked Washington to intervene and urge the Soviets to resume recruiting. And given the acute shortage of officers, Sikorski's government also asked the United States to inquire about the location of the approximately 8,000 missing Polish officers captured and held by the Soviets in 1939 and 1940.[23] The London Poles were unduly optimistic that a strong intervention by Washington with the Kremlin would be effective because of alleged Soviet dependence on American aid.

Neither the United States nor Britain was anxious to alienate the Soviets at a time when the Kremlin pressed for a second front in Europe that was unlikely to occur soon, and both powers feared that the Soviet Union, if sufficiently provoked, was capable of signing a separate peace with Germany. Moreover, Churchill and Roosevelt preferred to see the Poles get out of the Soviet Union anyway. Churchill could use the Poles in the Middle East, where he could feed and equip them. Roosevelt believed that if the troops stayed in the Soviet Union they would continue to be treated like "stepchildren."[24]

To Anders, the situation for his troops and Polish civilians was intolerable. He flew to England to urge Sikorski to authorize the complete evacuation of the remaining troops in the Soviet Union. In the interest of the thousands of civilians, the Polish cabinet preferred to keep an army in the Soviet Union. Sikorski had sound military reasons, too, for leaving a Polish force there. First, he needed a continued source of replacements for his forces in the West. Second, he did not want to concentrate too many Poles in any single theater and risk their annihilation. He told Anders: "I have neither the right nor the intention to risk the concentration of the whole or a major part of the Polish Armed Forces on the one theatre of war, where a possible misfortune could bring about their excessive, if not complete destruction." Kot believed that keeping a Polish army in the Soviet Union was "the last trump" the United States, Britain, and Poland had "against such a disloyal partner as the Soviet Government." If the troops left the country without the Kremlin at least restoring recruitment and allowing the evacuation of Polish children, who suffered particularly, Kot claimed that "more than 500,000 of our population will face destruction, and Poland's political interests in her relations with Russia will be seriously jeopardized." The Polish cabinet voted against Anders' proposal.[25]

But Anders was a headstrong leader, and he had strong support among Polish officers and troops who opposed leaving so many soldiers in the Soviet Union. Many of these men opposed Sikorski's policy of rapprochement with the Soviet Union and resented his government's soft pedaling references to Piłsudski, an avowed Russo-phobe, whom they considered a national hero. Sikorski's hold on Anders was tenuous, despite the fact that he was not only premier but also commander-in-chief of the Polish armed forces. For example, when Sikorski went to the Soviet Union in December 1941 he felt it was necessary to ask Anders if the Polish commander was loyal to him.[26]

When Anders returned to the Soviet Union, according to his own account, he came to the conclusion "that to remain in Soviet Russia would mean the eventual extinction of all the Poles." On his own initiative, he asked the Soviets to allow the remaining Polish troops to leave the Soviet Union. The Kremlin, never enthusiastic about having a large foreign military contingent on its soil anyway, readily agreed and with surprising speed did all it could to get its Polish visitors out of the country as quickly as possible. Anders even paid General Zhukov, the Soviet who supervised the expeditious evacuation, a compliment: "I owed it to his energy that the two evacuations [March and August] were carried out so efficiently, and it was thanks to him, also, that I succeeded in getting many thousands of men released from prisons and concentration camps who would otherwise never have been freed."[27] Approximately 115,000 troops and civilians joined the evacuation from the Soviet Union to Iran.[28]

One of the principal reasons the Polish government signed the treaty of July 1941 was to look after the needs of the large number of its refugees in the Soviet Union. The flood of deportees, amnestied by the decree of the Supreme Soviet in August, required food, clothing, footwear, and sanitary facilities which the Soviets had difficulty in providing at a time when they were fighting for their own survival. The embryonic Polish army, though seriously limited in rations and other supplies, shared what it could with the civilians.[29]

Although the Soviets suffered from shortages of all kinds of items, they were uncooperative with Polish and American agencies which sought to bring relief to the deportees. Three times the Kremlin rebuffed efforts of representatives of the American Red Cross to bring food, medicine, and clothing.[30] When the Polish American Council raised clothing and other articles for transport to the Soviet Union, the Soviet ambassador to the United States, Constantine Oumansky, raised objections on hygienic grounds. The Soviet government, moreover, said it would levy customs duties and charge the Poles for transporting the supplies from the United States to Polish centers of concentration in the Soviet Union. After weeks of delay, by October 1941, more than one hundred tons of supplies raised by the Polish American Council had piled up and awaited export from New York.[31]

The Polish Embassy, isolated from the mass of Poles in the Soviet Union, tried to locate some of its offices closer to the refugees, but the Kremlin opposed the idea. When Ambassador Kot talked with the vice-commissar for foreign affairs, Andrei Vyshinsky, on November 2, 1941, he got negative replies to two Polish requests—namely, refusing to transport the refugees from the north, where many were concentrated, to a more hospitable climate in the south, and denying the Polish government a loan to effect the transfer. Kot emotionally asked Vyshinsky to tell him at least where the Polish people were so his embassy could help them. "Of course I will do that," the Soviet promised. When Vyshinsky made the curious inquiry to the British Ambassador, Sir Stafford Cripps, why the Polish government was not looking after its own women and children, Cripps told him with uncharacteristic bluntness that the Soviet Union had removed the people from their homes and that they were in the Soviet Union now, not Poland. Cripps cited a case of sixteen Poles, transported from the northern part of the country, who had died of starvation upon arrival at their destination. Vyshinsky stoutly denied that they died of starvation. The British intervention brought some modest improvement in the situation: the Soviets approved three million rubles for the relief of Polish civilians. Since there were approximately 300,000 Poles in Uzbekistan alone and 100,000 of them were unfit either for military service or for work, Kot understandably complained that the meager sum would not solve the problem. Instead of being grateful, as Vyshinsky expected, Kot was "frigidly polite" when he heard about the Soviet grant.[32]

The situation for the Polish refugees was grim. Isolated from representatives of their government, people wandered around the country heading for the south, where they hoped to find the Polish army and join it or attach themselves to it for help and protection. Soviet authorities, in the midst of a catastrophic war that saw the enemy in control of so much of their country, had their own refugees to worry about and were not overly sympathetic with people whom they did not regard as friends anyway. The Soviets wanted the Poles to remain in special sectors; but the deportees, frequently without authorization, moved south to Uzbekistan, where authorities subsequently moved 36,000 people to Kazakstan ostensibly to find work for them. Despite the extremely difficult situation for the Poles, the Kremlin refused to allow relief workers from the United States and Britain to enter the country to help.[33]

Roosevelt, touched by the sufferings of the deportees, told the State Department that "the Polish population should be saved by all possible means." He directed Harriman to intervene with Stalin on the refugee matter. American intervention and the possibility that Premier Sikorski might cancel his visit to the Soviet Union unless something was done by the Kremlin to improve the lot of the Poles brought results. By the middle of November 1941 the Kremlin agreed to establish settlements with adequate facilities, to allow the United States and Britain to provide assistance to the refugees, and to hasten the release of Poles still in prisons and labor camps. Furthermore, Vyshinsky informed Kot that the Soviet government had no objections if Polish officials went to areas where there were concentrations of Poles, issued passports, and gave them aid. But the precise latitude the Polish representatives would have in their activities was never clearly defined—the Soviets tried to limit while the Poles tried to expand the freedom of these officials. The Soviets, for example, opposed the establishment of consular offices. After Sikorski visited the Soviet Union, the loose and disorganized system of relief for the Poles was firmed up, eventually resulting in a welfare network that linked the Polish Embassy with 2,600 Polish settlements in thirty-five oblasts.[34]

But the relief of Polish civilians inevitably got tied up with other issues that disturbed Polish-Soviet relations, taking on political overtones that unfortunately victimized thousands of innocent people. Some of the Polish officials had engaged in intelligence gathering activities unrelated to their relief work. The Polish ambassador admitted that Polish soldiers had talked irresponsibly about joining rebellious Turkmen and Kazakhs against the Soviets. He even admitted that there were unfriendly remarks about the Soviets in *Orzeł Biały (White Eagle)*, the Polish army periodical printed in the Soviet Union.[35] The NKVD dutifully reported what they saw and heard to the Kremlin, which swiftly reacted to what it apparently interpreted as a Polish conspiracy. By the summer of 1942, the Soviets arrested Polish relief representatives and closed down their operations in several locations throughout the country. Even embassy officials were declared *personae non gratae.* The Kremlin charged sixteen Poles with intelligence work hostile to the Soviet Union and an additional seventy-eight were compromised substantially enough in the eyes of the Soviets to be deported.[36] The Poles argued that the Soviets had overreacted. The Polish chargé d'affaires in Russia, Henryk Sokolnicki, told Vyshinsky on July 19, 1942:

> if this action on the part of the Soviet Authorities was aimed at the destruction of the entire welfare and relief organization for Polish citizens in the USSR, created with such difficulty by this Embassy in agreement with the People's Commissariat, then it would be better to state this clearly instead of creating a fictitious situation in which one cannot be certain of the fate either of people or of institutions.[37]

By the end of July 1942 eleven out of twenty Polish relief delegations had been closed, depriving 40 percent of the deportees of welfare services. Approximately 3,000 tons of commodities sent by the United States and Britain for Polish relief could not be distributed by July because of the closure of Polish delegations at Archangel and Murmansk. Kot, never liked by Stalin, who referred sneeringly to him as *vash Kot*, was a casualty of the crisis, and Sikorski replaced him with Tadeusz Romer who tried to normalize relations between the two governments. The Kremlin, perhaps realizing that it may have overreacted and responding to American intervention in the matter, promised Romer that there would be no public trial for the arrested men. The Soviets did not intend "to make too much of it," Molotov declared.[38]

Among the innocent victims of the Polish-Soviet imbroglio were Polish children who suffered an extremely high mortality rate in the Soviet Union. The Polish government, anxious to save the substance of its youth, proposed to evacuate 50,000 of them from the USSR. "A fantastic plan," Vyshinsky sighed when he heard it. And he reminded the Polish ambassador: "We are having a war by the way, and quite a hard one too." Kot, in one of his last meetings with Vyshinsky before he left the country, shot back that the Soviets had brought the children to the Soviet Union in the first place. Vyshinsky angrily replied: "You are heaping reproaches on us again." The Polish government was understandably concerned about the fact that the young Polish children, who were in centers run by the Soviets, would lose their Polish identity because instruction was given to them in Russian, not Polish. In desperation, Sikorski again turned to the United States to evacuate the children. Roosevelt, who took a personal interest in the matter, directed the State Department and Red Cross to try to get the youngsters, together with mothers and guardians, out of Iran once they got there. Thousands of Polish refugees, including children, were relocated from Iran to various parts of the world with American help in the following months. Although shipping shortages and immigration laws prevented large-scale immigration of Poles into the United States, Washington temporarily received 2,000 refugees into the country and loaned the Polish government $3 million to care for almost 1,500 more who went to Mexico in 1943. This was a fraction, however, of the nearly 100,000 refugees who by 1944 were dispersed throughout the world. By then there were heavy concentrations of Poles in Africa, especially Tanganyika, Uganda, and Northern Rhodesia. There was an ironic note to the Polish Diaspora too. According to one report:

In one spot in Tanganyika there was established a German Lutheran Congregation, with luxurious bungalows surrounded by beautiful gardens and orchards. It was soon discovered that these pious missionaries taught Negroes that Hitler is the only God and the Englishman the greatest devil. Now the Germans are in a concentration camp, and the bungalows are handed over to Poles, who are told to consider them as [the] first "reparations for destroyed Polish villages."

Far more impressive was American lend-lease aid to the Poles. Poland had been included under the lend-lease program even before the Soviet Union. Initially, the aid took the form of assisting the Polish training program that was carried on in Canada. Throughout the war the United States lend-leased articles of a military nature to Polish forces in England, the Middle East, and Italy. But the most unusual form of lend-lease aid to Poland was the assistance in feeding and clothing approximately 56,000 Polish prisoners of war held in Germany.

Since the beginning of the war, the British, and later the United States, had sent packages of food and other types of aid to their soldiers held by the Germans. But the Polish government-in-exile, hard pressed for funds, was unable to do so. The Germans exploited the situation, conspicuously pointing out to Polish prisoners that they had been abandoned by their government. After Washington learned of the problem late in 1942, the United States, with the help of the Red Cross, was able to furnish each Polish prisoner an eleven-pound food parcel every month and a complete set of clothing each year under the lend-lease program. The International Red Cross verified that the Polish prisoners of war received the goods.[39]

The end of relief activities by the Polish government for its citizens in the Soviet Union effectively came on January 16, 1943, when the Kremlin declared that all people who were present in Soviet territory— that is, land occupied by the Soviet Union—as of November 1939 were Soviet citizens. That also put an end to further evacuations of refugees, who were once Polish but were now considered Soviet citizens by the Kremlin.[40]

In retrospect, the destruction of the Polish relief organization in the Soviet Union and the subsequent Sovietization of Polish citizens in the Soviet Union appear to have been parts of Kremlin strategy to pressure the Polish government to recognize Soviet claims to eastern Poland, acquired by the Molotov-Ribbentrop Pact of 1939. The Soviet action of January 1943 dramatically revealed how far Polish-Soviet relations had deteriorated since the halcyon days of December 1941 when Sikorski had visited Stalin. Thus long before the public revelation of the Katyn Forest massacre in April, 1943 Polish-Soviet relations were at the point of rupture.

When the Kremlin granted its amnesty in August 1941, it made no distinctions among Polish citizens of different nationalities. Within three months, however, the Soviets, over the protests of the Polish government, differentiated between ethnic Poles and those of other nationalities. That meant that Jews, White Russians, and Ukrainians who were on the territory annexed by Russia in 1939 were now considered Soviet citizens and could no longer enlist in Anders' army. The Kremlin's action was intended to pressure the Polish government to negotiate a frontier other than the Riga Line between the two countries. The London Poles refused. When Sikorski saw Stalin in December 1941 he warned him: "One must not create 'faits accomplis' by force. Nobody in the West will agree to it." Sikorski's government, armed with American and British pronouncements of not recognizing territorial changes made by conquest, continued to oppose negotiations with the Kremlin on the prewar boundary between the two countries. The Riga Line "must not be questioned," Sikorski told Stalin.[41]

Meanwhile, the Soviets pressured Britain to recognize Soviet claims to the Baltic States, which created fear in the Polish government that its own interests would be seriously affected. Polish diplomacy successfully enlisted American help in preventing an Anglo-Soviet treaty that granted territorial concessions in the Baltic. Faced with setbacks in negotiating a postwar boundary with Poland and in getting the British to recognize its claims in the Baltic, the Kremlin confronted the Polish government and the West with a bold *fait accompli* in January 1943. It announced that ethnic Poles who were present on the Soviet side of the Molotov-Ribbentrop Line in 1939 were Soviet citizens.[42] The Soviet bombshell resulted in feverish protests and efforts by the Polish government to get the United States and Britain to denounce the Kremlin's unilateral action, obviously intended to force Sikorski to recognize its claims to eastern Poland. But this time Polish diplomacy failed to stir a decisive American or British response.

The Polish government, afraid that Britain would capitulate to Soviet demands for the acquisition of the Baltic States and areas like Bukovina, enlisted American diplomatic support to prevent the sacrifice of political principle to military expediency. The Poles opposed recognition of Soviet claims for practical reasons too. If the USSR succeeded in getting the Baltic States and slices of the Balkans, it would encircle Poland in the north and south and it would have an advantage in later discussions on the controversial Polish-Soviet frontier. Moreover, Soviet acquisitions north and south of Poland would compromise Sikorski's federalist plans for eastern Europe after the war. Sikorski, who once described himself as "the initiator of the federal conception in Eastern-Central Europe," saw a federation of states between the Soviet Union and Germany as a "natural rampart of security of Soviet Russia, always so uneasy about her Western security." As the nucleus of the federation a Czechoslovak-Polish agreement was concluded in London on January 23, 1942. The Soviets, predictably, opposed Polish plans because they understandably feared that the federation would be used against them, not the Germans. The Soviet ambassador to the Polish government-in-exile, A.E. Bogomolov, bluntly told Kajetan Morawski, Polish under secretary of state: "A time will come when the choice will be put before you: Russia or Luxemburg." Later, Bogomolov told the American ambassador to the exiled governments in London, Anthony Biddle, "Russia was utterly opposed to this idea, in fact Russia simply would not have it."[43]

Sikorski, convinced that Soviet military responses to the Germans in the winter of 1941–1942 emboldened the Kremlin to pressure the British to make concessions in eastern Europe, urged Britain to wait until the Germans resumed the initiative on the eastern front and then to extract concessions from the Kremlin. That is why he adamantly opposed the proposed visit of Molotov to England until military events on the eastern front were more favorable to the West. Sikorski told Eden on March 9, 1942: "I have not observed a decisive German defeat." So fearful was he that the British might sign away a large chunk of eastern Europe, Sikorski even threatened to release a "Red Book," then being prepared in the United States, which detailed alleged Soviet brutalities and cruelties to Polish deportees in the Soviet Union. Until then, the Sikorski government had not publicized Polish difficulties with the Soviets.[44]

Anxious to forestall a Soviet thrust for the Baltic States and perhaps part of the Balkans, Sikorski hoped to win the support of the leading states of eastern Europe to affiliate with a declaration of principles, similar to those of the Atlantic Charter, that looked toward postwar collaboration among them. Ambassador Biddle, who was against the Polish plan, informed the exiled governments of his views. He told them that Sikorski's plan had to be submitted to the "acid test"— namely, "could it in any way be construed by the Russians as a move directed against them in terms either of the near or long range outlook." The Czechoslovaks, with whom the Poles had long and tedious negotiations on a future pact, agreed with Biddle that any Polish-Czechoslovak agreement had to be contingent on friendly relations between Poland and the Soviet Union. Of all the exiled governments based in London, the Greeks and Yugoslavs were the most receptive to Sikorski's proposal of a joint declaration for the postwar status of eastern Europe. Both nations feared Stalinist ambitions in the Balkans, especially in Bulgaria.[45] Harry Hopkins, the president's advisor, told Roosevelt that Sikorski's proposal was "risky business." Roosevelt himself noted: "I think Sikorski should be definitely discouraged on this proposition. This is no time to talk about the post war position of small nations, and it would cause serious trouble with Russia." When he learned that Washington and London opposed the plan, Sikorski dropped it.[46]

It is not improbable that if the United States or Britain had supported a modest federalist scheme between Poland and Lithuania in return for Polish concessions to the Soviet Union on its eastern boundary, some basis might have been found for moderating Soviet acquisitions in eastern Europe during the early stage of the war.[47] Sikorski, who appears to have entertained the idea of such a *quid pro quo,* might have succeeded because federalism had a strong chance of winning over the conservatives to a plan that Piłsudski himself had espoused but had failed to achieve.

Polish anxieties about the implications of an Anglo-Soviet treaty gained intensity by the early spring of 1942, when Sikorski made another visit to Washington to assure himself that the president still believed that territorial questions should be deferred until after the war. Roosevelt reaffirmed the American position to Sikorski. The Polish premier had reason to be even more gratified to learn that later a declaration to that effect was made by the United States to Maxim Litvinov, Soviet ambassador to Washington. Roosevelt frankly told Sikorski that the Soviets should realize it was "premature to eat one's pie before it had been baked." Sensitive about the implications of an Anglo-Soviet deal on the Atlantic Charter, the president told Welles: "To enter this transaction would mean that I tear up the Atlantic Charter before the ink is dry on it. I will not do that."[48] All this allayed Sikorski's fears that the views of some high-ranking State Department officials, such as Assistant Secretary Adolf Berle, who forecast and endorsed a Soviet sphere of influence in eastern Europe, were representative of official American policy.[49] The Polish premier, who had left England depressed and apprehensive, returned "with a fresh outlook and reinvigorated" by his visit with Roosevelt.[50] He was convinced that now the United States and Poland were moving in lock step against wartime territorial revisions in eastern Europe.

When the Anglo-Soviet treaty was signed in May 1942 it did not include territorial clauses. That, of course, delighted the Poles, who attributed the final outcome of the treaty to the crucial role of the United States. During a conversation with Sikorski, Eden surprisingly gave the Polish premier all the credit for the way the treaty turned out. Sikorski said that Eden deserved "150%" of the credit for having the courage "to take a sharp turn." Eden replied: "Yes, but we succeeded because I took your advice. The Poles evidently know the Russians much better than we do."[51]

Polish euphoria did not last very long. By the summer of 1942 Polish-Soviet relations had deteriorated rapidly over Soviet policies regarding the supply and recruitment of Anders' army and the relief and care of Polish refugees. By August 1942, when the remainder of the Polish army had been evacuated and the Kremlin had virtually destroyed the Polish relief organization in the country, the Polish government sought renewed support from Washington and London. Churchill could not give Sikorski any encouragement. The British prime minister and the president of the United States had made two crucial decisions by July 1942 that they believed might threaten good relations with the Kremlin—namely, the suspension of convoys to the northern part of the Soviet Union because of the disastrous losses from Nazi U-boats and the postponement of the second front in Europe which Stalin expected and Roosevelt promised that year. In reference to a British intervention on behalf of the Poles with the Kremlin at that time, Churchill candidly told Sikorski: "I cannot risk a refusal." Churchill suggested that it would be easier for Roosevelt to intervene on behalf of the Poles.[52]

Sikorski put great faith in Roosevelt's ability to influence Stalin's behavior toward the Polish government. He told the commander of the Polish Home Army, or AK as it was known, "I hope to be able to convince Roosevelt of the necessity of keeping a joint and strong line of action with respect to Russia, should the latter try to infringe upon Polish territorial sovereignty." A few days later, on December 1, 1942, after a mishap that seriously damaged his plane, Sikorski came to Washington on his last visit.[53]

Although Roosevelt reiterated his friendly intentions toward Poland, there was none of the firmness and determination about the Soviet Union in Washington that Sikorski had witnessed during his visit in March. The Polish leader now had serious doubts about Washington's determination to deal effectively with Stalin. Ciechanowski, who accompanied Sikorski on his visits with various American officials, also shared the same doubts, observing that Roosevelt acted as if he were intimidated by Soviet military efforts against the Nazis.[54]

While in Washington, Sikorski specifically asked for an American endorsement of a resurrected Poland with its prewar boundary in the east, a Polish-Czechoslovak confederation and a future acquisition by Poland of lands at Germany's expense. Ray Atherton, acting chief of the European Division of the Department of State, deprecated Sikorski's nationalism and flatly opposed the restoration of the Riga Line, which he claimed would contain "the seed of continuing hostility between the Soviet Union and the new Poland."[55] All Sikorski was able to get from Roosevelt was an expression of American support for an independent Poland. Nothing was said about its future boundaries or its relationship to other states, like Czechoslovakia, in eastern Europe. In a letter to Sikorski on January 5, 1943, Roosevelt said: "I need hardly assure you of the determination of the United States Government that Poland be reestablished. This is implicit in Article 3 of the Atlantic Charter and the Declaration of the United Nations. The views of this Government moreover reflect the warm sympathy which the American people have always felt toward the people of Poland in their age-long struggle freely to organize their national life." And in order to offset Soviet claims that the Polish army in the Soviet Union had shown no desire to fight the enemy, Sikorski suggested that Roosevelt say something favorable about Polish military resistance. Roosevelt obliged with: "The magnificent and continuing resistance of the Polish armed forces and people to the German enemy in occupation of their country, and the Polish contribution to the prosecution of the war testify to the inextinguishable vitality of the Polish nation and constitute the best guarantee for the re-emerging of a strong and independent Poland."[56]

While in Washington, Sikorski repeated earlier Polish requests for six B-24s in order to carry out liaison between the Polish Command in London and the Home Army in Poland. Roosevelt was sympathetic, but the bombers were in short supply and the Joint Chiefs of Staff preferred that the Poles work with the British on the matter. Roosevelt suggested that the British give the Poles the six bombers out of nearly four hundred planes which were allocated to Great Britain out of American production.[57]

To Stanisław Mikołajczyk, who succeeded Sikorski as premier in the summer of 1943, Western responses to Polish pleas for diplomatic help against the Kremlin in 1942 showed that "appeasement of Russia grew by the hour in London and Washington." The London Poles, he complained, "were told not to make any move or release any statement that might anger Stalin or give him an opportunity to break off relations with the Polish government in London."[58]

Sikorski's difficulties were by no means confined to winning American and British support for his policies toward the Soviet Union. Sometimes members of his own government took actions which poisoned Polish-Soviet relations. For example, while he was in Washington, the Polish Council of National Unity passed a resolution which affirmed Polish commitment to the Riga Line. A few days later, the Polish minister of information, Stanisław Stroński, discussed openly in London Polish plans for federation with the Baltic States, which the Kremlin claimed for itself. Sikorski, indignant over such provocations at a time when Polish-Soviet relations slid dangerously toward rupture, fired Stroński. Even Ciechanowski, who had never been an enthusiast for Sikorski's Soviet policy, remarked that his compatriots had acted "as fools, more dangerous than the enemy."[59]

No sooner had Sikorski returned to his government than the Kremlin announced in January 1943 that all ethnic Poles in the Soviet Union were now Soviet citizens. The Soviet action put an end to all affairs involving Polish refugees in the Soviet Union—namely, further evacuation of deportees and relief efforts by Polish authorities. Biddle described the Soviet policy as *chantage*: the Kremlin was telling Sikorski, in effect, to deal with Moscow, not Washington, on Poland's future boundaries in the east.[60] Stalin had made it abundantly clear by then that he, not Roosevelt, was in the key position to determine Poland's future. Again the London Poles turned to Roosevelt and Churchill for help.

The United States and Britain believed they were at an extreme disadvantage vis-à-vis the Soviet Union to make an effective response to the latest Kremlin *fait accompli* concerning the Poles. Roosevelt told the Polish ambassador that the Soviet Union was winning battles, an obvious allusion to the Soviet victory at Stalingrad, while the Western allies experienced difficulties in North Africa. The time was not yet ripe for an American initiative, Roosevelt told him. He explained to Ciechanowski that the United States was reluctant to take an action that might be misinterpreted as American meddling in Soviet domestic affairs. At a loss about how to proceed without offending Stalin, Roosevelt asked Ciechanowski for suggestions. The Polish ambassador urged Roosevelt and Churchill to assert their principles and force the Soviets on the defensive instead of trying to find out what the Kremlin would do in a given situation before they acted.[61]

When the Polish government continued to press Washington to do something to help it, the president grew testy. Welles conveyed Roosevelt's admonition to the Polish government to "keep its shirt on." Washington, not Poland, Welles added, would be "the only judge" of what could be done to help in the crisis. Sikorski, who placed great reliance on Washington's intervention, stressed the need for it to act quickly because a delayed reaction would only "encourage the creation of accomplished facts detrimental to Poland's rights and interests and difficult to readjust in the future."[62] The failure of Roosevelt and Churchill to respond to the Kremlin's unilateral action, Sikorski complained, had serious consequences among the Polish people: "The difficulties thus provoked by the Soviets and the lack of appropriate reaction on the part of the great Allies are causing serious uneasiness and ferment in Poland and have deeply affected the spirit of the Polish Army."[63]

While Washington and London maintained their long silence about the Kremlin's Sovietization of Poles in the Soviet Union, Stalin kept the door slightly open to Polish-Soviet negotiations on the citizenship question. He suggested to Ambassador Romer late in February 1943 that Soviet officials might have gone too far on the citizenship matter and held out the possibility that individuals who found themselves in the lands occupied by the Soviet Union could decide what citizenship they wanted to claim. But Molotov, usually impatient when Romer sought clarification of Soviet policy on the question, suggested that the option of choosing either Soviet or Polish citizenship would be reserved only to people who were not permanent residents in the disputed territory.[64] That meant most Poles in the Soviet Union would still be considered Soviet citizens as far as the Kremlin was concerned. Polish-Soviet negotiations, extremely tense in the early months of 1943, dragged on without any prospect of resolution, convincing Polish officials that the Kremlin kept the discussions in progress on the controversial issue in order to stave off intervention by Washington and London.[65]

The Western capitals were fearful that a further deterioration of Polish-Soviet relations would occur if the Polish government publicized that the Kremlin had made Soviet citizens out of the Poles. Roosevelt personally asked Ciechanowski to tell his government not to release the information. Welles told the Polish ambassador that if the Poles publicized their problems with the Soviets, it would be more difficult for the president to intervene later. In England, the Foreign Office instructed the Censorship Bureau to refrain from discussing the subject of Poland's eastern frontier and to limit itself to publishing without comment statements issued by the Soviet and Polish governments.[66]

The Polish-Soviet impasse seriously undermined Sikorski's position. After all, his policy had been based on rapprochement with the Kremlin, and now he received much criticism from those who had opposed the 1941 agreement with the Soviet Union. One Pole was so distraught over Sikorski's conciliatory policy toward the Soviet Union that he challenged him to a duel. The criticism was particularly vocal within the Polish armed forces. General Anders, who had strong links with right-wing Polish leaders in London, wanted Sikorski replaced. Biddle observed that Sikorski held up well against the attacks because "he pictures himself returning to his country at the head of the Polish forces of liberation; hence he would more than likely recognize the importance of remaining Prime Minister if for no other reason than to ensure his remaining Commander-in-Chief." Sikorski's morale noticeably picked up after the publication of a cartoon in the *Evening Standard.* It depicted Sikorski as "John Citizen" standing over a Polish army officer aiming a machine gun in the direction of Russia. Sikorski stood over him, saying: "Hi! You can't do that there 'ere." Biddle saw Sikorski the next day and found the premier was uncertain at first if the cartoon had not taken a slap at him. After he explained the point of it to Sikorski, Biddle described the reactions of Sikorski and his colleagues:

> With an "Oh! I see," he turned abruptly to his associates, who still wore tense and decidedly dense expressions, and, before he could utter a further word, they had about-faced, and were scurrying off in a pandemonium of flying memoranda, and pince-nez's falling to the floor, to order the distribution of this cartoon throughout the Polish armed forces and political circles. I'd bet that, as a result, no issue of the *Evening Standard* has ever had such a notable and rapid rise in circulation.

Biddle conveyed his view, which proved to be incorrect, that the Kremlin would not press too far in its policy of antagonizing Poland for fear of causing Sikorski's downfall and ushering into power an intransigent Russophobe. But some State Department officials saw it differently. Elbridge Durbrow, for example, claimed that the Russians wanted to break relations with the Poles and to establish a Kremlin-controlled government in Poland.[67]

Neither Washington nor London showed eagerness to get involved in the Polish-Soviet crisis. The United States ambassador to the Kremlin, William Standley, cabled in March 1943 that an American intervention would only worsen matters. Some diplomatic officials in the Soviet Union believed that whatever the merits of the Polish case, Washington and London would not intervene by force on behalf of the Poles. Therefore, they even argued that the West should take a "realistic" approach and support the Soviets against the Poles.[68] By then Roosevelt himself had come to the conclusion that if the Poles got East Prussia and Silesia from the Germans, the Polish government would gain rather than lose by agreeing to the Curzon Line, now demanded by the Kremlin. In any case, during Eden's visit to Washington in March 1943 the president told him that the Big Three would decide what they considered was a "just solution" and Poland would simply have to accept it. Roosevelt, according to his friend and confidant, Joseph E. Davies, did not oppose what the Soviets wanted so much as their method of getting it.[69]

By the middle of March 1943 the Polish government concluded that unless the United States took a firm position with Stalin on the citizenship matter, the Soviets would increase their imperialism and Sikorski's government would collapse. To Sikorski, the situation was absolutely "hopeless" unless Roosevelt personally approached Stalin. Moreover, Polish officials no longer wanted to continue negotiations with the Soviets on the citizenship question because of their conviction that they were fruitless and harmful to Polish interests. The Polish government warned that it would terminate the discussions soon and Western intervention "alone can save the situation."[70]

To make matters worse, Polish-Soviet relations were further embittered over the arrest and execution of two Polish citizens, Victor Alter and Henryk Ehrlich, well-known leaders of the Jewish Socialist movement. The Polish government tried to get their release but failed. Ambassador Kot wired his government that without outside pressure, the Soviets would not release the men. Norman Thomas, William Green, and Mrs. Roosevelt took an active interest in the fate of the men. The Kremlin rejected American inquiries on the grounds that the Jewish leaders were not United States citizens. Norman Thomas told Hopkins: "Many Poles and Jews are much alarmed by this reasoning, which they believe denies the good faith of Stalin's assurances of independence to Poland." Releasing Alter and Ehrlich, said Thomas, was one of the few acts Stalin could perform that would abate suspicion and increase good will among large and important groups which make up public opinion in the United States and Europe. Kot reminded Vyshinsky about outraged Western opinion concerning the Kremlin's behavior in the matter and asked pointedly, "Will the common struggle against Germany benefit by it?" Vyshinsky declined to comment on the arrested men because, he declared, the Kremlin considered them Soviet citizens. Kot shot back: "Do you wish by any chance to annex Warsaw after the war? They cannot be your citizens, after all, being Warsaw town councillors, and in your prison already when you proclaimed the annexation of Eastern Poland." Neither the intervention of the Polish government nor of the United States did any good. The Kremlin executed Alter and Ehrlich in December 1942, and when the Polish government found out in March 1943, it protested to Soviet authorities.[71] Now the crisis in Polish-Soviet relations intensified even more.

By early April, Ambassador Standley changed his mind and advised that the United States government should intervene on behalf of the Polish government with the Kremlin. He declared that the London Poles had gone as far as they reasonably could with the Soviets and argued that if the facts concerning the Polish-Soviet crisis became public knowledge, Allied unity would be threatened. Finally, on April 8, 1943, after being bombarded by numerous Polish pleas to do something, Roosevelt promised Ciechanowski that he would send a special envoy to Moscow to try to improve Polish-Soviet relations. The President appointed Joseph Davies, former United States ambassador to the Kremlin and an avowed Russophile, to the job, but before he left for the Soviet Union in May the Kremlin had severed diplomatic relations with the Polish government.[72]

III

THE SHADOW OF KATYN

The Soviet Union had seized the military initiative on the eastern front at the Battle of Stalingrad, which ended in February 1943. The Soviet government no longer needed the support of the West to survive, though it still needed Great Britain and the United States to defeat Germany completely and to achieve its objectives in eastern Europe. No longer requiring the good will of the London Poles, however, the Soviet government could now even risk a rupture in Polish-Soviet relations which had seriously deteriorated by the spring of 1943. Almost anything could have triggered the final break. In April the Germans provided the catalyst which provoked the Soviets to cut off diplomatic relations with the Polish government-in-exile. Despite the efforts of the United States and Britain to try to heal the breach, Polish-Soviet relations were never restored again until an entirely new, communist-dominated government was recognized by the Soviet Union early in 1945.

Several times the Polish government had tried to find out from the Soviets what had happened to the 8,000 officers who had been confined in 1940 in prisons at Kozielsk, Starobielsk, and Ostashkov. Ambassador Kot did not raise the matter directly at first because the Soviet military had convinced him the Poles had a better chance of locating the men through army channels. When no positive results were forthcoming, Kot concluded that he had been deceived and brought up the matter with Vyshinsky and Stalin. Premier Sikorski pressed the issue in December 1941 during his visit to the Soviet Union. The London Poles also enlisted the help of the United States and Britain too. Even Mrs. Sikorski appealed to Mrs. Roosevelt to help. However, none of these efforts brought a convincing explanation of what had happened to the missing men. As early as the summer of 1942 General Anders confided to Field Marshal Sir Alan Brooke, chief of the Imperial General Staff, that the Soviets had murdered the men, a view shared by other Polish leaders.[1]

Polish suspicions about Soviet culpability were virtually confirmed in April 1943, when Radio Berlin announced the discovery of 3,000 corpses of Polish officers in the forest of Katyn and charged the Soviets with the atrocity.[2] The Kremlin promptly denied the allegation, but the Sikorski government asked the International Red Cross to investigate the matter. Stalin was furious with the Poles and told Churchill that the action was "completely abnormal and contrary to all the rules and standards governing relations between the two allied nations." Stalin promptly decided to "interrupt" relations with the Polish government. Churchill, explaining the pressures on Sikorski from those who claimed the premier had not reacted strongly enough to Soviet policies, expressed the hope that Stalin intended only to warn the Polish government, not to sever diplomatic relations with it. Churchill told Stalin that if Sikorski "should go, we should only get somebody worse." And he added: "The public announcement of a break would do the greatest possible harm in the United States where the Poles are numerous and influential." So anxious was he to avert a split that Churchill promised to censor the Polish press in Britain.[3]

Roosevelt, who had been out of Washington on a tour of war plants in the West, belatedly appealed to Stalin not to sever relations with the Poles. In his original draft to Stalin, the president had used the word *stupid* in describing the Polish action, but Hull edited it out before the message was sent to the Kremlin. Roosevelt made a special point of commenting on the large number of Polish Americans in the armed forces and told the Soviet leader that "the situation would not be helped by the knowledge of a complete diplomatic break between yourself and Sikorski." American Ambassador Standley and his English counterpart, Sir Archibald Clark Kerr, tried but failed to get the Kremlin to delay publication of the note severing relations with the Poles. Clark Kerr remarked grimly to Standley, "This is madness."[4]

Washington and London still hoped that if Sikorski denied the truth of the German allegation and withdrew his request to the Red Cross, Stalin might restore relations with the Polish government. Sikorski could not go that far. After all, there were many Poles in England and the Middle East who had relatives at Katyn. Moreover, many Polish military leaders, always an influential element in the determination of Polish policy, believed that Poland had been silent long enough and that it was time to stop hiding the truth about the Soviet government. But Sikorski, who now believed the cabinet had acted hastily, offered to broadcast a statement that his government considered its appeal to the Red Cross to have lapsed. That was unacceptable to the Soviets. Standley cabled that all hope of rapproche-

ment between the London Poles and the Soviets had ended when
Izvestiya (News), on April 28, 1943, published a diatribe by Wanda
Wasilewska, head of the communist-dominated Union of Polish Patriots, who accused the Polish government of being in league with
the Nazis and attacked Anders' army for anti-Semitism and coward-
ice.[5]

Leading American officials believed that the Kremlin exploited the
Katyn affair to establish its hegemony over Poland. Standley wondered
now if the Kremlin planned to surround itself with a belt of pro-
Soviet states in eastern Europe. Biddle put it more candidly: he believed the Soviets used the Katyn issue as leverage to get American
and British agreement to their territorial claims in eastern Poland.
Nevertheless, Biddle was angry with Sikorski's government for its
failure to consult Washington and London before releasing its communiqué to the Red Cross. That, said Biddle, "had unfortunately created the impression in my mind to [the] effect that when his
Government was making trouble it preferred not to consult us; when
it got into trouble it looked to us to get it out."[6] Davies was one of
the few American leaders who made it clear that his sympathies were
with the Soviets not the Poles:

> It is a devil's brew, out of which only good can come to the enemy, and pos-
> sibly much harm to the Poles themselves. Stalin has said repeatedly he wants
> a strong and independent Poland. Well he might come to the conclusion that
> there can be no strong, independent government, which is not controlled and
> dominated by Soviet haters who cannot be trusted to be fair or impartial. He
> cannot and will not permit on his border a State that is openly or secretly
> hostile to even friendly relations.[7]

Hope for Polish-Soviet rapprochement was bolstered when Sikorski
went on the radio on May 4, 1943, and stated that the Katyn tragedy
did not alter Poland's implacable hostility toward the Nazis and that
one of the guiding principles of his government was friendly relations
with the Soviet Union. The next day, Stalin, responding to questions
from Ralph Parker of the *New York Times,* stated that he wanted to
see a strong independent Poland reestablished after the war and echoed
Sikorski's sentiments that both countries should be friendly neighbors.[8] Lest anyone in the West get the idea that his statement was
intended to do anything more than to give the appearance of improvement in Polish-Soviet relations, Stalin had Vyshinsky a few days later
dredge up the controversial issues of the past that divided the two
governments,[9] thus confirming the first open split among the United
Nations of World War II.

Once all hope of healing the breach in the near future had dissipated, the Polish government wanted the United States to play at least a nominal role in looking after its interests in the Soviet Union. Washington and London played an Alphonse and Gaston act: neither government was anxious to assume the task for fear of getting directly involved in the Polish-Soviet dispute. Finally, the British persuaded the Australians to assume protection of Polish interests in the Soviet Union, but Sikorski emphasized the importance of American and British support to help the Australians in the task.[10]

As if to take the sting out of its policies toward Poland, the Kremlin announced on May 22, 1943, that the Comintern would be dissolved. The announcement came while Davies was in Moscow, originally sent there to improve Polish-Soviet relations, and he got credit for it. Davies was jubilant over the announcement. He indicated that it "was one of the most significant things that has happened during the war and one of the most valuable." He added: "It indicated a disposition of these people to play ball with those in whom they believe." Actually, the dissolution of the Comintern was totally meaningless. The functions of the Comintern were simply turned over to the Foreign Department of the Central Committee of the Soviet Communist party and George Dimitrov remained in charge. About the only tangible thing Davies came back to Washington with was the information that Stalin shared Roosevelt's desire to meet as soon as possible.[11]

Sikorski, convinced that the Soviets wanted to dominate Poland, asked Roosevelt and Churchill to help in bringing about a resumption of Polish-Soviet relations. Sikorski specified conditions he wanted the Kremlin to meet: to allow families of Polish soldiers abroad to leave the Soviet Union, to release able-bodied men from confinement, and to permit Polish authorities to resume relief work in the Soviet Union. The Kremlin revealed some but not all of its own conditions too: removal of key individuals from the Polish cabinet, suppression of anti-Soviet propaganda in the Polish press, and mitigation of the Russophobia in the Polish armed forces in England and the Middle East. There is no doubt about the depth of anti-Soviet feeling among Polish troops abroad. Bitter over Moscow's refusals to allow their families to leave the Soviet Union, they were at the point of rebellion in the Middle East in May 1943. So alarmed was Sikorski that he flew there to moderate the anger of the men.[12]

The State Department believed that an American approach to the Kremlin should avoid the two controversial issues in the dispute—the boundary question and the complexion of the Polish government. Hull felt that if the United States brought up these issues, the Kremlin would be encouraged to make even bolder demands. Rather, Hull wanted the American government to approach the Soviets to allow

Polish authorities to resume relief work in the Soviet Union on behalf of their citizens, to recognize racial Poles as Polish citizens, to permit nonracial Poles to opt either for Polish or Soviet citizenship, and finally, to evacuate orphans and families of members of the Polish armed forces who served abroad. This approach, Hull affirmed, was consistent with "the principles upon which we feel that understanding between the United Nations should be based."[13]

Ambassador Standley disagreed, pointing out to Hull that if the United States brought up the citizenship question the Soviets inevitably would bring up the Polish-Soviet frontier to which it was tied. "Our suggestions on the subject of citizenship relate to human beings—not to land or property," Hull snapped, declaring that the two issues should be separated. Moreover, Hull believed that a settlement on the citizenship question need not prejudice Soviet or Polish claims to the territories in dispute. The secretary of state was anxious to get the diplomatic wheels turning. And after the stunning news arrived in Washington on July 5, 1943, of Sikorski's death in a plane accident at Gibraltar, Hull told Standley that "it is even more imperative that we immediately take steps to make it clear to the Soviet authorities that we desire to assist in bringing about the resumption of relations between the Soviet Government and the Polish Government-in-exile." The British endorsed Hull's position and agreed that a joint approach along the lines he suggested should be made to the Kremlin.[14]

Stalin was in no hurry to receive Standley and Clark Kerr until August when he and Molotov listened to the Anglo-American proposals in silence. Obviously displeased with the Western initiative, Stalin did not reply to the proposals until the end of September 1943. The Soviet government angrily reacted to the Anglo-American proposals for settling the Polish-Soviet dispute, regarding them as unacceptable and implying strongly that Washington and London should mind their own business. The Kremlin regretted that the United States and Britain did not exert greater effort to prevent the hostile acts of the London Poles, considered that Soviet agencies adequately handled the relief needs of Polish refugees, and claimed that it never objected to the remaining Polish citizens in the Soviet Union leaving the country. As for the evacuation of orphans, who the Polish government alleged were not properly cared for, the Kremlin told Washington that it had "unreliable information." Regarding proposals on the citizenship question, the Soviets boldly declared:

> It is impossible, of course, to agree with arguments, such as those advanced to the effect that all persons of Polish nationality who were formerly Polish citizens and are now in the Soviet Union should be recognized as Polish citizens because they formerly were domiciled in Poland. Does the Government of the

United States of America consider as Polish citizens Poles who formerly were
domiciled in Poland, but who at the present time are domiciled in the United
States of America, any more than the British Government recognizes as French
citizens Frenchmen who are domiciled, for instance, in Canada?[15]

Washington had gone as far as it believed it could with the Kremlin.
Roosevelt bluntly told the Polish ambassador earlier that if Stalin
pressed for a rectification of Poland's eastern frontier, the United
States could not go to war with him over it.[16]

The Anglo-American proposals to the Kremlin came only one
month after the appointment of Stanisław Mikołajczyk, leader of the
Polish Peasant party, as premier of the Polish government. His appointment brought a political shift to the left in the Polish cabinet. Mikołajczyk's deputy, Jan Kwapiński, was from the Polish Labor party,
and the rest of the government had men of sufficient liberal tendencies
to offset the right wing, represented by the Polish president, Władysław
Raczkiewicz, and General Kazimierz Sosnkowski, supreme commander
of the Polish armed forces. In contrast to Sikorski's cabinet, the Leftist parties—Socialist and Peasant—in Mikołajczyk's government increased their strength from two to three representatives. The reactionary
National Democrats and the Christian Polish Labor party retained two
seats each. The number of nonparty members, however, dropped from
five to three members, and one of those was the foreign minister,
Romer. Anthony Eden, pleased by the changes in the Polish government, confided to Ambassador John G. Winant that "the reorganization of the Polish government was reasonably good."[17] Of the thirteen
members of the new Polish cabinet, there were two peasants, two
labor men, three professors, three newspapermen, one lawyer, one
soldier, and one career diplomat.

Mikołajczyk, a simple, direct man, had offered the olive branch to
the Kremlin shortly after he came to power, making a special point of
emphasizing Poland's commitment to democracy and following Sikorski's principles in foreign policy. On July 16, 1943, he declared: "We
sincerely desire good neighbourly relations with Soviet Russia." At
the end of the month, he again reiterated the Polish position in a
speech to the Polish National Council. Mikołajczyk's identificaiton
with Sikorski's principles of cooperation with the Soviet Union, her-
alded by Roosevelt shortly after the general's death,[18] obviously had
no impact on the Kremlin's consideration of Anglo-American proposals to reconcile the break in Polish-Soviet relations.

After the Hull-inspired initiative of the late summer had failed, the
White House had come to the conclusion that Britain, not the United
States, should assume the major initiative in trying to bring about a

Polish-Soviet agreement. Before the foreign ministers' conference in Moscow in October 1943, Roosevelt met with Hull and other advisors and revealed that he supported a Polish-Soviet frontier "somewhat east of the Curzon Line, with Lemberg [Lwów] going to Poland." He told his advisors that when he saw Stalin later in the year he intended to appeal to him to accept it on moral grounds, implying that Stalin had it in his power to do what he pleased in eastern Europe anyway. But, in any case, the president repeated what he had told the Polish ambassador earlier—that he had no intention of going to war with Stalin over Poland.[19] Admiral William Leahy, Roosevelt's chief of staff, shared the same awareness of Soviet power and the Kremlin's ability to draft a Soviet territorial map for eastern Europe: "It is inconceivable to me that Stalin will submit to the re-establishment of sovereignty in Poland, Latvia, Lithuania, and Estonia, and it appears certain that the Soviet Government with its superior military power and its possibility of making a separate compromise peace with Germany can force acceptance of its desires upon America and Great Britain."[20]

Again, before the meeting of the foreign ministers in Moscow, Hull affirmed the American policy on the Polish question by telling Eden that it was now a British problem. Eden, somewhat surprised, agreed but pointed out that he had always understood that Hull was friendly with the Poles and would support them at the conference. Hull agreed to support Eden after he introduced the subject during the conference with Molotov.[21]

The only part of the Moscow conference that dealt with the Polish problem came on October 29, 1943, and the discussion was brief. Eden, in accordance with his understanding with Hull, introduced the subject by expressing regret that the Soviet Union and Poland still did not have diplomatic relations. Molotov repeated what Stalin had said earlier—the Soviet Union wanted an independent Poland that was friendly to the Kremlin. But that was the problem, Molotov said, claiming that the Polish government was hostile to the USSR. Eden immediately indicated that Mikołajczyk wanted to restore relations with the Kremlin, to which Molotov replied that that was the first time he had heard of it. Hull, in sharp contrast to the initiative he had sponsored during the summer, was extremely reserved. He made only a few tepid remarks in support of a restoration of Polish-Soviet relations. Describing what he had said at the conference to Roosevelt, the secretary of state wrote: "I then said that when neighbors fell out without going into the causes of the dispute we nevertheless felt entitled to express the hope that these differences would be composed and the two neighbors would resume friendly relations." Hull

was greatly relieved that the Polish boundary matter did not even
come up at the meeting, a "Pandora's box of infinite trouble" as he
described it.[22]

When he returned home, the secretary of state found to his dismay
that the Poles did not join in the chorus of praise lavished upon him.
The Polish government, frankly displeased with the Four Power
Declaration that had been signed in Moscow, expressed its serious
concern that no steps had been taken by Hull or Eden providing for
Polish administration of territory liberated by the Soviets. Instead,
the administration of Poland would be in the hands of the Soviets.
The Poles had hoped, and made the request several times, that the
United States would send a military mission to Poland to avert a
Soviet occupation of Polish soil. Hull claimed later that he had raised
the question of Western forces accompanying the Soviets in the liberation of eastern Europe, but that the Soviets had refused.[23]

Ciechanowski told James Dunn, advisor on political relations in the
Department of State, that the Four Power Declaration was "equiva-
lent to delivering Poland to the USSR for immediate sovietization."
That was worse treatment than Ethiopia and Italy received, because
the Negus had already returned to his country and the Italians had
their own civilian administration, he added.[24] Mikołajczyk in one of
his sternest comments on American foreign policy during the war told
Biddle: "If it was right to proclaim the principle that the United
States would not agree to and would not recognize any territorial
changes made in the course of the war, it was inappropriate to assert
at the same time that the countries which had territorial disputes
would not recover sovereignty until the end of the war."[25]

The Polish ambassador to Washington conveyed to Hull in strong
terms the anxieties of the Polish government about what had been
done in Moscow and what might happen at the forthcoming meeting
of the Big Three at Tehran. Hull, at a loss to understand Polish dis-
satisfaction with the Four Power Declaration, claimed that it safeguarded Poland's real interests. It meant "everything to Poland in the
future," he asserted. On the basis of his conversation with Hull,
Ciechanowski now advised his government that Churchill, not Roosevelt, might be the key to a diplomatic initiative on Poland's behalf.[26]
H. Freeman Matthews, chief of the Division of European Affairs,
thought the Poles should have been grateful instead of critical of
Washington. Reacting to Ciechanowski's letter to Dunn, Matthews
said caustically: "This is pretty bitter stuff—and not one word for
Moscow Conf. or one word against the Nazis."[27]

The Polish government was in a panic over what Roosevelt might
do at the Tehran meeting. Mikołajczyk desperately wanted to see the

president and Churchill before the meeting: he telegraphed them while they conferred in Cairo with Generalissimo Chiang Kai-Shek. Neither Roosevelt nor Churchill wanted to see the Polish premier on the eve of the first Big Three meeting of the war because they feared Stalin might back down. Mikołajczyk was in despair, telling Biddle that "even a man condemned to death was granted a last word before the court." The Polish military even contemplated doing something desperate. General Sosnkowski told General Marian Kukiel, Polish minister of defense, that if the Big Three gave away Lwów, Wilno, and other parts of Poland to the Soviet Union, he thought the Polish Home Army should confront Moscow with a *fait accompli* after receiving the silent approval of England and the United States.[28]

Hull thought the Poles had overreacted and told Biddle to urge them to take a "calmer outlook." He also advised Roosevelt that the United States should encourage the Polish government to order an uprising behind German lines and to assist the Soviet army, an operation that the Poles had intended to launch anyway when circumstances were favorable. The secretary believed that a Polish uprising would give the United States and Britain greater leverage in dealing with the Kremlin on the Polish question. The Poles realized that they had no choice but to launch an uprising behind German lines in order to offset Soviet charges, repeated with monotonous regularity since April 1943, that the Poles were in collusion with the Nazis. But Mikołajczyk was upset to find that the Combined Chiefs of Staff would not make definite commitments to supply the AK with ammunition and arms because of Polish-Soviet tensions and the fear that the Poles would use the material against the Soviets. Instructions from the government to the AK, however, revealed that Polish underground units were ordered not to fight the Soviets.[29]

Neither the United States nor Britain had any illusions about the restoration of Polish-Soviet relations on the eve of the meeting at Tehran. The British had made it clear to Mikołajczyk that unless his government compromised with the Soviets on the boundary question, there was slight chance that the Kremlin would restore relations with it. On his part, Ambassador Harriman was doubtful that the Kremlin would recognize a Polish government that was not reformed to include Russophiles in it.[30]

By the time of the Tehran Conference, the United States had drawn back substantially from its earlier willingness to take initiatives on behalf of the Polish government in its dealings with the Kremlin. Washington was reluctant to act even as an intermediary now, urging Britain to assume that role because of its treaty commitments to the Polish State. American officials privately appeared to have come to

the conclusion that the United States could do little for Poland except exhort the Soviets not to be too hard on the Poles. As John
Gaddis correctly pointed out, the United States would not "fight
for self-determination in Eastern Europe. The one question still un-
settled was how to present this policy in the United States as anything
other than a violation of the Atlantic Charter."[31] Washington never
did find the answer.

In late November and early December 1943, Churchill, Roosevelt,
and Stalin met at Tehran, the first of three wartime conferences of
the great powers. During a dinner meeting on November 28 it was
Churchill who brought up the question of the Polish-Soviet frontier
after Roosevelt had retired for the evening. Churchill proposed a
formula which the British government had favored for some time—a
quid pro quo by which the Poles ceded land in the east to the Soviets
and received compensation in the west from the Germans.[32] It was
not until the tripartite meeting on December 1 that the wartime leaders tackled the Polish question. Stalin, echoing the familiar charge
that the Poles were in alliance with the Germans, demanded guarantees that Mikołajczyk's government would not kill partisans and
would stop its intrigues against the Soviet Union. He confirmed what
Harriman had reported earlier to the president: Stalin would not restore relations with the current Polish government because of its alleged pro-German and anti-Communist policies.[33]

After Stalin had finished, Churchill asked the Soviets to present
their views on the frontier question, and if a reasonable formula was
devised he would personally try to get Mikołajczyk's government to
accept it. If the Poles rejected it, the prime minister said he would
wash his hands of them. When the discussion turned to the Curzon
Line, Stalin showed great interest in the State Department maps
which showed the ethnic composition of eastern Poland. Roosevelt
was most reserved during the discussion, which Churchill and Stalin
completely dominated. Finally, Churchill offered a formula: the
Curzon Line as the Polish-Soviet frontier with compensation for
Poland to the Oder River in the west and also in East Prussia. Stalin
agreed, contingent on the Soviet Union's acquiring the northern part
of East Prussia.[34] In reality, Stalin wanted more than the Curzon
Line because he also claimed Lwów, which the Supreme Council of
the Allied Powers in 1919 left to the Poles. No definite understanding was reached concerning where Poland's western boundary would
be drawn—whether the eastern or western Neisse River.

Although Roosevelt maintained a curious silence during this meeting, he had met privately with Stalin that day and told him that he
agreed with Stalin's views concerning Poland's frontiers. Contrary to

what he had told his advisors before the conference, Roosevelt did
not appeal to Stalin on moral grounds to give Lwów to the Poles.
For domestic "political reasons," the president explained, he could
not actively participate in a decision at Tehran on Poland's boundaries. Roosevelt pointed out that he had six to seven million Polish
American voters whom he did not want to lose in the 1944 election.
Charles Bohlen, chief of the Division of Eastern European Affairs of
the Department of State, who was present at the Roosevelt-Stalin
meeting, believed that the president had made a serious mistake in being so candid with the Soviet dictator.[35] The president's revelations
meant, in effect, that Stalin was reasonably assured that he did not
have to worry about American opposition to the Curzon Line and
for that matter could probably depend on Roosevelt's reticence while
he settled other matters with the recalcitrant Poles. Eden, who had
been critical of Hull's behavior at the Moscow Conference, was equally
critical of Roosevelt's position on the Polish question at Tehran. Eden
complained that Roosevelt was so reserved on the Polish problem
that he was "unhelpful." The Poles, too, upset since the Moscow
Conference, were apprehensive that the Kremlin might interpret Washington's behavior as giving the Soviets a free hand in eastern Europe.
The Poles asked for, but failed to get, a statement from the United
States that it recognized the Polish government-in-exile as the legal
government of Poland.[36]

When Roosevelt returned from Tehran, he proclaimed his satisfaction with the results of the meeting but said nothing about the concessions he had made to Stalin on the Polish question. Despite the
loss of his longtime friend, Marvin McIntyre, the president was jocular
at his press conference on December 17, his first since the Big Three
meeting. The reporters asked banal questions and the president did
not offer any substantive information. The high point of the meetings,
according to Roosevelt, was that he counted 365 toasts at the banquet
hosted by the Soviets. "And we all went away sober," he quipped.
"It's a remarkable thing what you can do, if you try."[37]

After the Tehran Conference, the United States continued to be
reluctant to assume an active part in resolving the Polish-Soviet imbroglio, contrasting sharply with the American initiative toward the
Kremlin after the Katyn massacre. Roosevelt, convinced he had established rapport with Stalin, did not want to jeopardize the relationship
over an issue he knew Washington could influence only in a small way.
So sensitive was the president to Moscow's feelings in the matter that
Mikołajczyk's proposed visit to the United States was deferred several
times until Washington had no choice but to invite him finally in
June 1944 for fear that public opinion would conclude that the

Americans had abandoned the Poles. The White House scrupulously avoided any guarantees to the Polish government regarding its frontiers and restricted its role to a halfhearted offer of its good offices in resolving the Polish-Soviet dispute.

In the early months of 1944, Churchill, not Roosevelt, pressured the Poles to accept the Curzon Line, arguing that they would receive compensation in the west at German expense. On January 5 the Polish government issued a statement expressing its willingness to resume relations with the Soviet Union but not at the sacrifice of its eastern territory. Stalin reacted angrily to the Polish position, describing the Poles as "incorrigible" and "incapable of establishing friendly relations with the Soviet Union." Echoing a now familiar charge against the Poles, the Kremlin considered that they were equally incapable of fighting the Germans in Poland. The British continued the pressure on the Polish government to moderate its position, and by January 14, 1944, the Poles issued a conciliatory statement asking Britain and the United States to act as intermediaries in the dispute and holding the door open to discussions with the Soviets. The Soviet reply, Eden said, was "like a blow in the face." The Kremlin wanted the Poles to accept the Curzon Line as a condition for the resumption of relations. Churchill urged Mikołajczyk to accept Stalin's offer at least "in principle." On his part, the prime minister assured Mikołajczyk that he would ask Stalin to stop propaganda attacks against the Polish government and interference in the internal affairs of Poland. Mikołajczyk told Churchill that he first had to consult with his cabinet and government representatives in Poland, but he had a fairly good idea what their attitude would be toward accepting the Curzon Line. Mikołajczyk's primary concern was to determine if the United States would participate in and guarantee a settlement that might be worked out with the Soviets.[38]

Despite the fact that Roosevelt had implicitly gone along with the Curzon Line as the Polish-Soviet frontier at Tehran, Hull still proclaimed the official American policy line that there should not be Soviet territorial acquisitions by force. Secretary of War Henry Stimson told his colleague that the American position should be more "realistic" than that. Stimson claimed that if the Soviet Union took the lands up to the Curzon Line, and the Poles received compensation at Germany's expense, the Kremlin "might well think she had been more generous to Poland than anybody else. It was hard and an interesting subject and it shows what we've got before us."[39] Other State Department officials, though they often deplored Soviet methods, did not urge active American involvement in the dispute. Harriman did not think Washington could do any more for the Poles than it already was doing.

Adolf Berle, sympathetic to Soviet territorial claims, felt that the Soviet Union could show more "self-restraint" toward Poland. But Elbridge Durbrow observed that even if the Poles got lands from Germany, they still would lose more land to the Soviets in the east.[40]

Roosevelt was reluctant to go any further than to let the Soviets know that the United States hoped the Kremlin would open discussions with the Polish government and offered "its good offices." On January 18, 1944, Harriman conveyed the American position to the Soviets, who felt the time was "not ripe yet" for mediation. Molotov condemned the Mikołajczyk government for not dissociating itself from Sikorski's "fascist act"—i.e., the Katyn affair—and for not disavowing Russophobes like Ignacy Matuszewski, the former minister of finance under Piłsudski who wrote for two leading anti-Soviet newspapers in the United States. The Soviets now made it clear that they could no longer do business with the current Polish government and favored the creation of a new one, composed of Poles from Britain, the Soviet Union, and the United States.[41]

In the face of growing Soviet hostility toward the Polish government, the White House gave cautious responses to questions submitted earlier by Mikołajczyk concerning how much the London Poles could depend on Washington. The United States (1) retreated from its official position of settling territorial matters after the war and pointed out that it might be desirable for the Poles and the Soviets to settle their boundary dispute themselves, (2) suggested its "good offices" to the Polish and Soviet governments but was not in a position to guarantee any territorial settlement, and (3) supported Churchill's efforts to reestablish Polish-Soviet relations.[42] Whatever illusions Mikołajczyk may have had about American support for the Polish position regarding the disputed eastern frontier, Roosevelt's response should have put them to rest. The president had made it clear that the United States did not want to risk alienating the Soviet Union and therefore would not assume any other role but that of a neutral, and a tepid one at that, in the Polish-Soviet dispute.

The Polish cause was weakened further in the United States and Britain by the pro-Soviet policy of Eduard Beneš, the exiled president of Czechoslovakia. After the Soviet Union entered the war and Polish-Soviet relations deteriorated, Beneš abandoned his policy of close relations with Poland and strenuously courted the Kremlin with the objective of concluding an alliance. The British opposed Beneš' policy because it greatly complicated their efforts to mediate between the Polish and Soviet governments. To overcome British opposition, Beneš visited Washington where he received American blessings for the proposed Soviet-Czechoslovak alliance, concluded in Moscow in December

1943. American and British officials who favored close cooperation with the Soviet Union cited the Soviet-Czechoslovak Pact as proof of Soviet good will toward the smaller nations of east central Europe and inferred that if the Polish government failed to reach an agreement with the Kremlin the fault was obviously on the side of the Poles.

Meanwhile, while Churchill assured Stalin that the London Poles had not completely rejected the idea of making territorial concessions to the Soviet Union in the east, he pressured Mikołajczyk to accept the Curzon Line. At a tense and difficult meeting at Chequers on February 6, 1944, Churchill threatened Mikołajczyk that if he did not accept the line the Soviets wanted, then England and the Soviet Union would make a bilateral deal that would be imposed on the Polish government. Mikołajczyk, whose cabinet in London and representatives in Poland opposed acceptance of the Curzon Line, said he could not agree to it but suggested a demarcation line between the two countries until a permanent boundary was drawn at a postwar peace conference.[43]

Roosevelt lent his efforts to get the Soviets and Poles together by urging Stalin not to do anything hasty and by pointing out that if the Poles accepted the Curzon Line, there would inevitably be personnel changes in the Polish government who were so objectionable to the Kremlin. At the same time, the president told under secretary of state Edward R. Stettinius to tell the Polish ambassador before he left for consultations with Mikołajczyk that the Polish government should not make so much over the boundary issue, and that in order to mitigate Soviet suspicions the London Poles should promise to retire from office after elections were held in liberated Poland.[44]

Under the barrage of Anglo-American pressure, the Polish cabinet agreed on February 15 to the Curzon Line as a demarcation line, running east of Lwów and Wilno, during the period of hostilities. But it unwisely refused to cede part of East Prussia to the Soviet Union, as demanded by Stalin at Tehran. It also refused to make any changes in the cabinet. Mikołajczyk's government had gone as far as the major political parties would allow. On January 9, in a "Declaration Issued by the Political and Social Organization of Underground Poland," the major and minor political groups, except the Communists, who supported the government-in-exile, declared: "Only the nation, never the foreign agency, can decide about political questions." On February 15 the Council of National Unity in Poland told Mikołajczyk: "We object firmly to any discussions with the Soviets with regard to the revision of the Eastern boundaries."[45]

It was extremely agonizing for Mikołajczyk to compromise on any issue with the Soviets, let alone the emotion-charged boundary question. Mikołajczyk and other moderates in the cabinet were vulnerable to the extremists in and out of the government, especially the military, who hankered for the day of their return to the homeland. The moderates ever since Sikorski's day were understandably afraid of charges by the extremists of betraying Polish national interests. Though Mikołajczyk was a moderate he was not immune to the pressures of the right who might overthrow him.

Churchill, realizing the political difficulties that Mikołajczyk faced, proposed the demarcation line to Stalin, noting that the Polish government had made a major concession in no longer considering the Riga Line sacrosanct. He pointed out that the AK had been ordered to reveal itself to Soviet army commanders in Poland and to cooperate with them. Churchill assured Stalin that once diplomatic relations were established, the Polish government would include "none but persons fully determined to cooperate with the Soviet Union." Roosevelt endorsed the Churchill initiative, telling Stalin that it went "far toward furthering our prospects of an early defeat of Germany and I am pleased to recommend that you give favorable and sympathetic consideration of it." In order to make it easier for Stalin to accept the proposal, Churchill even told the House of Commons that his government endorsed the Curzon Line as the postwar boundary between the Soviet Union and Poland.[46]

Stalin rejected the Churchill proposal on March 3, 1944, in a note that Eden described as "discourteous in tone and abrupt in its misrepresentation of Polish claims." To Roosevelt, Stalin reiterated his stubbornly held position—the unequivocal acceptance of the Curzon Line by the Polish government. He observed tartly that even suggesting the demarcation line was "insulting" to the Soviet Union. Stalin told Harriman in Moscow what Molotov had suggested two months earlier: Poland should have a new government composed of Poles from Britain, the Soviet Union, and the United States. When Harriman demurred, Stalin shot back: "Poland needs democrats who will look after the interests of the people, not Tory landlords."[47]

Despite Churchill's pleas not to close the door to a settlement, Stalin with some justification accused the prime minister of welching on the Tehran deal regarding Poland's eastern frontier. In reply to the prime minister's statement that he intended now to tell the House of Commons that all territorial changes should be postponed until the end of the war, Stalin charged in one of the strongest and most undiplomatic documents of the war years: "I shall consider that you have committed an act of injustice and unfriendliness toward the Soviet Union." The Division of European Affairs of the State Depart-

ment, struck by the vehemence of Stalin's reactions, advised that
"the only positive course" for the United States to follow was "to
abandon" the London Poles and force them to accept the territorial
changes demanded by the Kremlin. It admitted, however, that the
pull of reality collided with the ideals of the Atlantic Charter: the
suggested policy "would expose this Government to the justifiable
charge of violating the principles for which this war is being fought."[48]

Churchill did not think there was any point for him and Roosevelt
to continue their correspondence with Stalin on the matter while the
Soviet dictator was so surly and "determined to find fault and pick a
quarrel on every point." Despite the low point in the West's dealings
with Stalin on the Polish problem, Churchill was still optimistic. "I
have a feeling that the bark may be worse than its bite," Churchill
told Roosevelt, "and that they have a great desire not to separate
themselves from their British and American allies." He advised Roosevelt that in the current situation, it would be helpful if Mikołajczyk
made his oft-postponed visit to Washington in order to "show the
Russians the interest which the United States takes in the fate and
future of Poland." Churchill tried to assure a skeptical Mikołajczyk
that there was even more support for Poland in the United States
than in Britain. "Is it so?" the Pole asked quizzically. Churchill urged
Mikołajczyk to go to the United States and fend off Soviet charges
that his government was composed of landlords and reactionaries.
Because the Kremlin was so sensitive to Western opinion, Churchill
warned that "the Poles must reckon with the possibility even of the
Soviets buying over Polish press organs in America."[49] Before Washington acted on Churchill's advice, an episode occurred which convinced
many people in the United States, especially Polish Americans, that
the administration had abandoned the Polish government to the
Soviets. That added special urgency for Roosevelt, so close to the
1944 election, to invite the Polish premier to Washington.

Since January 1944 the Soviets had made it clear that they wanted
to deal with a new Polish government, composed of Poles from Britain,
the Soviet Union, and the United States. The Union of Polish Patriots,
which claimed to be the true spokesman for Poland, was already
sponsored by Stalin in the Soviet Union. Its president, Wanda Wasilewska, had tried to establish direct contact with the United States as
early as June 1943. Stalin also had a Polish army, headed by General
Zygmunt Berling, that operated with the Soviets. According to one
high-ranking State Department official, there was "no justification in
international practice for one government to form an armed force on
its territory ostensibly composed of nationals of another state and to
send this force into battle under the flag of that foreign state without

the latter's consent."[50] By the spring of 1944 Stalin invited two well-known Polish American sympathizers with the Soviet Union for a visit to Moscow in order to lay the groundwork for a future new Polish government.

One of the men, the Reverend Stanisław Orlemański, a decent but naïve Catholic priest who was pastor of a church in Springfield, Massachusetts, was the organizer of the Kościuszko League, a leftist Polish American organization. Organized in November 1943, the Kościuszko League merged with a small Detroit group which called itself the "Committee to Combat Propaganda Inimical to the United States among Americans of Polish Descent." Stalin had every reason to be pleased with the Kościuszko League because it had formally resolved that the Soviet Union should have "what territories British and American authorities may regard as rightfully belonging to the Soviets." The league publicized its pro-Soviet program in *Nasz Świat (Our World)*, one of several Polish American newspapers in the United States.[51]

Oscar Lange, the other prominent Polish American whom Stalin invited to the Soviet Union, was professor of economics at the University of Chicago. Born in Poland, Lange had known Wanda Wasilewska since their student days. Lange, who was to become the first ambassador of postwar Poland to the United States, was one of a group of Polish democrats and socialists in the country who was critical of the policies of the Polish government-in-exile. Late in 1943, Lange signed an "Appeal to Reason" with twenty-nine other distinguished intellectuals and artists in which they expressed opposition to Mikołajczyk's policy on the question of Poland's eastern frontier.[52] Obviously, Stalin intended to exploit the reservoir of goodwill that existed among some of the Poles in the United States. Little did Stalin realize, however, that most Polish Americans, represented in the Polish American Congress that was organized in May 1944, were hostile toward the Kremlin and its policies toward Poland.

The invitation to Orlemański and Lange in March 1944 caused a stir in the State Department. Hull and his under secretary, Stettinius, thought that if the two Polish Americans went to the Soviet Union for political discussions, their visit would directly involve the United States in the Polish-Soviet dispute which Washington scrupulously wanted to avoid. Moreover, Hull told Roosevelt: "Their visit would be widely interpreted as the first step in this Government's abandonment of the legal Government of Poland." Yet, the State Department admitted that it might be "undesirable if not impossible" to deny American citizens permission to accept the invitation. Roosevelt allowed the two men to go to the Soviet Union as private citizens, but he made a

special point of emphasizing to Stalin that the United States assumed
no responsibility for their activities. There was an ominous sign for
the London Poles that while plans for the departure of Lange and
Orlemański were underway, General Berling conferred with representatives of the Union of Polish Patriots and the Polish army in Moscow
and talked about the necessity of establishing a government in Poland
that was representative of the people and armed forces.[53]

Lange arrived in the Soviet Union on April 23, 1944; Orlemański
came a few days later, flying over the famed Alaska-Siberia route.
Father Orlemański did not intend to stay in the Soviet Union as long
as Lange because he wanted to return to the United States in time to
offset the impact of the anti-Soviet Polish American Congress, to be
constituted formally in Buffalo, New York, at the end of May.[54]

Stalin gave both men a warm reception. Orlemański had the dubious
distinction of being the first priest to visit the USSR since the 1930s.
While in the Soviet Union, the two Americans visited Polish army
units, children's homes, and schools. They came away with the conviction that Stalin was sincere in wanting to create an independent
Poland. Lange, convinced that the Union of Polish Patriots was not a
Soviet puppet, revealed upon his return to America that Stalin preferred to see a coalition government in Poland which would include
some London Poles, like Mikołajczyk and Romer, and some pro-
Soviet Poles. Lange, who was the keener observer of the two visitors,
talked with Polish soldiers and learned that most of them admired
Mikołajczyk but did not care for other members of the government-
in-exile. Likewise, they did not particularly admire Wasilewska and
her cronies. Equally revealing was the fact that the Polish troops,
recognizing that some concessions in eastern Poland would have to be
made to Stalin, wanted to keep Lwów on the Polish side of any
frontier. Lange personally argued for including Lwów in postwar
Poland in his interviews with Stalin.

Apparently in an effort to use Lange to bridge the gap between the
London Poles and the Union of Polish Patriots, Stalin urged the professor to stop in London on his return home and to talk with
Mikołajczyk and other Polish leaders there. Before his departure,
Lange was asked by Molotov if his report on what he had seen in the
Soviet Union would influence Polish American opinion. Lange replied that Polish Americans had been "thoroughly prejudiced by
years of propaganda and will consider me a Soviet agent or communist." But, he added, what the Soviets did in Poland after they got
there could affect Polish American attitudes in a positive way.[55]

Orlemański, particularly impressed by the way the Soviets treated
Polish children, was so warmly received by Stalin that he came to the

conclusion that the Catholic church would have no problem with
the Kremlin in postwar Poland. He told an interviewer after he returned that he had gone to the Soviet Union without the permission
of his bishop in order to relieve him of responsibility. "I might [have]
come back a man or a goat," the priest said, "but I came back a man."
Although he had not yet seen the bishop, his parish had bought a new
bell and he thought that perhaps the bishop would come to bless it
and then everything would be fine again. But his bishop was very displeased. Four hours after Orlemański arrived in Springfield, he received
notice that he had been canonically suspended and was ordered to retire
immediately to a monastery of his choice. At first, Orlemański told
the bishop that he was not under the jurisdiction of the diocese but
under that of the Apostolic Delegate because of a document from
Stalin concerning the church that the priest originally intended to
convey to the Pope's representative in Washington. But Orlemański
published the gist of the document and later bowed to his bishop's
order.[56]

No event had unified Polish Americans against the Soviet Union
more than the Orlemański-Lange visit to the USSR. The newly organized Polish American Congress, which claimed to represent six million
such Americans, regretted that the American government facilitated
their venture "whose notorious un-American activities have been
condemned by every honest American of Polish descent." Orlemański
especially caught fire for his "unfriendly act" against the Catholic
church. The Polish American Congress dubbed his visit a plan "to
mendaciously represent several millions of Americans of Polish descent as idolators of Stalin." The Coordinating Committee of
American-Polish Associations in the East, the first major political
organization representing the opinion of Polish American communities in the eastern United States, sent a delegation to the State Department to protest the Orlemański visit. The Polish Roman Catholic
Union of America (PRCU) saw Orlemański's visit as both farce and
tragedy.[57]

The Polish government, too, reacted with hostility toward the
visit of the two men. Hull received so much criticism that he complained to Ambassador Andrei Gromyko that he spent most of his
time "defending Russia against the attacks" that followed in the
wake of the controversial visit. He admonished the Soviet ambassador: "If we are to go forward with the movement of international
cooperation to preserve peace after the war, it's highly important
that we should understand each other's situation and psychology
better." Despite the uproar of Polish Americans, Roosevelt seriously
considered inviting the Polish priest to the White House to talk with

him "off the record." A distraught Hull quashed the idea, telling
his boss that all the information Orlemański had was already in the
hands of the State Department.[58]

The angry outburst of Polish Americans about the Orlemański-
Lange visit strongly indicated that they felt the White House had
abandoned the Polish government-in-exile. The administration could
not allow these feelings to go unchecked, especially at a time when
the national elections were less than six months away. Mikołajczyk
had wanted to see Roosevelt before the president went to the Tehran
meeting, but Roosevelt, anxious to avoid a confrontation with Stalin,
told the Polish premier he could not see him until after January 15,
1944. Then Churchill intervened and asked Roosevelt to postpone
the scheduled visit until he had a chance to convince Mikołajczyk
and his ministers to reach an agreement with Stalin on the Curzon
Line, agreed upon by the Big Three at Tehran. As Polish-Soviet relations deteriorated in the early months of 1944, Hull advised the
president to postpone the visit indefinitely. In March, Mikołajczyk
persisted in his efforts, and again Roosevelt excused himself on the
grounds of having bronchitis and receiving Prime Minister John Curtin
of Australia. The earliest he could see the Pole, Roosevelt said, was
early May. By then the uproar over Orlemański and Lange convinced
Hull that Roosevelt should see Mikołajczyk. "Another postponement," he warned, "would tend to give credence to the various rumors to the effect that we are planning to abandon Poland for the
sake of placating the Soviet Union." The secretary of state worried
about the Polish premier's visit highlighting the meeting of the Polish
American Congress which might tend to indicate that the United
States identified with Poland against the USSR, but if the president
intended to meet Mikołajczyk in 1944, Hull thought it would be
better then than during the election campaign. The president agreed.
At the same time he extended an invitation to Mikołajczyk, Roosevelt
asked Harriman, who was on his way back to his post in Moscow, to
tell Stalin to give the Poles "a break" in settling the Polish-Soviet
dispute.[59]

The Mikołajczyk visit did not result in any new proposals for the
resolution of the Polish-Soviet dispute. Although Roosevelt at various times during his meetings with the Polish premier urged the
Polish government to compromise with the Soviet Union, he undermined his own advice by suggesting that the United States could and
would do more later in the war for Poland. The Big Three leaders
assured themselves that Mikołajczyk would not stir up a hornet's
nest while he was in Washington: Churchill told the premier to "play
straight" with the president and to refrain from political blackmail

on the eve of the presidential election. Roosevelt, in turn, assured the Soviets that as a condition of his visit, Mikołajczyk would avoid public discussion of the Polish-Soviet problem, even refusing to meet Polish American groups interested in the matter.[60]

Washington warmly greeted Mikołajczyk and from the president down the pecking order, government officials spoke with him on several occasions. Despite the long-awaited invasion of France, which occurred while Mikołajczyk was in Washington, the president found time to participate in conferences and dinners and even to engage in much small talk with the Polish premier and his delegation. This warmth and solicitude that official Washington showed the Poles was at least partially responsible for the conviction with which Mikołajczyk left Washington—namely, that the United States could be depended upon to lend its support for a fair settlement of the Polish-Soviet dispute.

Roosevelt told Mikołajczyk that the Polish government should make concessions to the Soviets because they could "swallow up" the Poles. Neither the United States nor Britain intended to fight the Soviet Union, the president declared. On the other hand, he took the Polish position of deferring definite territorial settlements with the Soviets until after the war when he expected to act as a "moderator" to effect a solution. Roosevelt conveyed the impression that if Mikołajczyk made some changes in the personnel of his government, that would be sufficient to pave the way for an understanding with Stalin who probably would not be so insistent about his territorial demands. At no time did Roosevelt unequivocally tell the Polish premier to agree to the Curzon Line, and he left the clear impression that he had even opposed that boundary at the Tehran meeting. The closest the President came to recommending the controversial boundary was when he told Mikołajczyk that he might be able to persuade Stalin to leave Lwów, Drohobycz, and Stanislawów in Poland's hands.[61]

After a dinner in Mikołajczyk's honor on June 7—attended by General Henry Arnold, chief of the Army Air Forces (AAF), and General George Marshall, chief of staff, before they flew to England to supervise the early stages of the invasion of France—Roosevelt listened raptly to General Stanisław Tabor, chief of the general staff of the Polish army, who had accompanied the Polish premier to Washington. Tabor in graphic detail described the operations of the AK. So impressed was Roosevelt that he thought cooperation between the AK and Red Army might be the needed step to improve Polish-Soviet relations.[62] Despite Tabor's efforts to get the Combined Chiefs of Staff to supply the AK with needed supplies, the Allied military leaders reiterated standing policy that Poland was in the Soviet

operational area and it was easier for the Soviets to supply the Poles.
When Tabor mentioned the subject of a general rising of the Poles
behind German lines, the CCS emphasized that its timing be coordinated with the Soviet High Command. But a few Americans, like General William Donovan of the Office of Strategic Services, favored the
use of bases in the Soviet Union by the AAF to supply the AK.[63]
Little did Donovan realize that in two months the Poles would rise
up in Warsaw against the Germans, and that the Soviets would deny
the use of their bases to the AAF until Polish defeat was a certainty.
The CCS did promise the Poles a $10 million credit to purchase sup-
plies for the AK, contingent on its cooperation with the Soviet army.[64]

   Although Mikołajczyk received no definite commitments from Roosevelt, the president suggested that although he could do nothing for
the Poles in 1944 because of domestic politics, he would be able to
take a more vigorous stand for Poland later. At one point the president
impulsively offered to send Stalin a cable, asking him to receive
Mikołajczyk for a frank discussion. Two days later he reconsidered
his suggestion and Beneš' name was offered as an intermediary.
Mikołajczyk's government was not fond of the Czechoslovak leader,
and the Pole did not accept the suggestion. When Roosevelt saw
Mikołajczyk on June 12, the president urged the premier to go to
Moscow to talk with Stalin and to remove some of the Russophobes
in his cabinet. He obliquely suggested that even though Stalin might
not insist on the Curzon Line, the Poles would get a good exchange
by trading land in the east for that in the west. Asked by Stettinius
after this conversation if he was encouraged, Mikołajczyk replied:
"Yes, I am." Two days later, Mikołajczyk asked Roosevelt whether
he could return again to Washington to discuss matters with him if
his talks with Stalin failed. The president replied expansively, "Of
course, my door is always open."[65]

   Mikołajczyk left Washington with the conviction, based on what he
had seen and heard in Washington, that the United States was for a
free and independent Poland, preferred to settle frontier questions at
the end of the war, and favored discussions between the Polish premier and Stalin. Mikołajczyk, heartened by the belief that Stalin had
failed to discredit the London Poles and to secure the collaboration
of enough Poles in the Soviet Union, told his representative in Poland:
"Russia's tendency towards normalization of relations with Poland . . .
will be probably reinforced by the support of Poland and her Government by America whose attitude she takes more and more into
account." Doubtless, too, the massive invasion of France at the time
of his Washington visit bolstered Mikołajczyk's conviction that the
West would no longer be at a military disadvantage in its political
dealings with the Kremlin on the Polish question.[66]

Not all observers were as optimistic as Mikołajczyk. Ciechanowski and Sosnkowski seriously questioned Roosevelt's sincerity about helping Poland, concluding that the president used the visit for domestic political purposes. Eden frankly concluded that Roosevelt had deceived Mikołajczyk: "The President will do nothing for the Poles, any more than Mr. Hull did at Moscow or the President himself did at Tehran." Churchill was put out with Roosevelt for inspiring illusions in the minds of the Poles. Roosevelt's messages to Stalin after the premier's departure sustained the skeptical assessment of Ciechanowski, Sosnkowski, Eden, and Churchill. Roosevelt assured Stalin that nothing had changed in American policy on the Polish question since the Tehran conference.[67]

If Roosevelt had dealt candidly with Mikołajczyk in June 1944, the Polish government probably would have been more resolute in trying to get the best arrangement it could with the Kremlin concerning the boundary question between the two countries. On the other hand, Roosevelt may have believed that later in the war, when Anglo-American armed forces made a larger contribution to the defeat of the Germans and Stalin was reassured that his security interests could be satisfied within a collective arrangement, he might be able to get the London Poles a somewhat better frontier with the Soviets than the one Stalin wanted. But Roosevelt never had intimated that he favored anything more than a modified Curzon Line. Roosevelt still hoped, because he had no other choice, to bridge the gap between American ideals and its ability to influence affairs in eastern Europe. To have suggested anything else would have undermined a major part of his policy and vision of the postwar world. In practical and immediate terms, it ran a risk of jeopardizing his reelection in 1944. Hull gave the most accurate account, as it turned out, of the spare results of the Mikołajczyk visit to a press and radio news conference: "There is not much to say on concrete questions except that there were no specific issues taken up for consideration. The Prime Minister made a thoroughly agreeable impression on all with whom he came in contact and he left that very agreeable impression with everybody here."[68] It was on that will-o'-the-wisp that the head of the Polish government left for England.

When Mikołajczyk returned to London, he resumed discussions, initiated in late May 1944 by Stanisław Grabski, a staunch supporter of the premier, with Viktor Z. Lebedyev, Soviet ambassador to the exiled governments in England. The talks started out hopefully enough, but the Kremlin's position noticeably toughened after Stalin had been reassured that Roosevelt had no intention of doing anything more than he had already done for Poland. Lebedyev presented a virtual *diktat* to Mikołajczyk: accept the Curzon Line; remove four Polish

leaders from the Polish government, including the president of the
Polish Republic; and form a new government with Poles from London,
the United States, the Soviet Union and the newly created *Krajowa
Rada Narodowa* (National Council of the Homeland), which was a
communist-dominated parliament in Poland. Finally, the new government should condemn Sikorski's government for its policy in the
Katyn affair. Mikołajczyk laughed when Lebedyev presented the last
demand because the premier was a member of the government the
Kremlin now asked him to denounce. Mikołajczyk immediately broke
off discussions.[69] One historian has suggested that the collapse of the
Lebedyev-Mikołajczyk talks ended the last chance for "an accom-
modation between Russia and the Polish government in exile."[70] The
facts suggest, however, that the London Poles received one year later
what the Kremlin had offered in May 1944.

Meanwhile, the *Krajowa Rada Narodowa,* constituted in January
1944, became more prominent in the eyes of the Kremlin. It even
asked for diplomatic relations with and military aid from Washington,
but the United States refused. The Communist Poles, obviously getting their signals crossed with the Soviets, even asked that an American military observer be sent to Poland. Molotov quickly amended the
Polish request to the effect that the *Krajowa Rada Narodowa* only
wanted a Soviet military mission attached to it. By July 1944 the
Soviets played up the resistance work of the *Rada* and repeated their
claims that the AK did nothing against the enemy. Then on July 21,
1944, the Kremlin announced the creation of the Polish Committee
of National Liberation at Chelm, which later transferred its activities
to Lublin. It was to this Lublin Committee, as it was called, that Stalin
gave the administration of Polish lands liberated by Soviet armies. Although the Lublinites were not yet considered a government by the
Kremlin, Stalin told Churchill that "it is possible that in the future it
will serve as a kernel for the formation of a provisionary Polish government from democratic forces." By the time the Warsaw Poles rose
up against the Germans in anticipation of the Soviet army, members
of the Lublin Committee had installed themselves in the building of
the former Polish Embassy in Moscow, a bizarre clue to its metamorphosis six months later into a provisional government of Poland.[71]

IV

THE WARSAW UPRISING

The destruction of twenty-five German divisions in Belorussia in June and July of 1944 opened the path for the Soviets into Poland. The rapid Soviet drive westward, which brought some units to the eastern bank of the Vistula by the end of July, and the evacuation of German civilians and soldiers from Warsaw gave rise to speculation that the city would soon be in Soviet hands. Varsovians, eager to revenge themselves against the people who had occupied them for five years, heard several Moscow radio broadcasts urging them to rise up. The Polish government saw the impending entry of Soviet troops into Warsaw as an opportunity to assert its political control over the capital through its military and political representatives on Polish soil, thus confronting the Kremlin with a *fait accompli.* The Home Army rose up against the Germans on August 1, and the Soviets halted their advance at the Vistuala, claiming for the next six weeks that they were unable to help the Poles.

The Warsaw Uprising revealed how far apart the White House and the Kremlin were on the question of Polish self-determination. The United States, reacting to strong public pressure, tried to get the use of Soviet bases for the Army Air Forces, essential for shuttle operations from England to Warsaw. But the Soviets refused to give their permission until Polish capitulation was a virtual certainty. The United States, however, did send the largest relief mission of any of the Big Three nations, but it proved to be too little too late.

After the Mikołajczyk government assumed power, it told the AK that if the Soviets entered Poland without prior agreement with the London Poles, an uprising was authorized only if substantial Anglo-American help was in the offing. Otherwise, only diversionary and sabotage activities–code named *Burza* or "Tempest"—would be launched against the Germans as they retreated from Poland. And if normal relations existed between the Polish and Soviet governments, then *Tempest* would be conducted in cooperation with the Soviets. But in no case did Mikołajczyk's government want the AK to face the Germans in an armed struggle if the Soviet government was hostile to the London Poles. This merely affirmed what Sikorski had once told the former chief of the AK: "If the Soviet attitude to us should show itself to be openly hostile, I will only order the coming out of the civil authorities, withdrawing all our armed forces to the heart of the country to avoid their destruction by the Russians."[1] Thus in the absence of diplomatic relations between the London Poles and Stalin, the AK was to confine itself to sabotage and diversionary activities against the Germans and not to expose itself to the Soviets. But General Tadeusz Bór-Komorowski, head of the AK, disagreed. Violating the instructions of his government, he ordered his commanders to come out into the open after taking part in actions against the retreating Germans. Admitting that his order was at variance with his government's, Bór saw "no reason to create a vacuum on Polish territory as a result of military inaction in the face of the Russians by the [Home] Army, which represents Poland and her legal authorities."[2]

Ever since the fall of 1943 the AK had operated under the *Tempest* directive, which did not originally envisage an insurrection in Warsaw itself because of the understandable concern for defenseless civilians and the numerous historic buildings which made the ancient city one of the most beautiful in eastern Europe. Premier Mikołajczyk even tried at one point to work out arrangements to make Warsaw an open city. In the event of Nazi disintegration in the east, however, the *Tempest* plan allowed the AK to rise up and control "at least part of the country." The appraisal of the possibilities would be up to officials in Poland, but "the final decision and selection of the moment was up to the Government." Until July 1944 arms and ammunition needed for *Tempest* operations in the east were even taken from available stocks in the capital.[3]

But by the middle of July the concatenation of military and political events had created a different situation. For some time before the summer of 1944, Radio Moscow had urged the Poles to rise up against the Germans. But the appeals that came during the last days of July, when Soviet forces were at the Vistula, had special significance. On July 25 the Union of Polish Patriots in a broadcast from Moscow stated: "The Polish Army . . . calls on the thousands of brothers thirsting to fight, to smash the foe before he can recover from his defeat . . . . Every Polish homestead must become a stronghold in the struggle against the invaders. . . . Not a moment is to be lost."[4] On July 29, the day the Soviets formally announced the shelling of Praga, a Warsaw suburb on the eastern bank of the Vistula,

Radio Moscow broadcast: "Fight the Germans. No doubt Warsaw already hears the guns of the battle which is soon to bring her liberation. Those who have never bowed their heads to the Hitlerite power will again, as in 1939, join battle with the Germans, this time for the decisive action." Again the next day, another impassioned plea, repeated several times on the Soviet-sponsored broadcasting station, "Kościuszko," called the Poles to arms:

Warsaw trembles from the roar of guns. The Soviet Armies are pushing forward and are near Praga. They come to us to bring us liberation. The Germans, when pushed out from Praga, will attempt to hold Warsaw and will try to destroy everything. In Bialystok they sacked everything for six days. They murdered thousands of our brothers. We must do everything to avoid a repetition of these horrors on Warsaw. People of Warsaw, to arms! The whole population should gather round the National Council and underground army. Attack the Germans. Stop the Germans destroying public buildings. Assist the Red Army in crossing the Vistula. Give it information and show it the best fords. The more than a million inhabitants ought to become an army of a million men fighting for liberation and destroying the German invaders.[5]

Even Churchill declared before the House of Commons that this was "a hopeful moment for Poland." After relating to the House the efforts of the British and American governments to promote Mikołajczyk's early August visit to Stalin, Churchill was almost ecstatic:

The Russian Armies now stand before the gates of Warsaw. They bring the liberation of Poland in their hands. They offer freedom, sovereignty and independence to the Poles. They ask that there should be a Poland friendly to Russia. This seems to me very reasonable, considering the injuries which Russia has suffered through the Germans marching across Poland to attack her. The Allies would welcome any general rally or fusion of Polish Forces, both those who are working with the Western Powers and those who are working with the Soviet. We have several gallant Polish divisions fighting the Germans in our Armies now and there are others who have been fighting in Russia. Let them come together. We desire this union and it would be a marvelous thing if it could be proclaimed, or at least its foundations laid, at the moment when the famous capital of Poland, which so valiantly defended itself against the Germans, has been liberated by the bravery of the Russian Armies.[6]

The apparent congruence of military and political factors convinced Bór's key lieutenants that Warsaw was ripe for a rising. During the last part of July, Bór's chief of staff, General Tadeusz Pełczyński (or "Grzegorz" as he was known), his chief of operations, General Leopold Okulicki, and also from the operations division of Bór's staff, Colonel Józef Szostak met secretly and agreed to approach Bór concerning the necessity to initiate hostilities in Warsaw. On July 21, a fateful meeting took place. Bór, Okulicki, and Pełczyński agreed that an uprising in Warsaw should take place, establishing Polish sovereignty over the capital before the Soviets arrived.[7] Okulicki, having earlier convinced Pełczyński of the desirability of the plan, took the initiative and convinced Bór at the crucial meeting. On that day Bór sent the first of several momentous messages to London. In this one he predicted a German collapse in the east and revealed that he had ordered the AK to be in a state of military readiness, effective July 25.[8] Meanwhile Bór and Jan Jankowski, the government plenipotentiary for the homeland, had sounded out members of the Council of National Unity. Two questions were asked: First, did the members believe that the AK should anticipate the Soviet armies by taking possession of the capital? The council unanimously agreed that the AK should take Warsaw before the Soviets did. Second, how much time should transpire between the seizure of the capital and the entry of the Soviets? The council recommended that at least twelve hours were necessary so that civilian authorities could begin their duties. The answers to these questions were crucial to Bór. After that, to him it was only a matter of selecting the hour for the uprising.[9]

The Germans were well aware of an impending upheaval. The Poles openly advertised it, repeating to the Germans: "The day is coming." Through its own network of informers, the Gestapo had been apprised of AK plans and preparations. In an effort to crush Polish hopes that they would be able to assist the Soviets from within the city, the Germans went on a spree of arrests, deportations, and executions. And just a few days before the uprising actually occurred, the Germans found an AK cache of 40,000 grenades, which reduced the number available to units on the day of the uprising by half. But most Poles, in anticipation of liberation, continued to train themselves in the use of weapons and ammunition. People who had never had military experience gathered in private homes, six or seven to a group, once a week. One man, for example, stood in front of a mirror for hours to see how he was demonstrating the use of a rifle; he did this repeatedly so he would be flawless in making a presentation to a group of neophytes.[10]

The imminence of a German collapse on the Vistula and an uprising of the AK brought the Poles to the most important stage in their struggle against the Germans since 1939. It required full discussion and investigation by Polish political and military officials in London and Warsaw. Unfortunately, it did not receive that kind of treatment in either place. The supreme commander of the Polish armed forces, General Kazimierz Sosnkowski, was not even in London at the time.

Instead, he was in Italy visiting Polish troops who fought alongside the British there and holding meetings with other generals. Despite the appeals of his chief of staff, General Stanisław Kopański, to return immediately to London, Sosnkowski refused. Had he returned, he might have used his considerable influence and intelligence to sway the Polish cabinet, and especially Mikołajczyk, not to sanction the uprising so quickly. He might have failed in his efforts, but he did not try.

Sosnkowski was a brilliant man. He had the intellectual's gift to see the subtleties and complexities of varying points of view but he did not always display the decisiveness and determination that a commander-in-chief must have in large measure to be successful. At no time did he categorically order Bór and his lieutenants to stop plans for an uprising in Warsaw. Fluent in several languages, including English, and well read in literature and philosophy, Sosnkowski had an Olympian detachment about himself that seemed to yearn for a quieter, more intellectual life. Vastly different from Mikołajczyk, of whom he was not fond, Sosnkowski was a follower of the Piłsudski political school and shared the suspicion and hatred of Soviets the old Polish dictator had. Stalin, well acquainted with Sosnkowski, wanted him removed from the Polish government.

Deluding himself that he could influence developments from Italy, Sosnkowski, still unaware of Bór's alarm order of July 25, drafted a message intended for the AK chief on the same day, telling him to divide his forces into two groups; one was to remain in Warsaw and act as a conspiratorial underground against the Communists, the second should retire southwest and be in position to continue fighting. When the message arrived in London for retransmittal to Warsaw, Kopański was told by President Raczkiewicz not to send it because Sosnkowski's instructions contradicted the position the government had already decided upon. Sosnkowski wrote another message for Bór on July 28 in which he affirmed that an uprising in Warsaw would be an act without political value, requiring unnecessary sacrifices. This message arrived and was decoded in London only hours before the uprising began. Even if the message had arrived earlier, it is unlikely that the Polish government in London would have forwarded it to Warsaw in view of its July 25 authorization of the uprising. Sosnkowski believed in an inevitable conflict between the Soviet Union on the one hand and the United States and Britain on the other, and he therefore desired to husband Polish forces abroad for their eventual return to liberate the homeland. That is why he urged the evacuation of Poles, especially younger ones, by way of Hungary and Slovakia so that this "biological substance" would return Piłsudski-style to Poland.[11]

Meanwhile Bór advised London on July 26: "We are ready to fight for Warsaw at any moment. I will report the date and hour of the beginning of the fight." Bór also asked matter-of-factly that the Polish Parachute Brigade be dropped and that RAF attacks be launched against German airfields near Warsaw.[12] This notion was the product of ineffective military coordination between the Polish military staffs in Warsaw and London. Ever since 1941, when the first plan for a general uprising in Poland had been drafted, the idea persisted in the AK that it could expect parachute drops and air support from the West. These exaggerated expectancies had never been decisively quashed by Polish officials in London until the eve of the uprising, and even then, the London Poles were not categorical in relating this information to Warsaw.[13]

The cabinet decision reached in London on July 25 did not reach Jankowski, plenipotentiary for the homeland, until July 28. The London Poles had granted Jankowski plenipotentiary power to decide, without consultation with the Polish government in London, when to launch the uprising. The next day Jankowski, who was as uncompromising as Bór in his dislike of the Soviets, learned of the premier's trip to Moscow. Bór ordered his impulsive commander in Warsaw, General Antoni Chruściel, or "Monter" as he was known in the underground, to be in a state of readiness by July 30.[14]

But during the morning of July 30 Bór displayed a very cautious attitude. The Soviets, he said, were not in Praga, a Warsaw suburb on the east bank of the Vistula. Colonel Janusz Bokszczanin and Colonel Kazimierz Pluta-Czachowski, both members of his staff, supported Bór by urging restraint. Bokszczanin wanted to wait at least until the Soviet artillery opened up on the city; Pluta-Czachowski pointed out that the Poles should rise up only after they had evidence of a Soviet crossing of one of the Vistula bridges. Even intelligence officers under Colonel Kazimierz Iranek-Osmecki, head of Bór's intelligence division, warned against the rising in view of German strength in the area. In the meantime, a Polish courier, Lieutenant Jan Nowak, parachuted into Warsaw with an important message: none of the outside support Bór had asked for earlier from London—namely, operations by Polish fliers in RAF units over Warsaw and landings by the Polish Parachute Brigade—was possible.[15]

The London government forced Bór and his staff, the group in the worst possible place to evaluate objectively the international situation, to make the crucial decision whether to rise up against the Germans.

The two most important leaders of the government were not even in London: Mikołajczyk was en route to Moscow and Sosnkowski was curiously reluctant to return from his visit to Italy. This conspicuous absence of leadership in the Polish government was to take a heavy toll.

After the cabinet decision of July 25, it became a matter of vital urgency for the premier to fly to Moscow and work out some kind of rapprochement with Stalin concerning the future of Poland. A successful grab by the AK for Warsaw while Mikołajczyk was conversing with Stalin was the kind of spectacular gambit that the Poles were so inclined to make. More importantly, it was the kind of thing that would vastly improve Mikołajczyk's bargaining power with Stalin.

While his comrades agonized over the timing of the rising, Mikołajczyk, appearing outwardly calm and self-possessed, departed London for Moscow via Cairo and Tehran. While at Cairo the premier met Tomasz Arciszewski, venerable leader for forty years of the Polish Socialists, who had been flown out of Poland clandestinely. They exchanged a few words and flew off in different directions— Arciszewski to England and Mikołajczyk to the Soviet Union. Mikołajczyk was accompanied by Stanisław Grabski, an aging academician, who served as speaker of the Polish parliament, and Tadeusz Romer, the Polish foreign minister. Mikołajczyk was confident that he had the strong support not only of Great Britain but also, on the basis of the very warm treatment he received on his visit to Washington in June, of the United States. Greatly encouraged by Churchill's and Roosevelt's messages to Stalin on behalf of the London Poles, Mikołajczyk arrived in Moscow on July 30 and met Molotov that evening.[16]

"Why did you come here?" Molotov asked icily. "What have you got to say?" The premier explained that he had come to see Stalin to discuss problems involved in fighting the Germans and to explore the possibilities of closer collaboration between the Soviet army and the AK. Molotov was aloof. But he admitted that the Soviets were only six miles away from Warsaw which, he asserted, would be taken soon. That revelation warmed Mikołajczyk, confirming the wisdom of his government's decision made only five days before. Then Molotov tried to get Mikołajczyk to see the Lublin Committee. "I can see them. But that is an internal question concerning only Poles," Mikołajczyk replied. "I'm here as Prime Minister of the Polish government to see the Prime Minister of Soviet Russia." The meeting ended as abruptly as it began.[17]

At ten o'clock the next morning, July 31, the high command of the AK assembled for its first staff meeting of the day. On the basis of the discussions at that time, Bór's staff was divided on the timing of the upheaval. Some wanted to initiate the uprising immediately, others urged delay. Bór asked the members of his staff whether the time for the uprising had arrived. They were to reply with a single *tak* (yes) or *nie* (no). Only three of the seven members who voted believed the time had come—General Okulicki, Colonel Szostak, and Colonel Jan Rzepecki. The others—Colonels Iranek-Osmecki, Chruściel, Bokszczanin, and Pluta-Czachowski—did not think so. Bokszczanin was the only high-ranking staff officer who warned Bór that the Soviets might stop at the Vistula. He urged Bór to choose a time for the rising when the Soviets were fully committed to the battle for Warsaw. When the meeting ended at noon, it seemed unlikely that there would be an uprising the next day.

In the meantime, Bór informed Jankowski and Kazimierz Pużak, chairman of the Council of National Unity, and a few other government leaders about the situation. German strength was still great, he explained, and the Polish munitions shortage militated against more than four days of resistance. The political leaders accordingly urged restraint. Thus for a brief afternoon the planned uprising appeared more remote than ever.

However, at a 5:00 P.M. staff meeting, attended only by Bór, Pelczyński, and Okulicki, Bór abruptly changed his mind. Chruściel had rushed into the meeting with an erroneous report that Soviet forces were in Praga and that they had already taken Radzymin and Wołomin. Without confirming Chruściel's report and despite the fact that several of his officers opposed the uprising, Bór hastily arranged a meeting with Jankowski to secure his approval for the rising. Jankowski listened respectfully until Bór made his presentation. Then he asked members of Bór's staff a few questions. Jankowski could do little but accept the faulty intelligence estimate of German and Soviet operations near Warsaw. Then he turned and simply said: "Very well, then, begin." The fate of one million people hung on that simple sentence. Bór ordered Chruściel: "Tomorrow, at seventeen hours [5:00 P.M.] precisely, you will start operation *Tempest* in Warsaw."

After this decision had been reached, Bór's intelligence chief, Colonel Iranek-Osmecki, presented hard evidence that the Germans were massing for a counterattack against the Soviets. Bór curiously ignored the information and fatalistically remarked: "It is done. It's too late already to change the decision." Later, Pluta-Czachowski reported to Bór that a German counterattack against the Soviets at Modlin had begun. Again Bór refused to change the order. When Colonel Szostak arrived later and heard the fateful order, he pointedly asked Bór why he had ignored the evidence which suggested a continuation of his wait-and-see policy, which was significant because Szostak had earlier endorsed an immediate rising. Bór lamely said he could not wait any longer to take the city before the Soviets arrived.[18] There was no turning back.

For years the Poles had plans for an uprising that included an upheaval in Warsaw. Developed by General Stefan Rowecki, Bór's predecessor, and Sikorski, the plan called for the destruction of German administrative, police, and army units, the capture of military warehouses, the occupation of the city and suburbs, the seizure of such key centers as railroad stations, bridges, radio stations, and public utility buildings. The plan also called for defensive lines to the east of Praga and on the west bank of the Vistula to seal off the city. It was an ambitious plan, and naïve, too, because it assumed American and English help, especially airpower, and aid from Polish forces fighting in the West. The plan, which would have tested the strength of several well-armed divisions, called for a surprise attack against the most critical objectives first and later, after the Poles captured enemy arms and ammunition, against more strongly fortified objectives. As George Bruce pointed out, "the uprising was first and foremost an 'equipment action'; and only secondly a battle for vital objectives."[19]

After the main forces completed their fighting inside the capital, they were supposed to defend Praga and the west bank of the river while reserves assembled for action to the north and west of the city. Of crucial importance were, of course, the efforts to prevent the Nazis from entering the city after the uprising began. And to that end Bór and his staff issued orders for the construction of antitank barricades at all important road junctions and access roads to Warsaw.[20] The plan for an uprising in the city had always been contingent on the collapse of the Germans on the eastern front. But as the Poles tragically found out, that was not the case.

On August 1, 1944, the AK rose up in Warsaw. The Warsaw Army Corps numbered approximately 25,000 men, although if one included civilians and reserves, the number was larger. But only about 2,500 soldiers were properly armed on August 1. Thus only a fraction of the AK could be used effectively against the Germans on "D" day. The Germans, on the other hand, had approximately 15,000–16,000 well-armed troops who were supplemented and strengthened as the uprising progressed.[21]

"Warsaw will be wiped out," was Hitler's laconic reaction when he heard of the outbreak in the Polish capital.[22] His order to destroy the city quickly filtered down to his henchmen. The Führer's new chief of staff, Heinz Guderian, quieted the serious concern of Hans

Frank, the governor general of Poland, who had once pompously remarked that "the whole Vistula shall be as German as the Rhine." Now he was not so sure and even contemplated moving his headquarters out of Cracow. Guderian reassured him on August 3 that the Polish uprising would be suppressed "with all means possible" and when it became clear which parts of the city were in German and Polish hands the Luftwaffe would start its air bombardment.[23] A few days later Frank's morale had improved because by then the Germans had forced the Poles on the defensive. "The town of Warsaw is in flames in almost all parts. The burning down of the houses is the best means to prevent the rebels from using them as shelter," Frank declared to Reichminister Hans Lammers. "After this uprising and its suppression Warsaw will meet its deserved fate; it will be completely destroyed."[24]

Meanwhile, Heinrich Himmler, head of the SS, assured his chief: "My Führer, . . . Warsaw . . . will be erased; this nation that has blocked our way to the East for the past 700 years and which has been a constant obstruction in our way since the first battle of Tannenberg." He added: "Then, historically, the Polish problem will be no great problem at all, neither to our children nor to all those who will come after us, and not even to us."[25] Then he went to Posen where he dispatched most of the police force of the city—some with artillery—together with the SS Brigade Dirlewanger and the SS Brigade Kaminski to Warsaw. All the units were under the command of SS *Gruppenführer* Heinz Reinefarth, who had the dual disability of lacking tactical training and despising the leaders of the SS brigades ostensibly subordinate to him. Confident that the whole affair would be over swiftly, Himmler gave his units carte blanche. They were told to shoot everyone, including women and children, and they were permitted to loot. The order to raze Warsaw to the ground was given in writing and was of course Hitler's will.[26] In reference to the implementation of Hitler's order, Himmler later told a group of generals, "At the same time I have moreover given the order to destroy Warsaw completely. You may now think that I am a terrible barbarian, as you please. Yes, I am a barbarian when I must be. . . . The order was: to set fire to every block of houses and blow them up."[27]

Thus, from the outset, suppression of the insurrection was an SS and police affair. The Wehrmacht was too busy trying to stop the Soviets at the Vistula. Field Marshal Walter Model, "the Führer's Fireman," did not want any part in the matter, advising that the Germans responsible for provoking the Poles to rise up—namely, Frank and his cronies—should handle it. His troops, Model sneered, were too good to quell insurrections.[28] Guderian, however, felt differently. He tried to have Warsaw included in the army's operational area since it was on the front line. But Himmler anticipated him.[29] The Poles fought desperately and held the military initiative until August 5. The Nazis, realizing now that they had a major crisis on their hands, appointed General Erich von dem Bach-Zelewski, SS *Obergruppenführer* and general of the Waffen SS, to suppress it.[30]

In his hasty decision on July 31 to order the uprising for the next afternoon, Bór failed to take into account intelligence information indicating that the Germans were still strong enough to counterattack.[31] The German response to the long successful Soviet advance resulted in a temporary setback for the Soviets near Warsaw. However, the Soviet government claimed unconvincingly that it was unable to render *any* military assistance to the Poles and refused to allow the United States to use Soviet airfields in its efforts to aid the Varsovians.

When the uprising broke out, it was quite natural that the Poles first asked the British for assistance against the Nazis. After all, London was the wartime home of the Polish government and it was the British who provided so much assistance through its Special Operations Executive to the Home Army. Churchill promptly telegraphed Stalin on August 2 and told him about British intentions to help the AK. He also related Polish appeals for Soviet help. Stalin's reply was "prompt and grim." The Soviet chieftain was unimpressed with Polish claims against the Nazis, expressing disbelief that there was a rising in Warsaw, and refused to aid the Poles.[32] Meanwhile, the Royal Air Force (RAF) and the Polish Air Force (PAF), its headquarters in England since 1940, began to fly to Warsaw and take the losses which made the operation so suicidal. During a series of missions involving seventy-nine planes between August 13–16, eighteen crews were lost.[33] After such catastrophic losses, it became urgent either for the Soviet Union to send the necessary assistance or to allow the United States with its large heavy bomber fleet to shuttle supplies which required the use of Soviet bases.

Despite the efforts of the London Poles to get Washington to help their underground before the summer of 1944, the United States had demurred. On their part the British preferred that the Poles work through them.[34] Thus the United States played no direct military role prior to the summer of 1944 in assisting the Home Army, though it did help by providing roughly $10 million in financial aid for the Home Army. The Poles tried to get larger financial support that summer, requesting $97 million largely for the operations of the AK. The president, however, authorized the allocation of $10 million for 1944 with the proviso that the Polish underground cooperate with

Soviet forces. But after the Soviet government created the Polish
Committee of National Liberation, the Joint Chiefs of Staff believed
that the condition could not be met and recommended that the fi-
nancial allocation be deferred. For almost three weeks after the
Warsaw uprising the matter rested there, until after it became apparent that Washington could do nothing else that month to help the
AK and the money was finally released.[35]

Neither Roosevelt nor the Joint Chiefs of Staff was excited about
the prospect of embarking on a large-scale supply operation in a
theater of operations which was unquestionably Soviet. Early in
August the Joint Chiefs deferred the matter of supply to the Poles
to the Combined Chiefs of Staff, who considered it a British responsibility.[36] American political and military officials preferred it this
way for several reasons. First, the United States and the Soviet Union
had just established a precedent in their wartime relations when the
Soviets allowed the Army Air Forces (AAF) to use bases in the U-
kraine in carrying out bombing missions against German targets in
eastern Europe. Eastern Command, the AAF headquarters in the
Soviet Union, began to supervise American missions in June 1944.
Second, the AAF bases in the Soviet Union were regarded by policy
makers as a stepping stone to the erection of similar facilities in
Siberia so that when the Soviets went to war against Japan the AAF
would have the installations to bomb the Japanese mainland. Then,
too, there was Roosevelt's design of establishing a constructive relationship with the Soviets that would spill over into the postwar era
during which the two titans, along with some minor constellations,
would maintain peace. For these reasons Washington was reluctant
to go too far in risking a confrontation with the Soviets over supplying the Poles. Some American military people even thought America's
involvement foolhardy, jeopardizing what they believed to be solid
gains in military collaboration with the Kremlin. A few even blamed
the British for pressuring Roosevelt to go as far as he did.[37]

The United States did nothing to help the Poles in Warsaw, not
even releasing the funds earlier promised by the president, until the
middle of August. By then, several heartrending pleas had come from
Polish officials, including President Raczkiewicz, who asked the
United States to send supplies to the Home Army.[38] While the Joint
Chiefs of Staff still held to their original policy, the president had
authorized Averell Harriman, the American ambassador to Moscow,
to get Soviet permission for AAF planes to use Soviet bases for a
supply drop to Warsaw. The Soviets replied on August 15 that they
could not go along with the American project and described what
was going on in Warsaw as "a purely adventuristic affair and the

Soviet Government could not lend its hand to it." Harriman pressed
strongly later the same day, but the Soviets were adamant. It astonished and depressed the easygoing Harriman, who wrote the president
on the evening of August 15: "For the first time since coming to
Moscow I am gravely concerned by the attitude of the Soviet Government in its refusal to permit us to assist the Poles in Warsaw (as)
well as in its own policy of apparent inactiviety. If Vyshinski correctly reflects the position of the Soviet Government, its refusal is
based not on operational difficulties or denial that the resistance exists but on ruthless political considerations."[39] The following day
Stalin confirmed his position to Churchill, describing the uprising as
"a reckless and terrible adventure" from which he dissociated himself.[40] Meanwhile, the United States Eighth Air Force on August 14
filed alternate plans with the Eastern Command, for clearance with
the Soviets—one for a bombing operation against Königsberg, the
other for a supply drop to Warsaw. General Carl Spaatz, commanding
general of the United States Strategic Air Forces, hoped to use
seventy bombers and one hundred fighters in the Polish operation.
He expected fifty bombers to drop supplies over the capital while the
rest of the planes bombed a German airfield near Warsaw, something
the Poles had requested earlier. With uncharacteristic Soviet prompt-
ness the Soviets on the following day refused both requests but had
no objection to American or British flights, provided Soviet airfields
were not used.[41] That put an end, at least for the time being, to AAF
plans for a relief mission, since American planes needed to land on
Soviet bases following a supply drop to the Poles.

   Secretary of State Hull played an unusually strong role in reminding the president that the United States and Britain could not abandon the AK "simply because such action might not accord with
Soviet political aims." Churchill a few days later said roughly the
same thing: "We are nations serving high causes and must give true
counsels towards world peace even at the risk of Stalin resenting it.
Quite possibly he wouldn't." Even before he received the message
from Churchill, Roosevelt wanted Harriman to continue to press the
matter with the Soviets and to try to get permission for the AAF to
use the bases. Failing that, Roosevelt wanted the Soviets to understand that his country planned to aid the Poles so far as was militarily
feasible.[42] During the evening of August 17 Harriman talked with
Vyshinsky, who reiterated the Soviets position opposing use of its
airfields to aid the Poles but quickly added that the Kremlin did not
care what Britain and the United States did independently. "This
conversation reinforces my conclusion," Harriman said grimly, "that
the Soviet Government has no present intention of attempting to

drop arms to the Poles fighting in Warsaw." Harriman was in despair.
"These men are bloated with power and expect they can force their
will on us and all countries to accept their decisions without questions,"
he wrote. Harriman urged the president to send Stalin a message immediately using the same kind of blunt language the Soviet dictator
used in his messages to Churchill and Roosevelt. The United States
could not allow Stalin to prevent the AAF from helping the Poles, he
declared, warning that if the Soviet Union persisted in its policy "American public belief in the chances of the success of (the) world security
organization and postwar cooperation would be deeply shaken."[43]
Harriman understood, as the British did, that Soviet refusal to aid the
Poles by air reduced the chances for a political settlement with
Mikołajczyk's government to a cypher.

American efforts to get the Soviets to budge from their obstinate
refusal to allow the AAF to use Soviet bases to supply the Poles had
special significance in view of the heavy losses sustained by the RAF
and PAF during the four-day series of missions beginning on August 13,
and the suspension of further missions by British and South African
crews. Polish crews, however, continued to fly the suicidal missions to
Warsaw. Secretary Hull realized an impasse had been reached and did
not want to press the Russians further. He believed that the United
States had made its point, that Washington had gotten Soviet recognition of independent American initiatives for the Poles. Harriman did
not agree since Soviet opposition to the use of the bases prevented the
United States from giving the Poles military assistance. Nor did he believe that other considerations, such as the AAF project in the Ukraine
or future Siberian operations, were worth allowing the Soviets to get
away with their political play in Poland.[44] Roosevelt made one more
effort to get the Soviet chief to change his mind by sending a joint
message with Churchill to him. They asked him to send aid to the
Poles or allow them to do so by using his bases. They pointed to outraged world opinion if the Poles were abandoned. Stalin was furious.
On August 22, in a reply to the two Western leaders, he described
Bór and other Polish leaders in Warsaw as "power-seeking criminals"
and did not even acknowledge the appeal to use Soviet bases.[45]

The Stalin reply to the Roosevelt-Churchill message at the very
time the Germans were making their final drive for Old Town, the
section of narrow, winding streets and ancient timbered houses of
Warsaw which hugged the Vistula, meant a standoff in the positions
of the Big Three. Roosevelt agreed with Hull and did not want to
press any further. He felt he did all he could without seriously jeopardizing relations with the Kremlin, a relationship he wanted desperately
to maintain not only to win the war against the Germans but also to

defeat the Japanese. Already the Soviets were making it very unpleasant for the AAF bombing program by refusing to clear targets which might permit aid to Warsaw.

Meanwhile, Mikołajczyk met several times with Stalin in an attempt to resolve the Polish-Soviet crisis and to get Soviet help for the beleaguered people of Warsaw. During his first meeting with Stalin on August 3, Mikołajczyk tried to break the ice between them by introducing himself as a peasant and a worker. Then he proceeded to outline his concept of a Polish-Soviet agreement which rested on the establishment of a coalition government in Poland, representing the five major parties, including the Polish Workers' party (PPR). This was formally endorsed by the Polish government in London and by its representatives in Poland by the end of August. Stalin was quick to indicate his recognition of the Lublin Poles. "Does this mean that in your view there is no room in Poland for anybody except the [Lublin] Committee?" Mikołajczyk asked him. "I do not think so," Stalin replied, indicating that it would be wise to unite both Polish factions in order to form a provisional government and that the Poles should do this themselves.[46] Little did Mikołajczyk realize that before he left for Moscow, Churchill had endorsed the idea of a fusion of Polish elements friendly to the West and to the Soviet Union, thus undermining the Polish premier's plan. Roosevelt told Stalin he hoped for "the formation of an interim legal and truly representative Polish Government." By the end of August, the president even suggested that Mikołajczyk make political proposals acceptable to the Committee of National Liberation. To Mikołajczyk, this "letter marked his [Roosevelt's] acceptance of the Lublin Poles as the bona fide leaders of the nation."[47]

Stalin, encouraged by what he had heard from Churchill and Roosevelt, showed no interest in the coalition described by Mikołajczyk because this would have left his Lublin protégés in a minor position. As for the postwar Polish-Soviet frontier, Stalin again reiterated his long-standing position on the Curzon Line.

As for the activities of the Home Army, Stalin chided:

> I have received reports from our military commanders on your Home Army. What is an army without artillery, tanks, and an air force? They are even short of rifles. In modern warfare such an army is of little use. They are small partisan units, not a regular army. I was told that the Polish Government has ordered these units to drive the Germans out of Warsaw. I wonder how they could possibly do this, their forces are not up to that task. As a matter of fact, these people do not fight against the Germans, but only hide in woods, being unable to do anything else.

Admitting that the Home Army had no artillery, tanks, and planes,

Mikołajczyk pointed out that these disabilities did not prevent it from fighting the enemy. This was proof, he said, of their courage and determination. For five years they have been continuously carrying out sabotage, Mikołajczyk added, indicating that some key communication centers had been recently destroyed by the AK around Lwów. Then he added forcefully:

> Today I received a telegram informing me that 40,000 men in Warsaw came out to wage an open fight against the Germans. They ask only for supplies of arms to be dropped on the posts occupied by them. It would be impossible to enumerate all the facts of sabotage but they are registered by the Inter-Allied General Staff and have certainly been made known to the Soviet authorities. I found myself in a tragic position when, because of the severance of direct relations, I had to insist on an indirect approach to Russia for the coordination of operations, as coordination is a primary condition of success.

"Can you see no possibility, marshal, of contributing on your part to the rearmament of the Home Army?" Mikołajczyk asked. Stalin dodged the question. He indicated that the Soviets would not permit any action behind their lines, and for that reason he told Mikołajczyk that he had to reach an understanding with the Lublin Committee. When the discussion got back to Warsaw again, Stalin told the Pole that he expected to be in the Polish capital by August 5 or 6 but said the Germans were strongly defending the area. That was the most encouraging thing Mikołajczyk had heard since he arrived in Moscow. Stalin went on to express his interest in aiding the Poles, and with Mikołajczyk's encouragement he planned to send a few of his communications officers to assess the situation.

Three days later Mikołajczyk met with the Lublin Poles, who had been treated with so much ceremony and respect upon their arrival in Moscow, contrasting sharply to the back-door reception the London Poles got. On July 27, Stalin gave a huge banquet for the Lublinites in the Kremlin, the kind of gala usually reserved for heads of great powers, not for a group of unknowns who had no political standing except in Stalin's own mind. Present at the conference were Edward Osóbka-Morawski, a member of the Polish Workers' party who had played no part in political life; Wanda Wasilewska, chairman of the Union of Polish Patriots and vice-chairman of the Committee of National Liberation; General Michał Rola-Żymierski, a former Polish deputy minister of war who had been involved in a scandal before the war; and Andrzej Witos, brother of the famous premier of Poland, Wincenty, who served as vice-chairman of the Committee of National Liberation.

To Mikołajczyk, these were renegades. Losing no time with diplomatic niceties, he got immediately to the point. "I spoke to Stalin the other night, and he expressed a willingness to help our forces in Warsaw," he said. Then looking at Rola-Żymierski, he went on, "As Commander-in-Chief of the Kościuszko Division you have good contacts with Red Army headquarters. It is now your duty—as a Pole—to bring help as quickly as possible. Our men are in desperate straits." Wasilewska, interrupting Rola-Żymierski as he was about to reply, contended: "There is no fighting in Warsaw." This was an unbelievable claim but one that Mikołajczyk heard several times during his stay in Moscow. Stalin had expressed the same doubt during his earlier meeting with Mikołajczyk. Rola-Żymierski, contradicting Wasilewska's claim, admitted that he knew about the uprising in Warsaw and promised to secure the release of a Polish colonel who had been arrested by the Soviets after he helped them to take Lwów.[48]

The next day Mikołajczyk had an equally unsatisfactory meeting with Bolesław Bierut, an able man who had served for years as a Comintern agent and was destined to become the president of postwar Poland. Mikołajczyk did not like him, but he respected Bierut's intelligence. Again it was apparent that the political compromise Stalin suggested would principally constitute concessions by the London Poles. Bierut offered Mikołajczyk's group four seats in an eighteen-seat coalition cabinet dominated by the communists. This was a significant departure from Stalin's earlier political demands. Before the creation of the Committee of National Liberation, Stalin had asked that the Polish government-in-exile get rid of certain members as the precondition of Soviet recognition of the Poles. Now the Soviet dictator wanted to ensure that the pro-Soviet elements would have the preponderant voice in a Polish regime.

"If you want to go to Poland as a friend in complete agreement with us, we will accept you," Bierut said. "If you attempt to go as Prime Minister of the Polish government that is no longer recognized by the USSR, we'll arrest you." This was a left-handed compliment to Mikołajczyk and a veiled admission that Bierut needed the respected Polish statesman in a new reconstructed government. "I have no business here. All I want now is to get back to London and report to my government what I have seen and heard in Moscow," Mikołajczyk replied angrily. Before he went out the door, he turned to Bierut and appealed to his patriotism: "Help Warsaw—and stop the Soviet arrests of the Home Army that is helping to liberate our country." Bierut was impassive, shielding his anger and disappointment.[49]

Before he left Moscow Mikołajczyk, already worn out by the round of conferences and meetings, met one more time with Stalin on August 9. He was dumbfounded to find Stalin still trying to establish definitely whether there was an uprising in the Polish capital. "Can

you give me your word of honor," Stalin asked, "that there is fighting going on in Warsaw?" "I can give you my word of honor that there
is a fight there," the Pole replied. "It is a desperate fight. I beg you—
who are in the strategic position—to give us aid."

Stalin was unimpressed. "I had two of my communications officers
dropped into Warsaw after I saw you the other day," Stalin claimed.
"The Germans killed both of them when they attempted to land by
parachute." However, both officers apparently did make contact with
the commander of the AK in Warsaw, General Chruściel, and sent
several messages to Moscow. During his meeting with Stalin,
Mikołajczyk gave him a message from Captain Konstantin Kalugin,
probably a member of a partisan detachment serving with the Polish
People's army, who urged Stalin to send aid to "the heroic population
of Warsaw."[50]

Mikołajczyk left Moscow in the early hours of August 10 with
Stalin's assurances that Soviet help for Warsaw would come. He arrived in London three days later. Despite the frosty meetings with
Stalin and the frostier ones with the Lublin people, Mikołajczyk returned manifesting an aura of optimism and confidence for the Poles
in Warsaw and for the future of Polish-Soviet relations.

In a message to Bór, he talked about Stalin's greater understanding
of the problems in Warsaw:

> During a one-hour leave-taking conversation, on the evening of the 9th
> August, held in a very friendly atmosphere, Stalin showed much greater under-
> standing of the problems concerning the fight for Warsaw.
> I represented to him the position emphatically. Stalin primarily counted on
> the entry of Soviet Forces into Warsaw on August 6th. This was prevented by
> a counter-attack from the Praga area by some freshly brought up German
> divisions, among them the Hermann Goering Division from Italy.

He told Eden, the British foreign minister, that he was optimistic
about Soviet help for Warsaw. Despite the dead-end talks with the
Lublinites, he told Harriman that he wanted to work out a compromise with the Lublin Committee. Mikołajczyk believed that Stalin
would use the Lublin Committee to extract concessions from the
London Poles, not sponsor it as a rival government. Harriman thought
Mikołajczyk was inclined to allow matters to run their course because
the Lublinites were inexperienced and unrepresentative. "I cannot
disagree too strongly with this reasoning," Harriman declared.[51]

After he returned to London, Mikołajczyk desperately tried to get
Stalin to follow through with what he had told him in Moscow. In a
long pathetic plea to the Soviet chief, Mikołajczyk said:

Marshal Stalin, I understand that the Soviet High Command is not responsible for Warsaw's uprising; which we know now was premature and therefore could not have been pre-arranged with your forces. If certain elements of the Polish press express their nervousness in connection with this, it is only because they are deeply concerned with the tragic fate of the inhabitants of Warsaw. I can assure you that in the spirit of our friendly talks in Moscow I have done my best to stop this and I would wish to have the same spirit shown in this matter by the Soviet side.

Stalin never responded.[52] Chagrined that he had been unable to bring effective help to Warsaw, Mikołajczyk told Eden that he might have to resign from office. Neither Churchill nor Eden wanted that to happen, and when Mikołajczyk again brought up the possibility early the following month, Eden was furious. Churchill had made it clear that if Mikołajczyk resigned, the British would wash their hands of the Poles.[53]

To Churchill, Roosevelt wrote fatalistically on August 24, "I do not see that we can take any additional steps at the present time that promise results." But Churchill did not want the matter to rest there. The prime minister picked up a proposal by Mikołajczyk, who repeated it twice to Eden in the preceding few days, and made it his own. Churchill wanted the president to gamble, to send American planes to drop supplies over Warsaw and land on Soviet airfields even without the Kremlin's clearance to use the bases. He doubted the crews would be mistreated or the planes detained. Roosevelt was not prepared to go that far because it risked rupturing an already strained wartime alliance. Churchill was disappointed with the president's decision to stop there, though later he defended his wartime friend and colleague by saying that "terrible and even humbling submissions must at times be made to the general aim."[54]

Failing to get the stubborn Stalin to move from his position, Roosevelt could do nothing but grant the Home Army something it had asked for since the beginning of the uprising. On August 29, the United States and Britain belatedly recognized the AK as a member of the armed forces of the United Nations which granted it the protection of being treated by the laws and customs of war.[55] The recognition came too late for those who had already died in the bloodbath in Warsaw, but it was a courageous step, nonetheless, since it disputed the Soviet claim that the Polish underground was a gang of criminals.

The prime minister and the president were not insensitive to the desperate struggle in Warsaw, but Churchill did more than Roosevelt to aid the city. The results of a technical investigation he ordered on September 1 revealed that the United States was in the best position to initiate a long range, massive supply operation. The British War Cabinet considered the matter on September 4, and Churchill could not remember another occasion when all the members—Tory, Labor, and Liberal—showed so much anger with the Soviets. Churchill and Eden even toyed with the idea of stopping the next supply convoy for Stalin until he changed his attitude toward the Warsaw Poles. Both men seriously discussed "gatecrashing" Soviet airfields. Churchill said he was sorely tempted to tell Stalin: "We are sending our aeorplanes [*sic*] to land in your territory, after delivering supplies to Warsaw. If you do not treat them properly all convoys will be stopped from this moment by us." But Churchill did not go that far. In one of his sterner messages to the Soviet chief, Churchill told him on September 4 that people could not understand why "no material has been sent from outside . . . . The fact that such help could not be sent on account of your Government's refusal to allow United States aircraft to land on aerodromes in Russian hands is now becoming publicly known." He reminded Stalin that Britain and the United States had obligations to help the Warsaw Poles and again appealed to him to open his airfields to the AAF.[56]

Not all American political and military officials were for AAF supply operations for Warsaw. Harry Hopkins, the close advisor and troubleshooter for the president, opposed them because he believed they might jeopardize Soviet-American relations. Hopkins felt the Warsaw problem would be disposed of by "the sure victories on Germany's eastern front." And he became livid when the Roman Catholic church took a strong stand in favor of American support for Warsaw. Cardinal Edward Mooney of Detroit urged his parishioners to vote against Roosevelt in the forthcoming elections because of the lack of American assistance for the Poles.[57] The shrewd presidential advisor could not ignore the potential danger to the reelection of the president if the Warsaw question exploded as a major campaign issue. Ever since the organization of the Polish American Congress in May the administration had actively courted Americans of Polish background and went out of its way to assure them that the White House had Poland's genuine interests at heart. Many of these leaders, like Charles Rozmarek of the Polish American Congress, strongly urged the president to do something to help Warsaw.[58] By the middle of September there were warnings from Polish American leaders in the Democratic party that the traditionally Democratic Poles were wavering in their party loyalty. Frank Nurczyk, a highly placed party leader in Chicago, warned Roosevelt: "Many Americans of other nationality, of other political connections, are talking to our voters this way— Where is your friend in need? You are voting straight democratic, and here is your reward: your brothers and sisters, your fathers and mothers are dying in Europe and still fighting on all fronts . . . and nobody is willing to help hard-pressed Poland." One Polish American organization even offered to purchase supplies for their kinsmen through war bonds.[59]

Churchill kept up the pressure on Roosevelt, urging him on September 4 to authorize the AAF to carry out the mission, and to land on Soviet bases without Stalin's consent. Churchill suggested that Stalin might even welcome such an American action to bail him out of an embarrassing situation.[60] Roosevelt replied the next day with a very strange message in which he said military intelligence had informed him that the Poles had left Warsaw and the Germans were in control.[61] By then, the Department of State had advised the president in an accurate assessment that Stalin did not aid Warsaw because he wanted to undermine Mikołajczyk's prestige and minimize the possibility of his return to Warsaw. "In any event," the department said on September 8, "the decision was clearly political and appears to indicate Stalin's determination that the Soviet-sponsored Committee gain as full control as possible of the country."[62] Meanwhile Hopkins did all he could to dampen the chances of American involvement in a relief operation that might hurt the White House relationship with the Kremlin. Hopkins confided his strong feelings about the matter to Major General F.L. Anderson, who served as General Carl Spaatz's deputy for operations. Hopkins told him that he would withhold cablegrams from Churchill to the president in order to ensure that the United States would stay out of the affair. Anderson shared Hopkins' sentiments and believed that the British were using the United States as a tool.[63]

A few days after this startling admission by a senior presidential advisor, the Soviets suddenly relented and agreed to concert plans with the Americans and British for a coordinated air drop over Warsaw.[64] Stalin seemed to realize that he could no longer refuse to help the beleaguered Poles. Western pressure on him was substantial, reaching greater intensity by early September. Then, too, he could not remain oblivious to his own Polish military and political protégés. After all, he had Berling's Polish army, which had distinguished itself with Soviet forces. These soldiers were Poles, not Soviets, and they were eager to help their kinsmen in Warsaw. He realized that the image of the Soviet Union as a friend and liberator of Poland was difficult to sustain in the face of Soviet military inactivity and refusal to allow the AAF to use Soviet bases to help the Poles. Ever since the end of August the Western press had revealed the uncooperative posture of the Kremlin. Stalin apparently decided that it was time to indulge in some image-changing.

On September 10 the Soviets launched a successful offensive against
Praga, throwing the German Seventy-third Infantry Division into re-
treat. Three days later, Polish-Soviet troops reached the Vistula
bridges which the Germans, having previously wired for destruction
in such an eventuality, destroyed, leaving the northernmost one open
for the evacuation of the Nineteenth Panzer Divison.[65] Accompanying
the Soviet advance on that day were planes which dropped, somewhat
ironically, American canned food to relieve the grave shortages of
food and ammunition. The Soviet air drop beat the AAF to Warsaw,
and the Soviets lost no time in propagandizing their assistance to the
Poles. The missions continued for the next four days, stopping on
September 18. The Soviets resumed them three days later and continued the flights until the night of September 28–29. During the
twelve nights of air operations over Warsaw the Soviets dropped about
fifty to fifty-five tons of supplies, fifteen tons of which were food.[66]
Unlike the RAF and PAF missions, the Soviet planes—they used a
plane called the *kukuruznik*—flew several times over the area but
frequently released their loads without parachutes, with the consequence the supplies were so damaged that they were often useless.
The Soviet missions, however, came in time: Bór told London on
September 13 that he would order on the following day the distribu-
tion of the last of the hunger rations. Two days later Bór credited the
Soviet drops with enabling the AK to continue further resistance
against German attacks.[67]

After learning about the dramatic change in Soviet policy concerning aid to Warsaw, Roosevelt asked General Marshall to look into the
matter of arranging a concerted effort to assist the Poles, as the Kremlin had indicated. Marshall did this. Late in the evening on September
13, however, Harriman saw Molotov, who granted approval for AAF
use of Soviet bases following an American supply drop over Warsaw.
When Eden learned of the news that day, he talked over the telephone
with Churchill, who was in conference with Roosevelt at Quebec, and
told him about it. Churchill was delighted.[68] Since the Soviets began
dropping supplies over Warsaw on their own, there was no need now
to work out coordinated plans with the Soviet Air Force and the AAF
as Stalin originally suggested. Frantic 7, the name of the AAF supply
operation, had several false starts, largely because of bad weather, before it was launched.

At 5:30 A.M. on September 18, 1944, a massive air armada, consisting of 110 B-17s and 3 groups of P-51s, took off from English
airfields. Eighty-six of the fighters escorted the air fleet only part of
the way and returned to England while the remaining 62 P-51s stayed
with the bombers all the way. The airmen spotted the flaming city

from a distance of forty miles. Except for the blazing inferno below, it was a beautiful fall day, sunny and cloudless. The planes, flying between 14,000 and 17,000 feet, dropped 1,284 containers from multi-colored parachutes. Approximately 288 of them reached Polish hands. Out of 110 bombers, 105 arrived in the Soviet Union—3 planes returned to base early, 1 was lost and 1 was forced to land in Brest-Litovsk. Fifteen of the Flying Fortresses received major battle damage. Of the total number of fighters employed in the operation, the AAF lost 4.[69]

The Americans were not jubilant about the results of the mission. Less than 25 percent of the supplies reached Polish hands at the expense of several planes lost and damaged.[70] On his part, General Spaatz was ready to order another operation if he was told to do so. But he wanted to know what higher authorities in Washington had in mind because if another operation were to be flown, it would have to be done before the AAF bases in the Soviet Union were closed for the winter.[71] General Marshall did not favor another operation and requested the president's authority to discontinue future missions. Roosevelt was inclined to await the outcome of Soviet operations near Warsaw. He told Harriman: "Whether or not additional operations for assistance to Warsaw will be undertaken by American planes is dependent upon date of relief of Warsaw and assistance given by [the] Soviets in the meantime." Meanwhile, after additional pleas from the Poles came to the president's attention, Roosevelt changed his mind and told his aide, Admiral Leahy, that he wanted another mission sent if possible.[72] The same day the president announced his views, Churchill had a telephone conversation with General Anderson who appeared to have retreated from his earlier position of strong opposition to AAF relief missions to Warsaw. Churchill told the general about a visit from Mikołajczyk which deeply moved the prime minister. Anderson told him that another mission would have to be completed before October 5 when AAF bases in the Soviet Union would be closed.[73]

But another AAF operation did not materialize. Spaatz scheduled a supply drop for October 1, but it had to be cancelled because of bad weather. Even if the weather had permitted another mission on that day, the Soviets opposed further AAF operations for Warsaw on the erroneous grounds that Polish insurgents had already been evacuated and that the supplies would end up entirely in German hands. The Soviets had anticipated Polish surrender, which did not come until the following day.[74] How much of Stalin's information about Warsaw was distorted by himself or by others is impossible to ascertain, but there is no doubt that much information was inaccurately served

up by his subordinates.[75] The effort of the United States to assist
Warsaw was too meager and belated to prevent the Germans from
succeeding in their relentless efforts to crush the insurrection. By
October 1, after repeated attempts to establish liaison with the Soviets
had failed, Bór arranged for a cease-fire.[76]

It was during the Warsaw uprising that Stalin for the first time in a
very clear and decisive way demonstrated how important it was to
him to have a political settlement in Poland on his terms. The argument often advanced that the Soviet armies had reached the end of
their tether and could do nothing in August or September to help
Warsaw ignores the areas in which the Soviet Union could have been
of greater assistance if it had wanted to—namely, to drop supplies to
the Poles from the outset of the struggle, to bomb German targets
which would have relieved the air and artillery bombardment on the
Poles, to allow the United States access to its bases earlier than it did,
and finally, to establish effective liaison with the Home Army. All of
these efforts would have helped the Poles, mitigated the severity of
their plight, and prolonged their defense until the Soviets resumed
their advance.[77]

In addition to sending the AAF mission to Warsaw, Washington had
bolstered the morale of the Poles by belatedly naming a successor to
Biddle, who had resigned as ambassador to the Polish government.
Biddle, who had wanted a commission in the armed forces, had resigned in January 1944.[78] Roosevelt delayed the appointment of a
successor until July 1944, but it was not until September 1944 that
the Senate confirmed Arthur Bliss Lane to the post.[79] In retrospect,
Roosevelt's delay in appointing a new ambassador to the Polish government-in-exile appears to have been partially motivated by Washington's conciliatory policy toward the Kremlin over the Polish question.
But the president could not delay much longer the appointment of a
replacement for Biddle in view of the Warsaw Uprising and the mounting doubt about American support for Poland in Polish circles in England and the United States.

Lane, a seasoned diplomat who once served as a junior secretary of
legation in Warsaw in 1919, was ambassador to Colombia when he received the news of his appointment to the new post. Lane arrived in
Washington in October 1944, assuming that he would soon depart
for London. But in view of the uncertainty of the Polish situation,
Roosevelt asked Lane to remain in the nation's capital pending further developments.[80] Thus during most of 1944, Roosevelt did not
name a new ambassador to the Polish government, and when he did
the president kept him under wraps for months in Washington instead
of sending him to his post. Embarrassed by his long stay in Washington,

Lane kept away from his foreign service friends in order to avoid the perennial questions about when he was leaving for his diplomatic post. As it turned out, Lane stayed in Washington, learning everything he could about the Polish situation, until July 1945, when he finally departed to present his credentials to the Polish government. By then, however, he flew to Warsaw, not London, to a Communist-dominated Polish government.[81]

V

THE UNITED STATES VIEWS THE SOVIET UNION
AND POLAND, 1941–1944

Although Americans regarded the Soviets with hostility and the Poles with compassion at the beginning of World War II, by 1944 the metamorphosis of American attitudes was remarkable. Communications media in the United States—newspapers, periodicals, books, movies, and radio—and the American government increasingly offered favorable impressions of the Soviet Union that eclipsed those of Poland, and Americans had become increasingly impatient with the Poles for failing to compromise with the Soviets, who, they believed, only wanted a more equitable boundary with Poland, not outright domination of the country.

Thus the American government and communications media considered Soviet claims to the Curzon Line, long opposed by the Polish government, not only justified but also equitable to both sides. By that time, even the character of the Polish government itself was seriously impugned by attacks against its alleged unrepresentative and reactionary composition. The Soviet Union's successful defense against the Nazis and its later seizure of the military initiative, which it held until the end of the war, were understandably the most important factors in modifying the once unfavorable image of the people, the government, and the policies of the Soviet Union.

Not many observers expected the Soviet Union to survive more than a few weeks of the Nazi onslaught. Poland and France had collapsed in a matter of weeks. The Soviet Union had a shabby military record in the war with Finland in the winter of 1939–1940, when a nation of 4 million people resisted a nation of 160 million for five months. Only a handful of Americans in official circles were optimistic about the Soviet Union's ability to resist. But as the weeks turned into months, it was not long before the Soviets and their leaders became heroes in the American press.

Some of the image-making after June 1941 was administration-inspired. After all, the Soviet Union had joined Britain in a war against the Germans, and the United States had already gone to considerable lengths to aid the British. Washington considered that it was in American self-interest to help the Soviet Union. Roosevelt promised to send stopgap aid to Stalin until a joint Anglo-American supply mission, headed by Beaverbrook and Harriman, went to Moscow in September 1941 and worked out a long-range program of aid to the Soviets. Even though the Anglo-American mission signed the first wartime supply protocol for the Soviet Union in Moscow on October 1, no method of financing it had been definitely decided. Roosevelt delayed the logical step of including the Soviet Union under the provision of lend-lease for a month, so sensitive was he to the residue of anti-Russian feeling in the country. But by then, the administration enjoyed broad popular support for its decision to aid the Russians against the Germans.[1]

Shortly before the signing of the Moscow Protocol, the Soviets allowed Catholic and Jewish chaplains to serve in the Polish army in the Soviet Union. Roosevelt was anxious to exploit the liberalization of Soviet policies to improve the Soviet image in the United States. He encouraged Ciechanowski, the Polish ambassador to Washington, to publicize the Soviet Union's new policy toward religion. Ciechanowski obliged by sending a letter to the Department of State, which promptly released it to the press. The Polish ambassador had exaggerated when he told Hull that members of the Polish armed forces and civilians had full religious freedom in the Soviet Union because only a handful of Catholic priests had been freed by the Soviets to tend to the spiritual needs of thousands of civilian refugees.[2] During a press conference on September 30, 1941, the president was asked about a statement in Ciechanowski's letter which referred to the Soviets' allowing the Poles to have their own churches in the Soviet Union. Roosevelt replied: "As I think I suggested a week or two ago, some of you might find it useful to read Article 124 of the Constitution of Russia." He went on:

> Freedom of religion. Freedom equally to use propaganda against religion, which is essentially what is the rule in this country, only we don't put it quite the same way. For instance, you might go out tomorrow on—to the corner of . . . Pennsylvania Avenue, down below the Press Club, and stand on a soap-box and . . . preach Christianity, and nobody would stop you. And then, if it got into your head, perhaps the next day preach against religion of all kinds, and nobody would stop you.[3]

President Roosevelt, encouraged by what appeared to be signs of a change in Soviet policy toward religion, even informed Pope Pius XII that churches in the Soviet Union "were open." The papacy was not impressed. It remained skeptical about Soviet efforts to alter its prewar image of persecuting the church.[4]

In 1941–1942, the Kremlin did soften its attitude toward the church by suspending publication of the antireligious newspaper, *Godless*, and employed its editor in writing articles against the Germans for their suppression of religion. The Orthodox church published a lavish, gold-encrusted volume entitled, *The Truth about Religion in Russia*, which proclaimed that religious freedom really did exist in the Soviet Union. On the twenty-fifth anniversary of the Bolshevik Revolution, the Soviet press even published greetings from Metropolitan Sergei of Moscow to Stalin. This was the first time since the November Revolution that the word God had been capitalized in the official press. By 1943 Stalin officially restored the church by allowing the election of a patriarch of the Orthodox church, opened a seminary to train priests, and even allowed the publication of the Bible in the Soviet Union for the first time since the Bolshevik Revolution.[5]

The Office of War Information, combining the functions of an information agency and a propaganda instrument of the government, reflected official American policy in refusing to deal openly with the outstanding issues which divided Poland and the Soviet Union and in proclaiming a postwar world too good to be true. OWI tried to be objective: "Utmost and constant objectivity, calmness and judiciousness should characterize all our output in reporting Polish developments, their ramifications, and implications." So sensitive was OWI to Soviet sensibilities regarding the hotly disputed Polish-Soviet boundary that broadcasts referred to the 1921–1939 boundary as the "1939" frontier rather than the "Riga Line" or "pre-World War II frontier." Broadcasters were urged not to inflect their voices when mentioning the troublesome question. So wary was the agency of Polish sensitivities about the much publicized visit of Professor Oscar Lange and Father Orlemański to the Soviet Union in 1944 that OWI said nothing about it in its broadcasts. In one exceptional case, OWI departed from its broadcasting guidelines by speaking favorably of Premier Mikołajczyk's statesmanship, a build-up which continued from the fall of 1944 through the Yalta meeting in February 1945.

By avoiding the issues dividing Poles and Soviets, OWI deluded listeners in painting too optimistic a picture of wartime and postwar Polish-Soviet relations. OWI told the Poles, just as their representatives found out from State Department officials, that allied unity and Anglo-American faith in the Soviet Union would bring the desired political benefits to Poland after the war. Soviet occupation of eastern Poland in 1944, OWI broadcasts declared, was only temporary, a necessary expedient for Polish liberation. The fact that the Soviet Union might be fighting for aims different from those of its Western allies was never stated in official American foreign policy pronouncements during the war. Little wonder that one OWI directive said in 1943: "Try to make America seem the realization of the ideals which the exploited and under-privileged have cherished through the centuries. Make this picture so vivid and beautiful that the Poles will feel that we and the Russians are not only working for the same end, but for the only end which worthy men and women cherish."[6]

The London Poles considered that OWI broadcasts to Poland "might well have emanated from Moscow itself." When Mikołajczyk visited Washington in June 1944, he complained to Stettinius about the agency, arguing that it followed the same line as Moscow and thus made it extremely difficult for the Polish government. Stettinius called Elmer Davis, head of OWI, who assured the secretary that his agency "will follow the policy of the United States for a strong and independent Poland."[7]

So angular was OWI policy that when Ciechanowski sought its help in getting a change in an atlas, published by *Encyclopaedia Britannica*, which depicted pre-1939 eastern Poland within the frontiers of the Soviet Union, OWI refused on the grounds that the intervention probably would alienate the Soviets. As it turned out, Polish Americans responded to the situation and managed to pressure Britannica to publish a corrected issue.[8]

Between 1941 and 1944, the image of the Soviet Union in the periodical press was generally favorable. American periodicals carried fewer anti-Soviet articles than pro-Soviet and neutral ones. In the liberal and moderate magazines that one historian surveyed, the percentage of pro-Soviet and neutral articles topped 75 percent. What was particularly striking was that in the conservative periodicals surveyed, 36 percent of the articles were pro-Soviet and 23 percent were neutral. Newspapers, too, reflected the same favorable swing of public opinion. An examination of the editorials of thirteen major newspapers during the war years revealed that by 1944, only three of them could be considered anti-Soviet—the *New York Daily News, Chicago Daily Tribune,* and the *Wall Street Journal.*[9]

As the image of the Soviet Union improved in the West, the image of Poland declined by comparison. To be sure, Americans regarded Poles as courageous allies, but they became increasingly aware that the Soviets were fighting Germans on the most active front in Europe and winning battles. Sikorski and Mikołajczyk tried desperately to remind their allies, including the Soviet Union, of the continuing Polish contribution to the war effort. Since 1939 the Poles had maintained an

active underground organization and boasted over 100,000 Polish
airmen, soldiers, and sailors fighting on various fronts by May 1942.[10]
Admirable as Polish sacrifices were, they did not have the crucial impact on the winning of the war that the Soviets' effort did. And everyone, including the Poles, knew it.

As Americans became more favorable toward their Muscovite ally,
the strong moral and political position that Poland enjoyed in the
West during the first few years of the war eroded. Official American
policy contributed to this decline because the White House assumed
the role of arbiter in the Polish-Soviet dispute, scrupulously refusing
to discuss the issues dividing the Soviets and the Poles and avoiding
an approach to the Kremlin that might suggest the United States was
an advocate for Polish interests. The communications media, wittingly
or unwittingly, contributed to the erosion of Poland's position by offering favorable impressions of the Soviet Union, interjecting more
negative comments than before about the London Poles, and increasingly taking the Soviet position on the controversial boundary dispute
and later on the complexion of the postwar Polish government.

In 1941 and 1942 Poland still enjoyed a high position in the United
States. The signing of the Polish-Soviet treaty in July 1941 was applauded by the *New York Times* as "a miracle of conciliation" and
its sympathies were clearly with the Poles.[11] Sikorski paid several
visits in 1941 and 1942 to Washington, where he was warmly and
graciously received. Even Poland's relations with the Soviet Union for
the remainder of 1941 and 1942 were at least officially correct, so
there was no Polish question to jostle the image of unity in the Allied
camp. Moreover, it took some time to overhaul the Soviet image in
the United States.

Much of the discussion in the press in 1941 and early 1942 concerned the question of aid to the Soviet Union. Liberal periodicals
like *Nation* and *New Republic* took the lead in urging aid to Russia
and pressing for a second front. Church-related journals, like *Christian
Register* and *Christian Century,* were naturally sensitive about the
persecution of the church in the Soviet Union.[12] But the most consistent opponent of the Soviet Union was *Catholic World.* Its editor,
the Reverend James M. Gillis, disturbed by the actions of American
officials in aiding the Soviet Union, asked in August 1941: "Why
don't they all come out and say point-blank, 'we have no scruple
about an alliance with the Prince of Darkness in the battle for light.'"
He declared: "The position taken in these editorials over the entire
period since Nazism and Communism came into the foreground is
that they are both essentially vicious and that there is little to choose
between them." By the end of 1941, *Catholic World* predicted that

a collapse of Germany would mean a major victory for communism with the Soviet Union getting a major slice of Poland.[13] *Commonweal,* another Catholic periodical, assumed a more realistic stance, urging a *modus vivendi* with the Soviet Union but without sacrificing national integrity. Nevertheless, *Commonweal* complained by February 1942 about the "concerted effort to 'sell' the Soviets to the public" by making Stalin's regime "something like a combination of Washington's, Jefferson's and Lincoln's, and functioning under a similar constitution."[14]

Newspapers, too, had to deal with the dilemma of justifying aid to a nation Americans had long considered a pariah. The *New York Herald Tribune,* echoing the sentiments of many, took the position that the Nazis were worse than the Communists. The *Detroit Free Press* came around by the end of 1941 in praising the Soviets and predicting that Britain, the United States, and the Soviet Union would defeat Hitler.[15]

By 1942 the American press was filled with favorable references to the courage of the Soviet soldier and the power of the Red Army. Former ambassador to the Soviet Union and Roosevelt's friend, Joseph Davies, assured Americans in June 1942 that Soviet resistance would continue. Once unfamiliar Soviet generals, like Semyon Timoshenko, now became known to Americans. And in January 1943 *Time* magazine converted Joseph Stalin from the tyrannical "Man of the Year" of 1940 to the able and benevolent "Man of the Year" of 1943.[16]

Once the Soviet Union seized the military initiative at Stalingrad and the Katyn affair exploded a few months later, the articles in the American press revealed just how much the Soviet and the Polish images had altered. By 1943 many Americans, perhaps a majority, said they respected and admired the Soviet Union.[17] Conservative periodicals, such as *American Mercury, Christian Century,* and the *Saturday Evening Post,* joined *New Republic* and *Nation* in frequently echoing pro-Soviet and anti-Polish sentiments. *New Republic* and *Nation,* impressed by the increase in Soviet power, argued that the Soviet Union had justified security needs in eastern Europe. But *New Republic* did not always make it clear whether the Soviets were entitled to the land for security reasons or because the editors were impressed by the enormity of Soviet power. In an editorial on October 18, 1943, *New Republic* declared: "It would be folly for the Soviet Union to give up the influence which is falling into her lap." *Christian Century* and *Saturday Evening Post* noted that Soviet expansionism in eastern Europe was a fact to be reckoned with in the postwar world, and the smaller countries of eastern Europe should realistically

face up to the new development. By the end of 1943, an article in
American Mercury stated that neither Poland nor the Baltic States
should disturb amicable Soviet-American relations. *Life* declared
blandly that Soviets were just like Americans and compared the
NKVD to the FBI.[18]

When Berlin announced the discovery of the corpses of Polish officers at Katyn and accused the Soviets of the atrocity, the Poles
asked the International Red Cross to investigate the allegation. The
Soviet Union, accusing the Poles of acting in collusion with the Nazis,
severed diplomatic relations with the Polish government. *Nation* ap-
preciated Soviet anger with the Poles in petitioning the Red Cross to
investigate the German report, which it considered phony, but regretted that the Kremlin broke relations with the Poles. The *New York
Times* said much the same thing. *Christian Century* said the Poles
made a mistake and predicted that the Soviets would establish a Polish
government of their own. *Saturday Evening Post,* reflecting the views
of many Americans, declared the German report had no truth to it
and was intended to sow seeds of discord in Polish-Soviet relations in
order to weaken the Allied alliance.[19]

New Republic, on the other hand, accused the Poles of using the
issue to secure Anglo-American sympathy in the boundary dispute
with the Soviet Union. Even Polish resistance to the Germans was
criticized for being more nationalistic than ideological. *New Republic*
was the first American journal to question the representative character
of the Polish government, suggesting that the current one was a de-
scendant of those which were "as illiberal as the Nazis themselves."
One writer scored what he considered to be the mediocrity, reactionism, and Russophobia of the Polish ministers in London.[20]

The Polish government recognized the serious repercussions of its
action and almost immediately tried to improve the situation by withdrawing its request to the Red Cross. But it was too late; the Soviets
refused to restore relations. Polish officials tried to offset the negative
publicity their government had received in the American press by
providing information on Poland under Nazi domination to sympathetic writers who published the accounts in American periodicals.[21]

But the main thrust of the Polish government was to exert more
effort and to spend more money through its public relations agencies
in the United States to improve its image. So concerned was the Polish government about the deterioration of its image across the Atlantic
that it sent the secretary-general of the Ministry of Information to the
United States early in 1944 to step up propaganda activities. There
was a widespread feeling among the London Poles by then that the
very existence of the Polish government depended to a large degree

on the support it received from Americans, especially those of Polish extraction.[22]

The Polish Ministry of Information officially spent $3,324,000 in 1944 on propaganda activities. One of the major beneficiaries of the funds was the government's propaganda agency in the United States, the Polish Information Center, located in New York. Its budget in 1943 was $500,000; in 1944, it doubled. Other agencies receiving funds from the Polish government to promote the Polish cause in the United States included: the Polish Labor Group, Polish Catholic Agency, Polish Telegraph Agency, and the Polish Consul.[23]

Much of the money was spent on publishing various pamphlets, periodicals, and other printed material in the English language. *Poland Fights,* published by the Polish Labor Group, was a periodical that reminded Americans about the contributions of Poles to the war effort. *Polish Review,* a more sophisticated periodical, blended history with politics. It not only detailed Poland's fight against the Nazis since 1939 through its underground but also subtly tried to offset charges of Polish anti-Semitism and to point out the historical and cultural reasons for the restoration of Poland's prewar frontier. Another regular publication was the Polish Information Center's *Polish Facts and Figures,* which acquainted the American public with the political and social facts of Poland and, like other publications, reminded Americans of Polish resistance efforts.[24]

Perhaps the most sophisticated pamphlets published in the United States were those by KNAPP, which had close connections with the Polish government and its agencies in the United States. KNAPP's publications, printed in English and in Polish, covered different topics but their focus was the territorial integrity and independence of Poland. Invariably, some of these publications were critical of Anglo-American policies toward the Soviet Union and almost all of them were anti-Soviet.[25]

The Roosevelt administration became very upset with the publication of such material by agencies directly or indirectly linked with the Polish government because the London Poles had received funds on a regular basis since 1942 from the President's Emergency Fund. The funds, intended principally to finance the operations of the Polish underground, totaled $25 million by April 1944. Administration officials wanted Roosevelt to do something about the use of funds to finance material which criticized the United States and the Soviet Union. "Certainly any connection between U.S. funds for Poland and the use of such funds for anti-Administration propaganda in the United States deserves attention," Jonathan Daniels told the president. And if the Polish government did not "clean up this situation," then

he advised that it could be handled under the terms of the Foreign
Agents Registration Act.[26] Congressman Emanuel Celler brought up
the matter in Congress, suggesting that the funds the London Poles
received from the White House had been misused. Instead of using
the money for the Polish underground, the Polish government, Celler
charged, put the money "to other uses in the United States."[27]

After May 1944 the London Poles could also count on the help of
the Polish American Congress, the gigantic confederation of fraternal,
church, and civic organizations in the United States, which constituted
a powerful bloc of pro-Polish government opinion in the United States.
Although the Polish American Congress promoted the Polish cause in
the press and in Congress, its efforts were too modest and too belated
to change substantially the generally favorable image of the Soviet
Union in the American public's mind.[28]

The attempts of the London Poles to influence American opinion
were futile. The Polish ambassador to Washington, Ciechanowski,
complained that as early as 1943, "In a bigger and better way this
pro-Soviet propaganda drive [in America] was reminiscent of the
artificially created psychosis for Russia which seized France in the
old days of the Franco-Russian alliance."[29] Premier Mikołajczyk
echoed the same sentiments, saying that raising embarrassing questions about the Soviet Union inevitably brought a charge of "Fascist
saboteur and German spy." Commenting on the erosion of confidence
in the Polish government-in-exile in Western opinion, Mikołajczyk
wrote: "Western public opinion had been wrongly shaped in such a
manner that it was generally agreed that London Poles, many of them
having been away from home for six years, no longer understood
Polish domestic problems and preferred to dissent in order to remain
in the comparative luxury of England."[30]

Wladysław R. Malinowski, an active member of the Polish labor
movement and a strong advocate of Polish-Soviet understanding, told
the European American Club of the Free World Association in September 1943 that an individual could attack President Roosevelt and
his policies without being attacked by American liberals. But criticism of the Soviet Union, which "is considered by some people as a
criterion of democracy and progress," he said, "is considered anti-
Soviet and reactionary." He scored this attitude because it prevented
much needed discussion of crucial wartime issues.[31]

Malinowski's criticism was a valid one because Western Allied policy
had opposed public discussion and debate of the issues in the dispute
between Poland and the Soviet Union. Although Roosevelt and
Churchill sympathized with the Poles, neither wartime leader wanted
publicity of the issues for fear of damaging the fragile alliance with

the Soviet Union. Roosevelt and Churchill, in Mikołajczyk's words, "continued to impose silence upon us."[32]

The situation for the Poles in England was not any better. Eden admitted the Poles did not get as good a press as the Soviets because the Reds were winning victories and the English public was getting impatient with the Poles.[33] The Polish government continually complained about what it considered to be unfair criticism in the English press. Even the usually balanced *Times* increasingly regarded the Poles, Count Raczyński claimed, as an "encumbrance." In January 1944 Raczyński recorded in his diary: "On January 6th I returned to London and immediately found myself once more in the thick of Polish-Soviet differences. The effect is made worse by reading the British press and broadcasting reports. Everything to do with the Soviet ally, and especially its relations with Poland, is enveloped in a dense fog of mendacity."

During the spring of 1944 the London Poles received unfavorable publicity following courts-martial of Polish Jews who had deserted from the Polish army. Polish authorities handled the matter in a clumsy way, and charges of anti-Semitism reverberated throughout England. In despair, Raczyński wrote: "We are the victims of a conspiracy of slander in which different groups of our adversaries combine: pro-Germans, Communists, some Socialists, Russophile conservatives, and former isolationists such as Lord Beaverbrook. Our critics point to our internal differences as proving that the 'Polish reactionaries' have not yet been tamed by more democratic elements and so forth."[34]

Unlike Soviet publications, which were free to publish anything that exacerbated the dispute with Poland, the Polish press in England was subject to wartime censorship regulations which prohibited the publication of material which might "cause disunity between the United Nations." Churchill had promised Stalin after the Katyn affair that "The Polish press will be disciplined in [the] future and all other foreign language publications."[35] The British press followed the admonitions of the government so faithfully that it failed to cover adequately the Warsaw Uprising until Churchill and Eden personally intervened and pleaded for more exposure of the event.[36]

The year 1944 was a high point in the Soviet Union's military and political fortunes. At Tehran Stalin had won recognition of the Curzon Line from Churchill and Roosevelt, and a few months later the Soviets entered Poland. The Red Army offensive of 1944 brought it to Warsaw, the last major capital east of Berlin blocking the Soviet path westward. By the summer of 1944 the Kremlin recognized the Polish Committee of National Liberation, or Lublin Committee as it was

popularly called, and turned over to it the administration of Polish
lands liberated from the Germans.

The American press in 1944 not only dealt with the boundary
question but also increasingly focused upon the political aspects of
Polish-Soviet relations. Despite the impatience attached to the Polish-
Soviet problem, for the most part few writers demanded that the
United States take an active role in the dispute. *New Republic* enthusiastically applauded the Soviet Union's growing influence in
eastern Europe and especially in Poland. Frederick L. Schuman,
writing in the *New Republic,* asserted that historically the United
States and Britain had supported Polish claims west of the Curzon
Line, acceptance of which would be expedient in the interests of Big
Three international politics. He admonished "that present troubles
with Russia are mostly the result of our own past mistakes, and that
you don't end up with good will if you start out with hatred." In an
editorial the same month, the editors argued that Soviet claims of
postwar cooperation with the West should be believed. To allay
Kremlin fears and suspicions, the Soviet Union's buffer in eastern
Europe should be secure. As for the Mikołajczyk government, according to *New Republic,* it was "so deeply reactionary, its recent instructions to the Polish Underground have been so equivocal, that one can
scarcely blame the Russians for insisting that there can be no boundary
discussions with the present Polish government." The theme of Polish
reactionism, the Soviet Union's legitimate need for a buffer zone, and
the Kremlin's sincere desire for postwar friendship with the states
bordering the Soviet Union and the great powers of the West was repeated with monotonous regularity in the pages of *New Republic.* [37]

Other journals, such as *Saturday Evening Post* and *Christian Century,* were far less certain that the Soviet Union would be satisfied
with mere boundary revisions in eastern Euope. *Saturday Evening
Post* was not opposed to some expansion of Soviet interests in Europe,
but it would "not endorse a series of Munichs with Stalin in the driver's
seat instead of Hitler." Although the periodical featured articles by
Forrest Davis, who expressed doubt about Soviet ambitions in eastern
Europe, it also published Edgar Snow's glowing account of the Soviet
Union and its relations with the Lublin Committee. Like so many
journalists who visited the Soviet Union and Lublin, Snow predicted
a Socialist Poland, not a Communist one dominated by the Soviet
Union. [38] *Christian Century* was not so sure that compensating a
future Polish Communist government for territorial losses in the east
by the annexation of east Prussia was consistent with the Atlantic
Charter. But the editors did not see what the United States and England could do about it. [39]

To be sure, there were outspoken critics of the Soviet Union and American policy toward it, but their voices were muted by the barrage of pro-Soviet accounts which appeared in the press. William H. Chamberlin, writing in *Christian Century,* gave a prophetic preview of postwar Poland. He was also angry with pro-Soviet apologists in the United States: "The more Stalin does to undermine our confidence, the more our publicists and statesmen insist on a blind, deaf and dumb cultivation of the quality of confidence." William C. Bullitt, another outspoken critic of the Soviet Union, wrote an equally prophetic article, "World from Rome," which appeared in *Life.*[40] Eugene Lyons, not to be outdone by Chamberlin, wrote a blistering attack against the left entitled, "Letter to American Liberals," which appeared in *American Mercury.* He declared: "You showed yourself willing to countenance and even applaud in Russia the very same crimes you denounced elsewhere, you revealed yourself as just a totalitarian of another stripe who used liberal lingo by way of camouflage."[41]

Newspapers, too, reflected a generally favorable view of the Soviet Union and its policy toward Poland. Eleven out of twelve newspapers this writer surveyed reflected essentially a pro-Soviet view in 1944. In July the *New York Times* admitted its apprehension about how the Soviet Union's recognition of the Lublin Committee could be reconciled with its pledge to consult with the United States and Britain. Despite occasional doubts about Soviet policy, the *New York Times* continued to be remarkably pro-Soviet in its characterizations.[42]

The *Boston Evening Globe* reflected the common belief that Soviet military might justified the Kremlin to do what it pleased in Poland and the rest of eastern Europe. Comparing Soviet policies in Poland to those of a composer of music, "Uncle Dudley" wrote poetically:

> To the tune of victory month after month, they write in under those triumphant themes the full harmonic structure of political consolidation behind their advancing armies.
>
> Land and tools are reactivated as fast as their soil is redeemed. The Curzon line between Russia and Poland is reestablished; a Polish Committee of National Liberation is empowered by the Russians to administer civil affairs in the territory liberated as fast as the Red Army thunders westward.[43]

The *St. Louis Post-Dispatch,* repeating a now familiar theme in the American press, criticized the alleged undemocratic character of the Polish government in London and claimed that Stalin had honored his pledges regarding Polish independence. It criticized the anti-Soviet prejudice of the London Poles and asked them to "bow out of the picture."[44]

Just like those correspondents who visited the Soviet Union and wrote so favorably about it, American newsmen who met and interviewed members of the Lublin Committee tended to be impressed by their reformist plans for postwar Poland and their desire to get along with the Soviets. Maurice Hindus, writing in the *St. Louis Post-Dispatch,* admired Berling's Polish army. M.T. Hanunian, writing in the *Washington Post,* extolled the virtues of Wanda Wasilewska, whom he described as the "real moving spirit" behind the settlement of the Polish-Soviet boundary dispute. Quentin Reynolds described Wasilewska as a "spellbinder." Andre Visson dubbed the Lublin Committee a "political rainbow" from which Stalin could choose Poland's postwar leadership. But he, along with other newsmen, admitted that Mikołajczyk's presence in any future government was important from the standpoint of political legitimacy.[45] One of the few newspapers consistently critical of American and Soviet policy toward Poland was Roosevelt's nemesis, the *Chicago Daily Tribune.* It declared in August 1944: "The cavalier treatment of the Polish government-in-exile, which he recognized, obviously makes a mockery of his Atlantic Charter." On September 1, the newspaper explained that the reason Stalin refused to aid the Varsovians during the uprising was because "he doesn't want Polish Nationalsits to have any conspicuous part in the freeing of their country."[46]

Perhaps the most astonishing indication of how the American alliance with the Soviet Union and Poland had changed is revealed by the coverage of the Warsaw Uprising in the American press during the late summer of 1944. There were only five articles listed under the heading, "Warsaw, Battle of" in 1944 in the *Reader's Guide to Periodical Literature.* There were three more articles listed under "Warsaw," and one article which dealt with the uprising that did not appear under either heading in *Reader's Guide.* In all, then, there were only nine articles in American periodicals on one of the most controversial events of World War II. And two-thirds of them were short news items that appeared in *Newsweek* and *Time* magazines. Most of the articles talked about Polish heroism, reserved judgment on Soviet responsibility in delaying assistance to the Poles or were critical of Polish authorities for prematurely ordering the abortive revolt.

Only two articles in American periodicals in 1944 on the Warsaw Uprising took a pro-Polish position. *Newsweek* dubbed the uprising "the final turning point" in Polish-Soviet relations, making it impossible for Mikołajczyk to reach a reconciliation with the Lublin Poles. *Newsweek* declared that the Soviet Union proved it did not really want a free and independent Poland by the way it acted during the uprising. Then the editors confidently but erroneously predicted that the United States and Britain would not waver in their support of the Polish government in London, "even if this should involve serious difficulty with the Russians." W.R. Malinowski wrote in the *Nation* of Polish heroism and criticized the Big Three for failing to send adequate help to the beleaguered Poles. But his ire also went to the liberal press for "almost completely" ignoring the fighters in the Polish capital.[47]

Predictably, *New Republic* saw the uprising as being launched without proper liaison with the Soviets, a familiar theme in the American press. The editors admitted that it was likely that the Soviets for the same political reasons which motivated the Poles to launch the revolt abstained from coming to Polish assistance. More than a year after the event, Anna Louise Strong, a leading apologist for the Kremlin, explained in an article in *Atlantic Monthly* that Bór's poor timing was largely responsible for the abortive uprising. The Soviets, she argued, could not render proper aid to the Poles because the supply lines of the Red Army were overextended. Moreover, she calmly asserted that the Soviet effort to help the Poles was greater than that of the Western Allies.[48]

American newspapers, too, did not give the coverage to the event, and when they did it was often confused and distorted. The *Detroit News* had Poles pelting Soviet soldiers with flowers as they broke through German defenses in Warsaw's suburbs on the first day of the upheaval. The communiqués of the Polish government dealing with Warsaw simply could not compete with the dispatches covering the Anglo-American drive through France and the liberation of Paris which occurred at the same time. Even domestic political news engaged the attention of columnists and editors more than the Polish upheaval, which to many people seemed a remote event in a distant land. Moreover, journalists had easier access to the Lublin Committee than they did to the political and military authorities in the Polish capital. The consequence was that their stories reflected pro-Lublin bias.[49]

The best newspaper coverage of the Warsaw Uprising was by the *New York Times.* In addition to publishing the communiqués of the Polish government in London, which maintained regular radio contact with General Bór and political representatives of the Polish government in the homeland, the *New York Times* published several editorials on the uprising.[50] Consistent with its position of not judging Soviet policies in Poland, the *New York Times* went so far as to say on October 3, 1944, the day after the Poles surrendered to the Germans, that the United States should not blame the Soviets for the debacle at the Vistula and admonished Americans to remember "that the prewar Government of Poland was Anti-Russian."[51]

The White House press corps seemed almost embarrassed to ask the president about the uprising during his press conferences. Roosevelt held nine of them during the period of the upheaval, but it was not until October 3, 1944, that a reporter asked him the first question about the event. The president casually disposed of the query: "I think that I had better set a good example. I suppose I know as much about that particular thing as any American, and I don't know enough to talk about it." Hull's press conferences were no more informative. A Polish American journalist asked him: "Why do the Allies allow these inhabitants of Warsaw to go down fighting the Germans without any ammunition?" Hull replied it was "a long story," but the United States was "watching every sort of an opportunity to be of any use."[52]

But several members of Congress felt they knew enough about what was going on in Warsaw to criticize the Soviet Union's refusal to help the insurgents and to allow the West the use of its air bases for the purpose. Congressman Thad F. Wasielewski of Wisconsin commented: "It is not my purpose to make any accusation, but it is reasonable, since both Russia and Poland are our allies, to raise the question: 'Why?'" Congressman George Sadowski of Michigan, at the end of his patience with those who argued the uprising was premature, shot back: "Only such people as had suffered for 5 long years under the brutal and savage Huns have the right to discuss the question of prematureness." Congressman Wasielewski joined Sadowski in expressing concern for Polish refugees interned at Pruszków, a detention camp outside Warsaw, where it was widely believed at the time that civilians had been victimized by Nazi cruelties.[53]

The political implications of Soviet behavior at Warsaw brought Congressmen Charles Wolverton, William Barry, and William Miller to express their fears about the restoration of Polish territorial integrity. Congressman Miller became lyrical when he stated that he refused to entrust the future of the United States "to those underhanded men who now are carving up the body of their ally, bled white in their defense."[54]

Popular opinion seems to have been more responsive than the communications media to specific events that precipitated favorable or unfavorable discussion of Soviet policy. For example, in January 1944, when the Red Army crossed into Poland, there was a drop in the number of people expressing confidence in Soviet policy. But on the eve of the Warsaw Uprising, popular trust in the Soviet Union soared to 55 percent, a high that had been achieved almost one year earlier at the time of the Moscow Conference. Yet popular confidence declined by October 1944 because of Soviet behavior during the unsuccessful Warsaw Uprising. By the time of the Yalta Conference, however, most Americans with opinions on international relations thought in positive terms about the Soviets.[55]

From the administration's point of view, the Warsaw Uprising represented a serious threat to the maintenance of amicable Soviet-American relations. The United States was anxious to get the Soviets into the Pacific war to defeat Japan and to continue the allied coalition into the postwar epoch. The press, Congress, and the public reflected the spirit of allied unity espoused by the White House and the State Department. So strong was that spirit that the Polish upheaval did not substantially shake American confidence in the Soviets.

Between 1942 and 1944 there were seven books dealing with the Soviet Union on the nonfiction best sellers list, and all of them treated the Soviets favorably. *Mission to Moscow* ranked second in 1942; *Under Cover* was first, *One World* second, *Journey among Warriors* third, and *U.S. Foreign Policy* eighth in 1943; *Under Cover* dropped to fourth in 1944, and *The Time for Decision* and *The Curtain Rises* were in sixth and ninth place, respectively, in 1944. No books dealing with Poland made the best sellers list.[56]

Joseph E. Davies, the wealthy Wisconsin attorney who served as ambassador to the Soviet Union in the late 1930s, said in *Mission to Moscow* that the Soviet Union was "operating on capitalist principles" and that "the Russian people, the Soviet government, and the Soviet leaders are moved, basically by altruistic concepts." In the epilogue to the book, added in 1942, Davies said, "It is bad Christianity, bad sportsmanship, bad sense to challenge the integrity of the Soviet Union."[57] Davies' book won acceptance among liberals whose confidence in the Soviet Union had been shattered by Stalinist policies before 1941. Even a respected scholar like George Vernadsky thought the book gave a realistic picture of the Soviet Union to Americans.[58] Roosevelt was so impressed by it that on the inside cover of his copy, he wrote: "This book will last." Critics like Eugene Lyons, on the other hand, could not believe Davies' "monumental innocence."[59]

Quentin Reynolds, one of the best-known journalists of the war, in *The Curtain Rises* painted an equally favorable picture of the Soviet Union, stressing his conviction that when the war was over, Stalin would be easy to get along with. Of all the best sellers in the period 1942–1944, Reynolds' book was by far the most critical of the Poles. Referring to the Katyn affair, he said he was shocked at how the London Poles "so stupidly walked into the Goebbels trap." He supported Soviet claims to eastern Poland, accepted the Kremlin position regarding the arrested Polish relief workers, and assumed that the Polish newspapers in London that attacked the Soviet Union represented the opinion of the Sikorski government. To Reynolds, the Poles were out of step with the Soviets and he warned: "Poland isn't big enough to get out of step. When you get out of step you march alone. No one is big enough to march alone in this year of our Lord, 1943."[60]

Although most journalists who traveled to the Soviet Union wrote in positive terms about their experiences there, Eve Curie's *Journey among Warriors,* though generally favorable to Russia, did not depict the Russians in the same exaggerated way that Reynolds and other American journalists did. Moreover, unlike Reynolds, Eve Curie, the half-Polish daughter of Marie Skłodowska Curie, touchingly described the cruel and paradoxical aspects of Polish-Soviet relations.[61]

Three of the best sellers in the period 1942–1944 were programmatic books. Wendell Willkie's *One World,* first published in 1943, sold more than two million copies, and abbreviated versions of it appeared in more than one hundred daily newspapers. It was dubbed "the most influential book" printed in the United States during the war, and in it Wilkie argued for coexistence with the Communists after the war. Impressed by the effectiveness of Soviet society, he described it as a force that could not be ignored in the postwar world.[62] Less simplistic than Wilkie's book were *U.S. Foreign Policy* by Walter Lippmann and *The Time for Decision* by Sumner Welles, both of whom predicted that Americans and Soviets would cooperate in the postwar era because it was in their mutual interests to do so. Welles endorsed the Curzon Line as the future Polish-Soviet boundary with compensations for Poland at German expense. In 1944, Lippman came out with *U.S. War Aims,* which endorsed a Soviet sphere of influence over Poland and eastern Europe as a way to ensure postwar peace.[63]

According to listings in *Book Review Digest,* three to four times more books were published on the Soviet Union in the period 1942–1944 than on Poland. Moreover, a large percentage of the books dealing with the Soviet Union were by well-known journalists whose publications were serialized in popular American magazines. On the other hand, books about Poland were written by lesser known writers, some of them by scholars, did not appear in serial form, and usually were printed in small quantities. The consequence was that these volumes did not have the wide public exposure that books on the Soviet Union had.

Of three books published on Poland in 1942, only two directly involved the war—Simon Segal's *New Order in Poland* and the Polish Ministry of Information's *Black Book of Poland.* In 1943, the year that saw three best sellers alone about the Soviet Union, only three books dealing with Poland at war were published. These included

Professor Oscar Halecki's *History of Poland,* which carried the historical survey to the German campaign of 1939; Stonisław Strzetelski's *When the Storm Broke,* which dealt with the origins of World War II; and M. Kridl's *For Your Freedom and Ours,* an edited collection of historical material which attempted to disprove the oft-repeated depiction of Poland and its society as a nest of reactionary landlords.[64]

Nineteen forty-four was the best year for the Poles in the American book market. Seven books appeared, and six of them concerned Polish resistance against the Germans, beginning with the September campaign through the activities of the Polish armed forces in the West and the Polish underground at home. Predictably, many of them tended to be either implicit or explicit in their criticism of the Soviet Union. They included: *Story of a Secret State,* written by an officer of the AK who served as liaison between the Polish underground and the Polish government in London; *Forgotten Battlefield,* written by a poet who related the experiences of his compatriots in the September campaign; *Poland Fights Back,* which described the activities of Polish airmen, soldiers, and sailors on the various fighting fronts in the West; *Black Book of Polish Jewry,* which documented the extermination of Polish Jews by the Nazis; *We Stood Alone,* written by an American woman who married a Pole, gave a close look at events leading up to the outbreak of the invasion of Poland; and *Poland and Russia,* written by an American who lived for seventeen years in Poland, which was the most anti-Soviet account of the books published.[65]

Academicians contributed to the Americanization of the Soviet image in the United States. Leading scholars, such as Professor Foster Rhea Dulles in *The Road to Teheran*, told readers that historically Soviets and Americans fought as allies but never as enemies. He assured Americans the major objectives of each country's foreign policy was the preservation of peace. Dulles admonished Americans, in the words of Professor Ralph Barton Perry of Harvard University, that the United States could not first try to destroy the Soviets, then ignore them, and finally treat them "as poor relations." Pitirim Sorokin, a Soviet-born sociologist who taught at Harvard, also stressed the similarities between the Soviet Union and the United States, emphasizing the basic values that both countries allegedly shared as a key to understanding the long period of peace and cooperation between them.[66]

Professor Samuel N. Harper, the first leading American scholar of the Soviet Union in the United States, left his memoirs which echoed a deep affection for the Soviet people and sympathy for Soviet foreign policy. Max Lerner, professor of political science at Williams College, excused Stalin's purges, reminded his readers that the West had to share responsibility in driving Stalin to Hitler in 1939, and chided those who thought the Soviet Union would be aggressive after the war. Professor George Vernadsky assured Americans that the Soviet Union, by successive steps, culminating in the abolition of the Comintern, had become a national state.[67]

Sir Bernard Pares, one of the best informed students of the Soviet Union in the West who lectured in the United States in 1943 and 1944, attempted in *Russia and the West* to calm Americans who still were afraid the Soviet Union would export communism after the war. Pares claimed that revolutionary ideas in the Soviet Union were "dead as a doornail." One of the most significant things Pares saw emerging from the Soviet Union was "that material of character and purpose out of which a true democracy can be made." He denied Stalin had any territorial ambitions at Polish expense and besides, Pares confidently declared, the morale of the Poles would be sufficient to resist Soviet domination. Pares felt there was not too much one could do when the Soveit Union registered its *faits accomplis* by military force: "If Russia is to come out of this war as one of its principal winners, she is hardly likely to regard the moment of her greatest weakness as fixing the measure of her rights, or be prepared to give up her conquests for some new general formula of world peace."[68]

Not all scholars of the Soviet Union took so sanguine a view of Soviet policies. David Dallin of Yale University was the most persistent academic critic of the Soviet Union in the United States. In *Russia and Postwar Europe,* published in 1943, he analyzed the Polish-Soviet imbroglio and commented on Soviet shrewdness in separating the question of Poland from the question of the future of Soviet security. He asserted that Stalin's severance of diplomatic relations with the Polish government that year "was the first step, cooly calculated if not free from risk, by which the Soviet Government attempted to organize its sphere of influence." In two articles published the same year in *American Mercury,* he pointed out the Soviet intention to dominate eastern Europe and recommended an Anglo-American military strike through the Balkans to offset it. The eminent scholar, John Dewey, joined Dallin in decrying the idealization of Stalin and his policies and warned of its dangerous implications for the West after the war.[69]

Even the motion pictures, one of the most influential of the mass media, during the period 1942–1944 depicted an overwhelmingly favorable image of the Soviet Union. "After 1942," said one historian of the subject, "the American movie-going audiences, which numbered many millions per week, saw only the admirable side of life in the Soviet Union." One expert has estimated that 85 million Americans saw one movie per week in more than 17,000 theaters. There were newsreels, which usually included the Soviets battling the Germans on the eastern front, and Soviet-made documentaries, often narrated by well-known personalities like Edward G. Robinson, Edward R. Murrow, and Brian Donlevy, which impressed Americans. Most important, of course, were the five major motion pictures Hollywood produced that offered warm treatments of the Russian people at war— *Mission to Moscow, North Star, Song of Russia, Three Russian Girls,* and *Days of Glory.*[70]

Although most of these films were well received, *Mission to Moscow,* billed as "One American's Journey into the Truth," was controversial, prompting a critic to comment "that the Stalinists here stole or were handed such a march that the film is almost describable as the first Soviet production to come from a major American studio." The reviewer probably was unaware at the time that there was close cooperation between OWI and some Hollywood film-makers who on at least two known occasions submitted their scripts to the Soviet embassy in Washington for technical advice.[71]

One of the most powerful Hollywood films was Frank Capra's *Battle of Russia,* which one reviewer called "the best and most important war film ever assembled in this country next to *Birth of a Nation.*" Obviously pleased with Hollywood's films, the Soviets imported several of them. *North Star,* for example, played to 50,000 people over a three-week period in a theater in Siberia.[72]

During a typical week in 1943 in New York City, moviegoers had a choice of four different films about the Soviets but none about the Poles. In addition to motion pictures, the famed impressario, Sol Hurok, brought *Russian Ballet* to theatergoers in New York in 1943 and 1944. During one week in 1944, three Soviet-made films, Hollywood's *Song of Russia,* and a play, *Catherine the Great,* were featured. The same week saw one of the rare occasions that films about Poland were also offered to moviegoers—a *Free Poland* film festival was advertised in a small New York theater and *Madame Curie,* starring Walter Pidgeon and Greer Garson, was shown.[73]

One of the most remarkable phenomena of World War II was the dramatic change in American attitudes toward the Soviets and the Poles. The Soviet Union, considered a pariah in the eyes of Americans before Hitler unleashed "Barbarossa," emerged by the end of the war as an admired and respected nation. Poland, sympathized with more than supported by Americans, came to be characterized as the enfant terrible of the Allies, threatening to wreck the wartime alliance and to lessen the chances of Soviet-American postwar collaboration. In the favorable image-making of the Soviet Union, the government and the press exaggerated the flattering descriptions of the Soviet Union, but even worse they created the illusion that a genuine ideological unity existed among the Big Three. This led to idealistic expectancies in the public's mind that later were frustrated and resulted in bitterness.

While the Soviet Union was depicted as a democratic nation with a constitution similar to the one Americans had, the Polish government increasingly came to be seen as antidemocratic and reactionary. The Polish government, in reality, was more representative and less reactionary than its critics claimed. After all, except for the Communists, all shades of Polish political thought had representation in the Polish government in England and its agencies in the homeland. These characterizations of the Soviet Union and Poland prepared the Americans to accept the Curzon boundary between the two countries and the establishment of a provisional government, dominated by the Communists, in postwar Poland.

VI

POLONIA AND THE POLISH QUESTION

Before 1944 most Polish Americans identified with the Polish American Council which supported the government-in-exile but primarily concerned itself with charitable and humanitarian work on behalf of refugees. As early as the spring of 1942, however, nationalistic Polish Americans in the east, impatient with the Polish American Council for being too timid in political matters and critical of Sikorski's policy of reconciliation with the Kremlin, organized the *Komitet Narodowy Amerykanów Pochodzenia Polskiego* (National Committee of Americans of Polish Descent), known as KNAPP after its Polish words. KNAPP arrogated to itself the role of Polish American spokesman for a free and independent Poland. But KNAPP's members were ultra-nationalistic and Russophobic—some of its leading personalities were former "Colonels" in Piłsudski's government—and it did not have the support of the Catholic church, a major weakness in any organization that presumed to speak for Catholic Polish Americans.

In the spring of 1944, KNAPP leaders joined with moderate midwestern leaders and helped to create the Polish American Congress, a huge federation of fraternal, church, and professional organizations representing 6 million Americans of Polish extraction. The primary purpose of the new organization was to pressure the American government to establish a free and independent Poland after the war. The Polish American Congress became a force in American politics that seriously alarmed the Roosevelt administration, which feared that traditionally Democratic Polish voters might defect from the party in 1944 because of the president's policies toward Poland. The fear proved to be unfounded: Polish voters supported Roosevelt in 1944, but they grew disillusioned with him after the revelations of what transpired at the Yalta conference.

Polish Americans had a rich variety of organizations and newspapers that originated in the last half of the nineteenth century: There were

approximately ten thousand fraternal, religious, literary, and civic
societies in the United States. Among the largest were the fraternals.
The Polish Roman Catholic Union of America (PRCU), a fraternal
insurance organization originated in 1873, was primarily interested
in maintaining the Polish language and culture and the Roman Catholic religion. As a consequence, it was especially active in the establishment of schools and seminaries. During World War II, PRCU was
interested in both the humanitarian and the political side of the Polish question and contributed substantially to war relief for Poland.
As early as March 1942 the PRCU began to see that there was a need
for America's Polonia not only to send relief to Poles abroad but
also to organize a program of action to meet the diplomatic and political challenges that would confront Poland. "Is American Polonia
ready for action?" an editorial in *Naród Polski* asked.

In 1880 refugees of the Revolution of 1863 organized the Polish
National Alliance (PNA) and worked for the restoration of the Polish state. Unlike the PRCU, PNA's membership was not limited to
Poles of the Roman Catholic faith. Like the PRCU, however, PNA
was a fraternal insurance organization, boasting a membership of
300,000 by World War II. Because the PNA was the largest of the
fraternals and open to all Polish Americans, its activities were broader
than those of PRCU, covering a wide range of benevolent, educational,
social, and cultural areas. During World War II the PNA contributed
$1.6 million to the National Fund for Poland and to other agencies for
Polish war relief. The third major mutual aid society was the Polish
Women's Alliance. During World War II, there were approximately
one hundred Polish language newspapers and nine of them were
dailies, two of which were published in Chicago, two in Milwaukee,
and one each in Cleveland, Boston, Buffalo, New York, and Detroit.[1]

In 1941 the major Polish fraternals, along with several smaller ones,
organized the *Rada Polonii Amerykańskiej* (Polish American Council),
or popularly known as the *Rada.* Primarily a relief organization which
unified the humanitarian effort in the United States on behalf of
Polish war victims, the *Rada* did not directly engage in political activity on behalf of Poland. It was, however, the only national federation
which represented the moderate nationalist views of the fraternals.
Dean Francis X. Świetlik of Marquette University Law School, who
was grand censor of the PNA, also headed the *Rada.* Representing
approximately 5 million Polish Americans, the *Rada* expressed its
views through the *Dziennik Związkowy (Alliance Daily),* official
organ of the PNA. The *Rada,* although supporting the Sikorski and
later the Mikołajczyk government, eschewed intruding the Polish
question into American politics and was content to accept Roosevelt's

promise, delivered in a message to its 1942 convention, that "Poland shall rise again."[2]

As early as the summer of 1942, more nationalistic and anti-Soviet Polish Americans grew increasingly critical of the leadership and policies of the *Rada*. They believed that Polonia needed an organization which would speak aggressively for the resurrection of Poland with its prewar frontiers. They criticized the *Rada* not only for failing to provide that role but also for limiting its humanitarian appeals to Polish American citizens instead of making them to all Americans. Meeting in New York on June 20–21, 1942, Polish Americans in the east established the Komitet Narodowy Amerykanów Pochodzenia Polskiego (National Committee of Americans of Polish Descent), or KNAPP. The convention chairman, Franciszek Januszewski, publisher of the Detroit *Dziennik Polski (Polish Daily News)* and one of the five founders of KNAPP, assured Roosevelt of the organization's support, describing the president as "the Commander-in-chief of all free nations of this earth," and pledged the full involvement of Polish Americans in the war effort "to the highest pitch of productiveness and self sacrifice."[3] But KNAPP's president, Maximilian Węgrzynek, editor of *Nowy Świat (New World)* and exclusive importer of Polish hams to the United States, reflected the impatience of his organization when he declared that the time had come for Polish Americans to "stop asking others permission to speak." Now, he vowed, "we shall begin independently and with the greatest strength tell the truth about Poland." Like most KNAPP members, Węgrzynek was a devoted Piłsudskiite who believed that Poland should follow the former dictator's principles in rebuilding the nation after the war. This meant, among other things, implacable hostility to the Soviet Union. Because of KNAPP's narrow political base, most Polish Americans regarded the organization as a small group of followers of Piłsudski. Even the Catholic church was unsympathetic to it. The consequence was that KNAPP, though articulate and vociferous, remained a small organization, numbering only two thousand members by 1943.[4]

As followers of Piłsudski, KNAPP was critical of the policy of the Sikorski and Mikołajczyk governments toward the Soviet Union. It especially criticized the Sikorski-Maisky treaty of 1941 which had not secured Soviet recognition of the Riga Line as the postwar Polish-Soviet frontier. KNAPP believed that Sikorski and his government did a disservice by remaining silent concerning Soviet annexationist designs on Poland, thus giving the impression to American and English citizens that the claims of the Kremlin were justified.[5] Impatient with criticisms of his government's policy of rapprochement with the

Soviet Union, Sikorski tactlessly told an American audience in 1942 that whoever criticized his eastern policy was "an agent of Goebbels." Sikorski's comment provoked a storm of criticism from KNAPP.[6]

KNAPP constantly urged the American government to support Poland against the Soviet Union. Shortly after hearing the news of the Katyn massacre, Węgrzynek expressed the hope to Hull that the American government "will use all its means to verify the revelations of our enemy . . . . A moral Pearl Harbor of the world has been in the making. The United States, alone, has kept the moral conscience of the world alive. This may be the last straw and I pray that God may give our President and you, my dear Sir, the strength to endure and preserve unimpaired our moral leadership to which the faith of mankind is anchored." Hull's reply was vague and noncommittal.[7]

Through its *Biuletyn Organizacyjny (Organization Bulletin)*, KNAPP informed its membership that the problem of Polish refugees in the Soviet Union was not material but political. A vast amount of supplies for Polish refugees piled up in Iran, KNAPP argued, while the Soviets confiscated the supplies for the Poles that got to the Soviet Union. "That is Soviet politics," KNAPP declared. While the Polish government hid these facts, KNAPP announced in May 1943 that it intended to inform the American public of the true state of affairs by publishing a series of advertisements in the nation's newspapers. In July 1943 the congress of KNAPP resolved in a petition sent to Roosevelt and to Congress that the United States government had the right and was in the position through lend-lease aid to the Soviet Union to demand that the Kremlin release the thousands of Poles in the Soviet Union.[8]

Long before the Germans publicized their allegations that the Soviets were responsible for the mass murders at Katyn, KNAPP had concluded that the Kremlin was guilty of the atrocity. One respected member of the organization asked in a letter to the *New York Times* on January 3, 1943: "Has the act of exterminating 7,000 Polish officers, prisoners of war, been paralleled anywhere else?" In March 1943 KNAPP sponsored a Mass for the thousands of Poles, including the officers, allegedly killed by the Soviets. Predictably KNAPP blamed Sikorski for hiding the story of the murdered officers, thus allowing Soviet guilt to go unnoticed and unpunished. In the end, the Soviet Union, not Poland, benefited from the shortsighted policy, said the *Biuletyn Organizacyjny* in May 1943.[9]

The rupture in Polish-Soviet relations in the spring of 1943 appeared to vindicate KNAPP's criticisms of Sikorski's policy toward the Soviet Union and its oft-repeated exhortation that Polonia needed a strong and decisive spokesman. "Where is the voice of American

Polonia?" KNAPP asked. And in a direct slap at the *Rada,* it responded: "There is none." KNAPP claimed that the *Rada* had consistently failed to fill the void of spokesman for Poland in the United States and asserted that it would perform that role. As people tied by blood and culture to the motherland, Polish Americans had a special obligation to speak out loudly about what the Poles were fighting and dying for, an article in the *Biuletyn Organizacyjny* declared. After all, it went on, American and Polish interests were the same—"the triumph of western civilization, of right over might, of Christianity over barbarism, of human freedom over human bondage."[10]

With the entry of Soviet troops into Poland in January 1944 and the aggressiveness of the Kremlin on the Polish question, KNAPP felt that there was now a special urgency for the United States and Britain to confront the Soviet Union firmly. But Węgrzynek despaired of either the United States or Britain doing anything to stop the expansion of the Soviet Union. To dramatize the Polish cause, KNAPP inspired and organized massive religious observances in 341 Polish parishs from Maine to Virginia. KNAPP told Roosevelt in January 1944 that "at this very moment the truth of the Atlantic Charter is being determined." In a speech on March 11, 1944, Węgrzynek attacked British capitulation to the Soviets by agreeing to the Curzon Line and American silence and passivity in the face of the Kremlin's aggressiveness.[11]

By early 1944 KNAPP leaders were convinced that a major Polish American organization with political clout had to be organized in order to influence Washington to take a stronger position toward the Soviet Union over Poland. In March 1944 KNAPP played a crucial role in the creation of the Coordinating Committee of American-Polish Associations in the East, the first major political organization which represented the opinion of Polish American communities in the eastern United States. Even after the creation of the gigantic Polish American Congress in May 1944, the Coordinating Committee continued to function, linking Polish Americans along the eastern seaboard.[12]

Despite its small size, KNAPP's propaganda activities were impressive. It published sixty issues of the *Biuletyn Organizacyjny* from 1942 until 1948. Even more impressive were the seventeen pamphlet-length studies dealing with various aspects of the Polish problem, with special emphasis on Poland's relations with the Soviet Union, that it published. These were not typical propaganda broadsides. Respected writers wrote them, and the tone although obviously pro-Polish was sophisticated and intended for a knowledgeable audience.

Among the best were Ignacy Matuszewski's *What Poland Wants* and *The Western Frontier*; F.A. Voigt's *Poland, Russia, and Great Britain*; John McKee's *Poland, Russia, and Our Honor*; and Stanisław Strzetelski's *Bitwa o Warszawe*,[13] the first historical study in the United States on the Warsaw uprising of 1944.

The most brilliant writer associated with KNAPP was Ignacy Matuszewski, a former minister of finance in Piłsudski's cabinet who published frequently in the two leading rightist newspapers, *Nowy Świat* and *Dziennik Polski* (Detroit). A prolific writer, Matuszewski authored 401 signed articles and 130 unsigned pieces.[14] Matuszewski, who wrote in Polish and English, had no doubt that the Soviet Union intended to obliterate Poland as an independent nation. Therefore, Sikorski's policy of reconciliation with the Soviet Union was anathema to him. In December 1942 Harold Callender, a *New York Times* correspondent, described Matuszewski as "the animating mind" behind the anti-Sikorski press in the United States. He claimed that the Polish writer's motives were not impersonal because he was one of the "Colonels" of Poland "from which General Sikorski became alienated long ago." After Matuszewski rebutted Callender's assertions of his alleged ulterior motives, he asked why should not the Polish opposition express itself. After all, he said, it was Poland, not its government, that was a member of the United Nations: "For this reason one must grant the same rights to the Polish Opposition as one would to any opposition in a free country according to the American pattern, which does not eliminate Republicans from the family of the United Nations when the Democrats are in power." Matuszewski went on to repeat his familiar theme that Sikorski had misled the public about the true state of Polish-Soviet relations and had himself succumbed to illusions about the motivations of Soviet policy. "The peoples of Europe are fighting for freedom," Matuszewski proclaimed, "and not for a change from German to Soviet leadership."[15] Matuszewski bemoaned the fact that American public opinion accepted the Soviet argument that land to the east of the Curzon Line justifiably belonged to the Soviet Union. In an article published in *Nowy Świat* on January 7, 1944, he persuasively argued that the territory claimed by the Soviets in eastern Poland contained 5 Poles for every .005 Soviets.[16]

In seven articles entitled "Your Sweat" which appeared in *Nowy Świat* and *Dziennik Polski* in February 1944, Matuszewski argued that since 4 percent of lend-lease produced for the Soviet Union was the product of the labor of American Poles, Poles sweat only to enslave their own relatives by the Soviet Union. He took the title of Stettinius' book, *Weapon for Victory,* and asked Polish Americans if they were not forging a "Weapon for Defeat." He also charged that Roosevelt gave a higher priority to the lend-lease needs of the Soviet Union than to those of the United States. He satirized: "All American gramophones and political gramaphones are playing an identical tune: 'After the war Russia will be the greatest world power.' May be—if you will make her so. You—Americans. Is Russia winning? Yes—thanks to Polish blood, English stout heart, and your sweat." He concluded the installment of articles by pointing to the obligations imposed on the Soviet Union by her adherence to the Atlantic Charter and posing two questions to his readers: "First, does Russia carry out her obligations under which America had extended her aid? Second, what to do if she doesn't? It isn't my business to answer these questions, but it is yours, as it concerns your sweat."[17]

Because he claimed that the Soviet Union had violated its agreements, including the Sikorski-Maisky Treaty, Matuszewski could not understand why the Roosevelt administration wanted to weaken the Atlantic Charter by appeasing the Soviet Union. To him, such a policy was not only foolish but also dangerous because the Soviet Union wanted to dominate Europe.[18]

Matuszewski considered Mikołajczyk's policy toward the Kremlin even worse than Sikorski's because he was prepared to negotiate Poland's eastern frontier. In an article in *Nowy Świat* in April 1944, Matuszewski roared: "One can not negotiate the death of one's own nation. Whoever starts such negotiations condemns that nation to death." He told Mikołajczyk in July 1944 that the premier did not have the support of the Polish people for his policy of rapprochement with the Soviet Union: "Mr. Mikołajczyk says that he is certain of the support of a majority of Poles. No, Mr. Premier! If, sir, you are going to capitulate, openly or furtively, all Poles will give you, sir, a 'veto.'"[19]

Shocked by the Yalta agreement and the highly touted Hopkins mission to Moscow to end the East-West deadlock over Poland, Matuszewski described the coalition that comprised the provisional government of Poland as a group of "traitors and executioners" and erroneously predicted that "America will turn away from such a government with contempt after the flashy publicity of Mr. Hopkins' mission dies down and the appalling truth becomes known."[20]

Matuszewski's writings provoked a storm of protest from moderate Polish American organizations, the liberal American press, and the administration. The Polish National Alliance declared: "The American Polonia does not need teachers and leaders like Matuszewski." One Polish American group called for the writer's arrest. Another Polish American organization even branded Januszewski, Matuszewski's

publisher, a non-Pole.[21] I.F. Stone, the prolific liberal writer, characterized Matuszewski as "a first-rate mind in the service of reaction"
and wondered disapprovingly why so many Polish intellectuals were
rightists.[22] Peter Davenport, writing in the *Nation,* accused the Pole
of causing disunity among the allies. Eric Estorick, also writing in the
Nation curiously blamed Matuszewski, Węgrzynek, and Januszewski
for causing the Soviet Union to sever diplomatic relations with the
Polish government-in-exile in April 1943.Estorick suggested that the
Polish writer's articles on lend-lease were subversive, a view held by
some in the administration, and claimed without offering proof that
they were responsible for slowdowns in war industries which heavily
employed Polish Americans.[23] Philip Adler sneeringly described
Matuszewski's pamphlet, *What Poland Wants,* as "the bible of the
Polish fascist, anti-democratic, anti-semitic, anti-Soviet intrigants! "[24]

Ever since Pearl Harbor, the American government had been
nervous about the possible disruptive impact of ethnic groups and
newspapers in the United States. Out of 215 major organizations "of
foreign political import," the Poles tied for sixth place with the
Yugoslavs with 13 groups. Polish Americans probably had even a
higher percentage of the ethnic press. Early in the war, Roosevelt
had authorized the Department of Justice to investigate the ethnic
press in an "organized way and as soon as possible." As early as
December 1941 the Department of State made it clear that it dis-
approved of criticism of American foreign policy: "The first concern
of the United States must always be the unity of the country."[25]
Hull was troubled by Americans who continued to have some feeling
for the land of their ancestors: "Men and women who have left other
countries and chosen the United States as their home should think
of foreign policy not in terms of the land they left behind them but
in terms of the land that is giving them refuge and sustenance."[26]

So concerned was Washington about the loyalties of ethnic Americans on national unity and morale, it paid close attention to Americans of foreign origin. It was not surprising, therefore, that the
Roosevelt administration was apprehensive about Matuszewski's
writings and the newpapers that published them. As a consequence,
Matuszewski was forced to register under the Foreign Agents Registration Act, even though communists and fellow travellers were
spared that harassment. One government official described Detroit's
Dziennik Polski,[27] to which Matuszewski often contributed, as one
of "the two most violent 'nationalist Polish' papers in the United
States." The other, he added, was *Nowy Świat.* The Office of Emergency Management was upset over the possibility that the president,
as a matter of routine, planned to send a congratulatory message to

the publisher of the *Dziennik Polski,* Januszewski, on the fortieth
anniversary of the newspaper because "even the barest congratulatory
note, will be taken as an endorsement of the paper and so understood
by its readers." It added patronizingly: "The foreign language audience works that way." But after Congressman Sadowski assured the
White House on March 7, 1944, that Januszewski's newspaper had
supported Roosevelt in 1936 and 1940 and would support him in
1944, Roosevelt sent the note of congratulations, conspicuously
avoiding as he had been advised, "the controversial Polish-Soviet situation."[28]

As Soviet armies swept across the prewar Polish-Soviet frontier,
Polish Americans became more apprehensive about the likelihood
that Poland would be reestablished as an independent nation after
the war. The policy of moderation, espoused by the *Rada,* became
less convincing to Polish Americans confronted almost daily by
evidence of Soviet aggressive ambitions at Poland's expense. KNAPP
had long argued that there was a vital need to create a strong organization in defense of Poland's rights, a need that it had been unable to
fill. By early 1944 events moved swiftly to mobilize a national federation of Polish American organizations. On January 29, 1944, the
Rada declared that as a relief organization it could not engage in
political activity, thus abdicating the field to others. The *Rada* had
no alternative: political activity by relief organizations receiving
funds from the National War Fund was forbidden. On March 4–5,
1944, fifty delegates met in Chicago as a Conference of Representatives of Polish Mutual Aid Organizations, Clergy, and the Polish Press.
The meeting, dominated by the three largest fraternals, included
representatives from the clergy and eight of the nine Polish dailies.
Charles Rozmarek, president of the Polish National Alliance, delivered
the keynote address. He emphasized the need for American Poles to
coordinate their activities in the defense of Poland and called for a
Congress of Polonia to accomplish the objective. Peter Yolles, former
editor of *Nowy Świat,* suggested that $100,000 be raised to tell
"the truth about Poland" and that the signatures of 5 million Americans of non-Polish origin be gathered to impress Congress with the
grassroots support in the United States for a free Poland. The conference called for a Congress of Polonia "for the purpose of supporting
the efforts of the American Government to win the war and the peace,
to support the Atlantic Charter and the Four Freedoms of President
Roosevelt as well as to come to the aid of democratic Poland, represented by the legal Government in London." The declaration left no
doubt that the Congress would also be "a gigantic manifestation for
the cause of Poland, and at the same time an evidence of the strength

and solidarity of Americans of Polish descent." The delegates appointed an executive committee, consisting of Rozmarek, John Olejniczak, president of the Polish Roman Catholic Union, and Honorata Wołowska, president of the Polish Women's Alliance, to make the necessary arrangements for the forthcoming congress.[29]

Meanwhile, KNAPP planned a conference of its own in the east. On March 11 and 12, 1944, 170 delegates representing 2 million people, established the Coordinating Committee of American Polish Associations in the East. Rozmarek attended the meeting and was one of its principal speakers. He paid tribute to Węgrzynek, head of KNAPP and the Coordinating Committee of American-Polish Associations in the East, whose political activities "splendidly filled out the gaps in activities in times when Polonia was not yet organized as an entity in defense of Poland's rights." Rozmarek appealed to the New York–based group to work "together, unitedly and harmoniously" with the Chicago-based Polonia. A few of the delegates suspected that Rozmarek wanted to hamper the activities of the Coordinating Committee, but Rozmarek, a suave, friendly man, managed to persuade the New York organization to appoint representatives to the executive committee of the Polish American Congress.[30] Rozmarek's role in bringing together the two centers of Polonia on the eve of the official convocation of the Polish American Congress was crucial in forging the united front that Polish Americans needed in order to speak with authority on behalf of Poland.

To be sure, the conferences in Chicago and New York in March 1944 had their critics in the Polish American community. The *Przewodnik Katolicki (Catholic Guide),* a Catholic weekly which originally supported the Chicago meeting, was critical that only three delegates represented thousands of Polish Roman Catholic priests. The newspaper left no doubt, too, what it thought of KNAPP's leaders:

> It is difficult to believe that such disrupters of American Polonia as Yolles, Wegrzynek, Matuszewski, Januszewski . . . should suddenly without any motives, burn with disinterested love for the Polish cause. For this reason so many of the present leaders of KNAPP, seeing that the future Poland will no longer be that of the Sanacja, that they will not have a monopoly of hams, or free trips, and that they are losing the ground under their feet, are trying to save themselves by joining the ranks of national and Catholic leaders.

Polish American leftists also attacked the union of the Chicago Polonia with KNAPP. The Kościuszko League, organized by Father Stanisław Orlemański, condemned Rozmarek's claim that an alliance with KNAPP was necessary for the future of Poland. The league congratulated Świetlik, head of the *Rada,* for opposing the involvement of Polonia in Polish politics.[31]

The organizational efforts of American Polonia brought concern to Washington. Administrative officials viewed with alarm the forthcoming conclave of the Polish American Congress in Buffalo at the end of May 1944. As early as June 1943, the Foreign Nationalities Branch of the Office of Strategic Services had concluded that the rupture of Polish-Soviet relations had resulted in greater Polish American political awareness. But it warned: "Coupled with the numerical strength of the Polish American community this may make Polish aspirations in Europe a matter of some consequence in American politics during 1943 and 1944."[32] White House adviser Oscar Cox told Harry Hopkins early in February 1944 that the Polish-Soviet dispute had reached the point that it might have undesirable domestic repercussions. "The Polish-Americans," he said, "may be able to start enough of a rumpus to swing over other groups before November of 1944."

Roosevelt himself was concerned about what was going on in American Polonia. Four days after the Chicago conference, Roosevelt in a message to Churchill conveyed his anxiety about "our Polish complications here." Polish American Congressmen also put pressure on Roosevelt to do everything he could for Poland. In late October 1943 ten Polish American legislators, joined by the speaker and majority and minority leaders, made a special appeal to the president on behalf of Poland. Four months later, Congressman Joseph Mruk of New York caustically asked the president: "Do you think, Mr. President, that the Atlantic Charter can still be saved from the world's great heap of well-intentioned 'scraps of paper'?"[33] On their part, the president's assistants paid more attention than before to the anniversaries of Polish parishes, schools, and newspapers by sending greetings and congratulatory messages on the president's behalf.[34]

The Office of Strategic Services recognized that American Polonia was not "at heart anti-Administration," but it was apprehensive over what could happen at the forthcoming meeting of the Polish American Congress in Buffalo. On April 1, 1944, the Foreign Nationalities Branch told the director of Strategic Services:

> Concrete manifestations of a new united movement taking form, which after the mammoth meeting in Buffalo next month may become seriously disturbing in American politics, include a shoving aside of the moderate leadership in the Polish-American fraternals and the alignment of these powerful organizations with the ultra-nationalist, openly anti-Russian leadership of the numerically small National Committee of Americans of Polish Descent (KNAPP).

The Congress, it warned, was "expected to bring to full flood a tide of Polish nationalist sentiment in the United States."[35]

Even before the Buffalo conclave, Polish Americans left little doubt about their political awareness and organizational talent. In commemoration of Poland's Constitution Day on May 3, the White House was inundated with thousands of printed postcards urging the president to oppose another partition of Poland. One clerk in the White House asked his superior in despair: "What do we do with the 4,000 that arrived by May 8?" They were sent to the State Department.[36]

The Polish American Congress met in Buffalo during May 28–30, 1944, the largest gathering of Poles in the United States. More than two thousand delegates from twenty-two states attended. Most of the delegates were middle-class men and women; almost one-third of them were clergy who represented not only the Roman Catholic church but also the Polish National Catholic church. Before the convocation of the Congress, a huge parade, consisting of twenty-five thousand participants, marched through Buffalo's business district.[37]

Rozmarek, who delivered the keynote address, dispelled fears in Washington that the Congress had gathered for political purposes. "The Polish cause is too sacred to be used for partisan politics," he declared. The Congress had two major objectives, Rozmarek said: to cooperate with the government to end the war and to support American foreign policy based on the Atlantic Charter which would ensure a just peace for Poland. Rozmarek, echoing the strong anti-Soviet line of KNAPP, condemned Soviet expansionism and decried those who argued that the Kremlin needed eastern Poland for security reasons. The Soviet Union did not have to fear Poland, he said, and reminded his audience that it was the Soviet Union which had participated in the partitions of the eighteenth century.[38] So unified was the congress in its anti-Soviet position that when Adam Kujtkowski, a delegate from Detroit who represented the Polish National Alliance and who also was a supporter of the Kościuszko League, rose to speak, he was booed and shouted down with cries of "Bolshevik." Other speakers, too, echoed the strong anti-Soviet tone of the Congress and urged the administration to restore the Polish state with its prewar frontiers.[39]

Lest anyone accuse Polish Americans of disloyalty, Rozmarek emphasized their sacrifices in the war, their record of purchases of war bonds, and their noninvolvement in even a single case of sabotage. Rozmarek had elements of the press in mind when he condemned them for "waging a campaign of villification not only against Poland but against native Americans of Polish descent."[40] So sensitive was the organization to charges of being half-American or, worse, un-American that it did not hyphenate its name. The Polish American Congress released a statement which read: "We maintain our filial love for Poland does not in any way alter our loyalty to the United States. We are Americans first and last." Although the speeches at the meeting revealed doubt about the administration's foreign policy, the delegates applauded Roosevelt's name whenever it was mentioned. And when the president's greetings were read to the convention, the delegates rose to their feet in applause.[41]

Rozmarek kept administration officials informed about the meeting of the Polish American Congress before it even convened. He assured the delegates, "We are not doing anything objectionable to American authorities." Before the convention assembled Assistant Secretary of State Breckinridge Long had advised Polish American leaders to set an American rather than a Polish direction in their discussions in Buffalo. The organizers of the conclave followed his advice because they conspicuously did not invite the Polish ambassador or any of the Polish consuls to Buffalo. Even the Polish Telegraph Agency did not send an observer. Ciechanowski and Victor Podoski, his counterpart in Canada, told the press that they had nothing to do with the congress, saying: "It is entirely the affair of Americans of Polish descent, and it is our policy to have nothing to do with it."[42]

The constitution adopted by the congress was a victory for those who controlled the machinery of the convention. The document stated seven basic aims of the Polish American Congress. The crucial one read: "To unify action by Polish Americans consistent with their rights and privileges as citizens of this country." This, in effect, gave a clear mandate to the Congress to pressure the administration to support Poland against Russia. The constitution provided for an executive committee, consisting of a president, five vice-presidents, an executive secretary, and a treasurer. It consisted of Charles Rozmarek, president; Maximilian Węgrzynek, Jan F. Mikuta, Teofil Starzyński, Franciszek Januszewski, and Honorata Wołowska, vice-presidents; Stanisław Gutowski, executive secretary; and Jan Olejniczak, treasurer. KNAPP influence on the executive committee was strong: three of the people were either members or supporters of the organization.[43]

The congress adopted a memorial to President Roosevelt on May 30, 1944. The original draft was revised, eliminating irrelevancies and some of the strong language. In its final form, the memorial urged Roosevelt to continue to aid Poland, emphasized the importance of the triumph of the Atlantic Charter after the war, endorsed the continued recognition of the Polish government-in-exile, admonished the United States not to surrender its ideals to "any of her

Allies by accepting exigencies which violate our honor or sense of justice," emphasized that the permanency of the postwar peace depended upon a just solution to the Polish problem, and appealed to the President not to recognize Soviet *faits accomplis* affecting Polish independence and territorial integrity.[44]

On the same day, the congress approved a memorandum to Secretary Hull which expressed the basic principles that guided its opinion. Endorsing the Atlantic Charter as "the supreme achievement of our international political activity," the Polish American Congress told Hull that it saw these principles not as abstractions but as vehicles to achieve American security. To Hull, the congress was more candid in expressing its suspicion and doubt about American policy toward the Soviet Union. Efforts to reconcile the system represented by the Atlantic Charter and that represented by the Soviet Union had led to "the obscurity of the present foreign policy of the United States which is giving rise to much well-founded criticism." Convinced that the Soviet Union could not continue its fight against the Germans without American lend-lease aid, a commonly held view in Polish American circles, the congress told Hull: "As regards the war period, it is apparent that, due to the development of its military strength, the United States has become the world's greatest military, sea, and air power. As, at the same time, America is the arsenal of the United Nations, none of those nations can successfully continue its military operations without our help."[45] The implication was clear—cut off American lend-lease to the Soviet Union and thus force the Kremlin to honor the Atlantic Charter.

One of the largest contingents at the congress was the Roman Catholic and Polish National Catholic clergy. The Roman Catholics were concerned that KNAPP leaders might seize control of the congress and push the organization too far in an extreme direction and also that the Polish National Catholics were given equality with the Roman Catholic clerics at the convention. There was a sticky moment when one delegate moved that a bishop of the Polish National Catholic church address the conclave after a Roman Catholic hierarch had done so. Rozmarek denied the motion, stating that there were too many prelates to allow all of them to speak. A serious crisis was averted when a Roman Catholic bishop spoke on behalf of the motion and the Polish National Catholic prelate was allowed to say a few words. But a more significant conflict arose over a resolution of the Committee on Religious Affairs which had recommended support of the League for Religious Assistance to Poland, an organization associated with Catholic Action. After heated discussion, the resolution was sent back to the committee. In its revised form, the resolution mentioned the league as one of several organizations worthy of support and affirmed Poland's traditional freedom of religion. The Polish National Catholic church had won a victory.[46]

One of the most important meetings during the congress was that of the three Polish American organizations of journalists—the Polish National Union of America, the Guild of Polish Newspapermen, and the Alliance of Polish Journalists—which established the Union of the Polish American Press. The purpose of the new organization was to act as a news gathering agency for the Polish press in America and to improve the interpretation of news about Poland through a representative in Washington. The Polish government had long believed that the American public should be better informed about Poland's postwar goals and hoped the Polish American press, unified in one syndicate, would meet that challenge. Among the motions presented before the new organization was a protest to be sent to the British government for suspending publication of the rightist, anti-Soviet newspaper, *Wiadomości Polskie (Polish News)*. Almost one hundred Polish American newspapers, including the nine major dailies, affiliated with the Polish American Congress during the years 1944–1948.[47]

Even Polish businessmen met in Buffalo in several conferences as the Federated Merchants Organizations of America. Ignacy Nurkiewicz, who headed the group, warned the American business community about the economic impact of the Soviet Union in European markets. He admonished:

> If this is true concerning Europe, it is particularly true concerning Poland— that any curtailment of whose boundaries, we warn our fellow Americans, will have a definitely detrimental effect upon the economic life of the United States . . . . It is obvious, therefore, that should the Eastern territory of Poland be annexed to Soviet Russia, half of the Polish market will be lost to American trade.[48]

The fears of the government that the Polish American Congress would have a disturbing political impact proved to be groundless. Though its resolutions were anti-Soviet and expressed doubt about American policies toward the Soviet Union, the congress had gone out of its way to assure the administration that the Polish question was not an issue of partisan politics. One White House official, obviously relieved by the moderate position of the congress on American foreign policy, confidently observed: "I think we sort of handled the Buffalo conference so that we pulled some of the fangs out of it." Washington officials even had grudging admiration for the Polish conclave: one report said it "will go down in history as the most colossal piece of organizational work."[49]

To be sure, the Polish American Congress had its critics. Long was disappointed that the congress "popped off" too much in the direction of Polish nationalism. The *New York Times* warned the delegates in Buffalo not to follow a line that "would merely emphasize the first part of its hyphenated name and raise suspicion that an intransigent Poland is dearer to it than either America or victory." *Pravda* labeled the congress "a comedy of Polish fascists,"[50] a view endorsed by the pro-Soviet Kościuszko League and the American Polish Labor Council.

One week after the Buffalo convention, Rozmarek wrote to Roosevelt and requested that a delegation of the Polish American Congress meet with him in order to present the memorial which the conclave had adopted. Despite assurances from Congressman John Dingell and Senator James Mead, both of whom had addressed the Buffalo gathering, that the Polish American Congress was friendly to Roosevelt and that Rozmarek would be an influential delegate to the Democratic Convention, the president was not so sure that it was a good idea. He asked his aides, Stephen Early and Judge Samuel Rosenman: "What do you think?" Rosenman immediately sought State Department guidance.[51]

Elbridge Durbrow, the department's expert on Polish affairs, admitted that the president was in a bad position. If he agreed to see the delegation of Polish Americans, Durbrow feared that considerable anti-Soviet publicity might follow because of the tone of the memorial. Yet, Durbrow admitted that if the president refused to see the Poles, he would probably be subjected to criticism from most Polish Americans. Presidential advisors Jonathan Daniels and David Niles erroneously concluded that "most" of the members of the delegation selected to present the memorial to the president were unfriendly to him and that if he received the group from the Polish American Congress, he should also see the representatives from the American Polish Labor Council, which was pro-Roosevelt. They said, "Inasmuch as he probably would not want to see both, we do not think he should see either." Early and Rosenman therefore advised the president that General Edwin Watson, one of Roosevelt's secretaries, should receive the memorial and that he should also see a delegation from the American Polish Labor Council.[52]

There the matter rested until early September 1944, during the height of the Warsaw Uprising, when Rozmarek again repeated his request for the delegation to deliver personally the memorial to the president. This time Rozmarek enlisted the help of Mayor Edward Kelly of Chicago who told Watson that Rozmarek "is probably the most influential Pole in this area" and urged that the president receive him. Kelly, uncertain about the Polish vote in Illinois in 1944, thought the visit would help the Democratic party's chances. By then most of the administration officials who originally opposed the idea of the visit now had changed their minds. Niles now told Rosenman: "I am certain the President should see Rozmarek. The Labor Poles are not pressing at this time so I'd forget them for the present—Remember October 11 is a Polish Holiday." The State Department, too, had changed its opinion on the advisability of the visit. Attorney General Biddle, reacting to the Polish plight in Warsaw, told the president, "This would afford you an excellent opportunity to meet the Committee and say something that would hearten the Poles. You need not, of course, commit yourself to any line."[53]

By September, the Warsaw Uprising and the upcoming presidential election were the crucial factors in convincing the president's advisors that he should see the Polish American leaders. By then, Polish Americans were outraged by Soviet inactivity at the Vistula while the Germans slaughtered their kinsmen in Warsaw. They had serious doubts, too, about American failures in helping the Varsovians. Rozmarek asked: "Why haven't we the moral strength to give voice to our abhorrence? Our silence augments the cry of Warsaw." In a speech over the Columbia Broadcasting System, Rozmarek expressed concern about the 150,000 Poles in the detention camp at Pruszków, outside Warsaw, who he claimed were "doomed to extermination." Olejniczak and Wołowska, leaders of the other two large fraternals, joined Rozmarek in appealing to Roosevelt to prevent the mass murder of Poles at Pruszków by the Germans. *Naród Polski*, PRCU's weekly, declared its conviction that Roosevelt, whom it once described as a "providential president of America and the entire world," did all he could to aid Warsaw.[54] During the uprising, countless Polish American groups drafted petitions and resolutions opposing another partition of Poland and urging the United States to be firmer toward the Soviets.[55] Congressmen, too, expressed sympathy for their constituents. Philip Philbin of Massachusetts declared that in view of Soviet behavior toward Poland, "is it surprising that our Polish-Americans are so disturbed and upset over the events transpiring in Europe?"[56]

By then the White House was keenly aware that none of the major Polish American fraternals had endorsed Roosevelt yet for a fourth term. Washington officials, moreover, were frankly concerned about the efforts of the Roman Catholic church and Catholic labor unions who interjected the Polish issue in the campaign and urged Polish Americans to be more aggressive on the Polish question. Hopkins observed: "I confess I have no great patience with the efforts which the Church inspires by what amounts to almost secret and devious methods to control the political affairs of the world."[57] Accordingly, the administration tried to appease Polish American voters. Under the circumstances, one wonders whether the AAF relief mission to Warsaw on September 18 was not at least partially motivated by domestic political considerations.

Roosevelt asked Hull if he would paraphrase the messages of gratitude from Mikołajczyk for sending the aid and release them to the press.[58] When Arthur Lane's nomination as the new American ambassador to Poland became known during the same month, people close to the president pointedly asked the Polish ambassador to the United States if the appointment would help Roosevelt politically. Ciechanowski, no child to politics, wrote later: "I answered jokingly that it would largely depend on whether Arthur Lane was sent to London in time to present his credentials to the President of Poland before the November elections." To dramatize American concern for Poland, one of the presidents's advisors suggested that cities in the United States provide skills, supplies, and other assistance to rebuild Warsaw after the war. Since several other European cities had suffered as much as Warsaw, the proposal was primarily politically, not altruistically, motivated. The president was so concerned about his Polish American constituency that he agreed not to retire the only Polish American general then in service, Joseph Barczyński, from the army because of age. Finally, on October 2, 1944, the day the Poles surrendered to the Nazis in Warsaw, Roosevelt recognized that it was good politics to see the delegation representing the Polish American Congress, which had tried to see him for four months.[59]

On October 11, 1944, nine Polish American leaders met President Roosevelt in the White House. They included the three presidents of the major fraternals, Rozmarek, Olejniczak, and Wołowska. In addition, there were Teofil Starzyński, president of the Polish Falcons of America; Walter Pytko, president of the Polish Beneficial Society; Thaddeus Adeszko, a prominent attorney from Chicago; Stanisław Gutowski, executive secretary of the Polish American Congress; Jan Mikuta, treasurer of the Polish National Union of America; and B.L. Smykowski, president of the Polish American Council, District 2. Rozmarek, spokesman for the delegation, presented the memorial to the president and asked for his assurances that the principles of the Atlantic Charter still constituted the basis of American foreign policy. He pointedly asked that "neither an alien nor a puppet system of government shall be imposed upon Poland nor that any part of her population will ever be disposed of or transferred against the really freely expressed will of the Polish people."[60] In reality, the Polish American

Congress had adopted a position on Poland's frontiers considerably more extreme than that of Mikołajczyk's government which had already conceded that a demarcation line be drawn during the war, pending a permanent determination of the Polish-Soviet boundary after hostilities.

The president did not made any definite commitments to the delegation. "You and I," Roosevelt replied, "are all agreed that Poland must be reconstituted as a great nation. There can be no doubt about that." He conspicuously avoided saying anything about Poland's future government or boundaries, which was precisely what the Polish Americans wanted to hear. Roosevelt delivered his general remarks before a backdrop of a huge prewar map of Poland, thus strongly implying that Poland would be recreated with the Riga Line as the Polish-Soviet boundary.[61]

Roosevelt's meeting with the Polish American leaders was not entirely a success. Rozmarek was a Democrat but he had not endorsed Roosevelt for another term yet. Neither did he make any deal to support Dewey, as had been alleged.[62] Although a few of the leaders of the Polish American Congress were Republicans, especially those with KNAPP connections, most were Democrats, thus reflecting the prevailing political views of most Polish Americans affiliated with the congress. Even the strongly Republican KNAPP, for example, recognized this elemental fact about the Polish American voter and did not take an active role against Roosevelt's reelection. Rozmarek simply bided his time, waiting for a stronger statement by Roosevelt in support of Poland before he endorsed him. And he got it. On October 28, 1944, a week away from the election, the president invited Rozmarek aboard the presidential train in Chicago and promised him that the principles of the Atlantic Charter and the Four Freedoms would not be abandoned concerning Poland. On the basis of Roosevelt's promises, which went considerably farther than what he had told Rozmarek two weeks earlier in the White House, Rozmarek endorsed the president for reelection on the following day, an endorsement which was widely publicized in the Polish American press before the election.[63]

During the campaign of 1944, Dewey tried to convince Polish voters that if he was elected president he would follow a tougher policy toward the Soviet Union. Januszewski, one of the vice-presidents of the Polish American Congress and a Republican, complained to Senator Arthur Vandenberg about Dewey's concentrating his attacks on the New Deal, which had helped the Poles, instead of on Roosevelt's foreign policy. But Vandenberg pointed out that the Republicans could not yet prove that Roosevelt had failed to live up to American commitments to Poland. Moreover, Vandenberg confided his doubt that Dewey, if elected, could get a better settlement for Poland from Stalin than Roosevelt.[64]

Dewey's strongest statements in support of Poland came at the Pulaski Day celebration in New York City early in October when he expressed his doubts about Roosevelt's commitment to restore the Polish nation to its prewar boundaries and urged Polish Americans "to bring discussions of Poland's fate from the dark to the light." Former President Hoover, who privately said to Ciechanowski that Roosevelt had "double-crossed" Poland, told the same audience in New York that he thought the administration had engaged in arrangements with the Soviets that might be detrimental to Poland. Mayor Fiorello LaGuardia, who was also on the program, described the Pulaski Day parade as a protest against the lack of support to the defenders of Warsaw who had been forced to capitulate.[65]

Administration fears about the Polish vote in the election proved groundless. Over 90 percent of Polish Americans voted for the president. Table 1 lists the eighteen states with the largest Polish American population and the election results in those states.[66]

No sooner was the election in the United States over than Churchill made his famous speech to the House of Commons in December 1944 which endorsed Soviet claims to eastern Poland. The Polish American Congress reacted strongly against British policy and opposed Churchill's efforts to pressure the Polish government to compromise with the Kremlin on the Curzon Line. Rozmarek described Churchill's policy as a recognition of "his impotency to deal with an ally turned aggressor." Then, in the sternest criticism he had màde about Roosevelt's policy, Rozmarek stated: "The American people are entitled to receive a more clarifying analysis of their government's foreign policy than any heretofore given."[67]

At the end of December 1944 Rozmarek called for an extraordinary session of the Supreme Council of the Polish American Congress to meet in Washington and urged Polish Americans to flood Congress, the White House, and the State Department with protests against the Soviet Union's policy toward Poland. The administration, alarmed by the increasing sharpness of Polish American criticism, tried to stifle it by appeals to patriotism and the need to maintain Allied unity in order to win the war.[68]

Despite the outpouring of support for the Polish government-in-exile and the reconstruction of Poland with its prewar frontiers, Polonia had no direct influence in changing either American public opinion or Washington's policy toward the Soviet Union over Poland. Its impact was more moral than political, as an advocate, and often a very eloquent one, of the ideals contained in the Atlantic Charter.

STATES WITH LARGEST POPULATIONS OF POLISH DESCENT

State	Population of Polish Descent[1]	Percentage of Total Population	Total Vote 1944[1]	
			Roosevelt	Dewey
New York	689	5.0	3,304	2,988
Illinois	422	5.0	2,079	1,939
Pennsylvania	398	4.0	1,940	1,835
Michigan	294	6.0	1,107	1,084
New Jersey	219	5.0	988	961
Ohio	157	2.0	1,571	1,582
Massachusetts	156	4.0	1,035	921
Connecticut	121	7.0	435	391
Wisconsin	118	4.0	650	675
Indiana	49	1.0	781	876
Minnesota	39	1.0	590	527
California	37	1.0	1,989	1,513
Maryland	34	2.0	315	293
Rhode Island	19	3.0	175	123
Missouri	19	1.0	807	761
Texas	14	0.2	822	191
Nebraska	13	1.0	233	330
New Hampshire	9	2.0	120	110
Total of 18 states[2]	2,807		18,941	17,100
United States total	2,906	2.0		

[1] In thousands.

[2] These 18 states contained 97 percent of the population of Polish descent in the United States.

To what extent the activities of American Polonia may have suggested to the Polish government in London that it had more support for its policies in the United States than it really had is difficult to assess. But there is no doubt that the Polish government-in-exile expected American Poles to play a greater political role in 1944–1945 than they had in previous years in counteracting the pro-Soviet image in American public opinion.

VII

THE ROAD TO YALTA

Despite the fact that the Warsaw Uprising had demonstrated that the United States could influence affairs in Poland only in a limited way, the United States did not alter its basic goal of supporting the establishment of a free and independent Poland after the war. However, until the Yalta Conference in February 1945, the American government continued its public policy of favoring a postponement of the settlement of territorial issues until after the war and, in general, of opposing active involvement in Polish internal affairs. At Yalta, President Roosevelt, in sharp contrast to his passive role on the Polish question at the Tehran meeting, took the initiative and sought to resolve the territorial question and the complexion of the future government of Poland. To American officials, the arrangements made at Yalta on the Polish problem were consistent with American principles and promised to ensure postwar collaboration with the Soviets. But the euphoria accompanying the Yalta agreement soon dissipated when it became evident in the weeks that followed that the Soviet Union relied on traditional methods of ensuring its security in eastern Europe. The consequence was that Poland slipped into the Soviet sphere of influence, thus colliding with American policy which had been committed to the restoration of a free and independent Polish state.

By the time of the Warsaw Uprising, the Department of State began to see that American influence in determining Polish affairs would be limited. Charles Yost of the Division of Central European Affairs commented in mid-October 1944 that American policy was not likely "to ameliorate, or even substantially to affect" conditions in eastern Europe. He added: "The American people as a whole are frankly not interested in Eastern Europe or the Near East." Stettinius told Roosevelt that Soviet influence in Poland would be great and that the United States could make its presence felt "only if some degree of equal opportunity in trade, investment, and access to sources of information is preserved."[1]

At the end of October 1944 the Policy Committee of the Department of State initially proposed that the United States endorse the Curzon Line as Poland's eastern frontier and support a reorganization of the Polish government-in-exile. Harriman, who was in Washington and participated in these discussions, endorsed the proposals because the compromise promised that the Polish people might be in a position to select their own government. On the other hand, Harriman was adamantly opposed to the Kremlin's simply forcing the Lublin Poles on the people of Poland. He had made it clear that if the Soviets should force a communist regime on Poland, the United States could not "stand aside without registering the strongest of objections." These proposals, if adopted by the State Department, would have significantly departed from previous American policy and would have gone far toward meeting Stalin's oft-repeated demands. But in the end even the State Department did not endorse the proposals. As one historian of this period has commented: "Apparently, it seemed easier to revert to previous policy statements than to achieve agreement on the proposed changes."[2] Even if the State Department had accepted the proposals, the president probably would not have seriously considered them at that time since the national election was only one week away.

Meanwhile, as a gesture of compromise toward the Kremlin, Mikołajczyk persuaded President Raczkiewicz to remove Sosnkowski from his position as commander-in-chief of the Polish armed forces. Under the threat of Mikołajczyk's own resignation, Raczkiewicz reluctantly agreed and appointed General Bór to replace him. But Bór's appointment did not bring the desired results: the Lublin Poles attacked him as "a criminal against the Polish people." Mikołajczyk found himself under attack from the Soviets and from his own kinsmen who opposed Sosnkowski's dismissal.[3] Ciechanowski, shaken by Warsaw's defeat and Soviet attacks against Bór, was convinced Stalin did not genuinely want to work out a political compromise with the London Poles. He urged a strong American reaction against the Kremlin and especially, "no weakening of the 'moral support'" that Roosevelt had promised Mikołajczyk during the premier's visit to Washington in June.[4]

A short time later Mikołajczyk, pressured by Churchill, flew to Moscow to participate in talks between the prime minister and Stalin. Before he departed London, Mikołajczyk was led to believe that his conversations in the Soviet Union would be based upon the Polish proposals of August 30 which envisaged the establishment of a

government based on the five major political parties, including the
Communists, in Poland. But when Mikołajczyk got to the Soviet
Union, Stalin made it clear that he wanted unconditional acceptance
of the Curzon Line, and he rejected the August proposals on the
grounds that they ignored the Lublin Committee. Mikołajczyk coun-
tered by saying he was not authorized to accept the Curzon Line and
suggested that the Polish proposals of August were intended to go
considerably farther than a settlement between the London and Lublin Poles. At a conference on October 13, 1944, attended by Mikołajczyk, Churchill, Stalin, Eden, and Harriman, Molotov shocked the
Polish premier by revealing that Roosevelt had agreed to the Curzon
Line at Tehran. Harriman, convinced that Molotov's contention was
erroneous, later told Mikołajczyk that the Russian foreign minister
had acted disloyally and had misinterpreted the President's remarks.
Harriman explained that the reason he did not correct Molotov at
the time he made the remark was because the ambassador did not
want to risk an incident which might cost Roosevelt votes in the
1944 election.[5]

Stalin and Churchill exerted enormous pressure on Mikołajczyk to
accept the Curzon Line. Even Harriman urged the Polish premier to
come to an agreement with the Soviets. Churchill, who had publicly
endorsed the Curzon Line as Poland's frontier with the Soviet Union,
pleaded with, cajoled, and even threatened the Poles to accept the
controversial frontier, which the prime minister considered the key
to the solution of the Polish-Soviet problem. During a meeting with
Mikołajczyk on October 14, Churchill criticized the London Poles
for not coming to an agreement with the Soviets before the creation
of the Lublin Committee. At one point, Churchill claimed that if
Mikołajczyk accepted the Curzon Line the Soviets would withdraw
support from the Lublin Committee. "You *must* do this," Churchill
urged. "If you miss this moment everything will be lost." Contradicting what he had said earlier, Churchill suggested that acceptance
of the line might enable him to get the London Poles 60 percent of
the seats in a coalition government with the Lublinites. When the
Polish premier showed no inclination to agree to the boundary,
Churchill angrily told him: "I wash my hands off; as far as I am concerned we shall give the business up. Because of quarrels between
Poles we are not going to wreck the peace of Europe. In your obsti-
nacy you do not see what is at stake. It is not in friendship that we
shall part. We shall tell the world how unreasonable you are. You will
start another war in which 25 million lives will be lost. But you don't
care." When Mikołajczyk bemoaned that Poland's fate had been decided at Tehran, and that he was not about to hand over half of

Poland to the Soviets, Churchill shot back: "You are absolutely crazy." Churchill grimly warned Mikolajczyk that unless he accepted the Curzon Line, "The Russians will sweep through your country and your people will be liquidated. You are on the verge of annihilation."[6]

After the conference was over, Churchill told Roosevelt that if the London Poles accepted the Curzon Line, then "in the next fortnight we may get a settlement." Churchill and Eden tried to convince Stalin to leave Lwów to the Poles in order to make it easier for Mikołajczyk to accept the Curzon Line, but Stalin would not budge. As for the composition of the future government of Poland, Stalin was receptive at first to 50 percent of the seats going to the London Poles with Mikołajczyk as the premier of a coalition government, but later he corrected himself to a ratio in favor of his Lublin protégés. Churchill was optimistic that if the London Poles accepted the boundary Stalin wanted, the composition of the Polish government would not "prove an insuperable obstacle."[7]

Although nothing of substance had been resolved in the Moscow talks, the official communiqué summarizing the discussions reflected Churchill's optimism: "Important progress was made toward solution of the Polish question, which was closely discussed between the Soviet and British Governments. These discussions have notably narrowed differences and dispelled misconceptions." Roosevelt was "delighted" to hear Churchill's optimistic assessment of the talks and told the prime minister on October 22 that, if a solution was found soon, he wanted to be consulted in order to delay possibly the publication of the news for a few weeks because of the national election on November 7.[8]

After he returned to London, Mikołajczyk met with the Polish Council of Ministers and told them what had transpired in Moscow. Before reaching a decision on Stalin's terms, Mikołajczyk wanted to know where the American and British governments stood. He specifically asked the British government: (1) Would it support the extension of Poland's frontiers in the west, even if the United States opposed it? (2) Would it support the extension of the Polish frontier to the Oder River? (3) Would it guarantee the frontiers and independence of the Polish state? On November 2 the English responded favorably to Polish questions concerning the frontier extensions in the west, but they would guarantee Poland's territorial integrity only jointly with the Soviets.[9] The American reply, which came at the end of November, was very general and constituted a reaffirmation of principles that had guided American policy toward Poland for some time. Roosevelt told Mikołajczyk that the United States supported "a strong, free and independent Polish state," would not oppose frontier arrangements made by the Poles, Soviets, and British, and restated American inability to guarantee specific frontiers.[10]

Mikołajczyk had also appealed to Roosevelt to try to get Stalin to give the Poles Lwów and the East Galician oil fields. The Polish premier needed these areas to win acceptance of the Curzon Line from his cabinet and to maintain the support of the Polish people. Initially, the State Department supported the Polish request, noting that the areas had never belonged to the Soviet Union before 1939. But when it became obvious that the Big Three would meet again soon, Stettinius advised Roosevelt not to raise the question of Lwów until he saw Stalin. Meanwhile, Harriman had been instructed to return to Moscow by way of London and inform the Polish premier what Washington's policy was toward Poland. If after talking with Mikołajczyk, Harriman believed that it would be advisable for the United States to take up the question of Lwów with Stalin before the Big Three meeting, he was authorized to do so. By the time Harriman arrived in London to see Mikołajczyk, the Polish leader was at the point of resigning from office.[11]

Mikołajczyk, convinced that acceptance of the Curzon Line was the *sine qua non* of an agreement with the Soviets, was unable to win the support of any political party except his own in the Polish government. He told the delegate of the government in Poland that Britain and the Soviet Union pressed for an agreement and the United States was "passive." Most of the members of the Polish government believed that the Soviets intended to communize Poland and therefore hoped that when the United States and Britain built up their strength in western Europe, they would exert their influence on the Kremlin to allow the Polish people to choose their own government. That was why many Poles preferred that the Soviet Union simply take eastern Poland without the approval of the Polish government. This was not an entirely new view: Sikorski had expressed the idea once to Adolf Berle that a workable arrangement with Stalin would eventually be realized when the West established a balance of power vis-à-vis the Soviet Union in Europe. Mikołajczyk, on the other hand, believed that the only way to prevent the communization of Poland was "by pitting oneself against the task on the spot, in Poland, notwithstanding the enormous risks and hazards." Mikołajczyk therefore felt that he had no alternative but to resign and keep himself in readiness for the future. Less sanguine than his opponents about future Anglo-American help, Mikolajczyk was keenly aware of the growing diplomatic isolation of Poland. He wrote: "We were becoming increasingly isolated. The Big Three regarded us either openly or

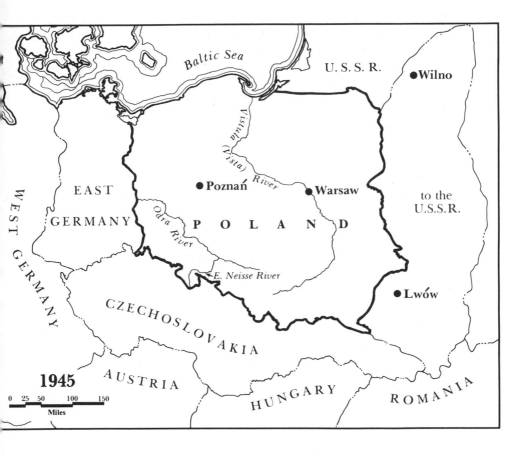

privately as saboteurs of their unity because of our refusal to yield on all points."[12]

Mikołajczyk's resignation on November 24, 1944, brought the more nationalistic and Russophobic government of Arciszewski to power. By early December the British, dramatizing their disapproval of the Arciszewski government, refused to allow it to communicate with Poland by using its own coded messages, a privilege enjoyed by Mikołajczyk's cabinet. However, the British reversed themselves by February 1945 and allowed cypher communications between the Arciszewski government and Poland.[13] The British press alleged that Mikołajczyk's resignation was a consequence of America's refusal to guarantee Poland's frontiers. That was untrue since Mikołajczyk could not convince his own government to accept the Curzon Line. Mikołajczyk himself admitted the guarantee of Poland's frontiers by the United States had never become the issue. The American press joined the British, however, in seeing Mikołajczyk's departure from the Polish government as virtually ending any hope of a satisfactory settlement between the London Poles and the Kremlin.[14]

A few weeks after Mikołajczyk's resignation, Churchill reaffirmed his government's recognition of the Curzon Line, including Lwów and the oil fields, and expressed regret that "the difficulties inherent in the forming of a Polish Government in harmony with the Lublin Committee" had not been overcome. The United States government, reacting to criticism in the American press even from commentators who favored the Curzon Line but objected to an imposed settlement on the Poles without their consent, issued a statement reaffirming American commitments to a free and independent Poland.[15]

Roosevelt had good reason to fear that the Soviets might go on and recognize the Lublin Committee as a provisional government, now that Mikołajczyk had left the scene and the Soviets had little to stay their hand. Ever since Mikołajczyk resigned, the Soviet press began to refer to the Lublin Committee as a "government." By early December 1944 the Moscow newspapers carried references to alleged demands by the people of Poland that the Lublin Committee transform itself into a provisional government. As George Kennan put it, this was an obvious "build-up for the final act." Roosevelt personally appealed to Stalin not to take any action before the Big Three meeting, scheduled after the president's inauguration. But Stalin unconvincingly claimed that the Kremlin would have no choice but to recognize the Lublinites when they constituted themselves as a provisional government. Roosevelt expressed dismay when Stalin claimed he could not delay the recognition and told the Soviet dictator that the United States had no intention of following suit. The President even impugned the claims of the Lublin Committee to represent the Polish people by telling Stalin that "it is therefore an unquestioned truth that the people of Poland have no opportunity to express themselves in regard to the Lublin Committee."[16] But to no avail. On December 31, 1944, the Polish National Council decreed the transformation of the Lublin Committee into the Provisional Polish Government. Soviet recognition followed on January 5, 1945. And the Kremlin lost little time in pressuring the Czechoslovaks and the French to do likewise.[17] A turning point had been reached on the Polish question: The United States could either abandon the Poles to the Soviets or take the initiative in trying to preserve Polish independence. The president chose the latter alternative and went to Yalta with that objective in mind.

Despite failing health, Roosevelt traveled halfway around the world

to meet Stalin and Churchill for the last wartime conference among
the leaders who had led the Allied cause since 1941.[18] On February 4,
1945, the first day of the conference, Stalin frankly told Roosevelt
and Churchill that since the great powers had borne the brunt of the
war, they should write the peace settlement without any interference
from the small nations. Churchill observed that the Big Three should
use their power with moderation and respect the rights of the smaller
states. "The eagle should permit the small birds to sing and care not
whereof they sang," Churchill quipped. When the president said that
Polish Americans were very interested in the future of Poland, Stalin
shot back with conviction: "But of your seven million Poles, only
seven thousand vote." Stettinius commented later: "The inaccurate
information that the Soviets had about the United States was a source
of continual amazement to us." He added: "Possibly, of course, their
representatives in the United States sent home only what they thought
the Kremlin wanted to hear." At one point in the discussion, Charles
Bohlen emphasized the President's position to Vyshinsky, who argued
that Americans should obey their leaders. Bohlen challenged Vyshinsky
to come to the United States to tell that to the American people, a
challenge the Soviet official accepted.[19]

During the plenary session on February 6, Roosevelt took the initiative and introduced the Polish question at the conference. He made
it quite clear that the United States was favorable to the Curzon Line
as the Polish-Soviet boundary, but he urged Stalin to make a concession to the Poles by giving them Lwów and the oil fields south of it.
"Most Poles," Roosevelt observed, "like the Chinese want to save
face." But the president timidly presented his position, noting that
he advanced the proposal as a suggestion and would not insist on it.
Recognizing that it was now impossible to form a coalition between
the London and Lublin Poles, the president offered the first concrete
proposal for establishing the mechanism by which a new Polish government could be formed, a proposal that had been originally suggested by Mikołajczyk prior to the conference. Roosevelt suggested
that a presidential council be established which would then create a
government based on the five major political parties in Poland. Again
Roosevelt indicated that he was not wedded to this proposal either.
Churchill endorsed the idea of Stalin making a magnanimous gesture
to the Poles by giving them Lwów and the president's proposal for
an interim government for Poland.[20]

After a ten-minute recess, Stalin astutely argued the Soviet case.
He pointed out that it was both a matter of honor and security for
the Soviet Union to have a strong and independent Poland so that
future invasions of his country could be avoided. Thus, he declared,

in sharp contrast to the Russia of the czars "who had wished to suppress and assimilate Poland," the Soviet Union "wants a strong, independent and democratic Poland." But he refused to offer territorial concessions to Poland, asking "Should we then be less Russian than Curzon and Clemenceau?" Then he cleverly assumed the posture of being more of a democrat than either Churchill or Roosevelt by suggesting that he had "enough democratic feeling not to set up a Polish government without Poles." Polish participation was necessary, he stated. Then he confirmed what the Western leaders already knew, that the time for a compromise between the London and Lublin Poles was over. But he made it clear, too, that the right of the Poles to govern themselves, a basic goal of the Western powers, was in serious jeopardy by claiming that the Lublin, now Warsaw, government was as democratic as de Gaulle's regime, and that there were only two aged Poles in the West—Stanisław Grabski and Lucjan Żeligowski—who would be acceptable to the Lublinites for inclusion in the Warsaw government. The Warsaw regime, Stalin asserted, "won't hear of Mikołajczyk." Stalin convincingly argued that the Red Army needed a secure rear, provided by the new regime in Warsaw, which it allegedly would not have if the London Poles and the AK were ensconced in the Polish capital. He sneered at the AK: "We have had nothing good from them but much evil."[21]

The next day Roosevelt completely demolished the claims of the Polish government-in-exile to political legitimacy and the basis upon which the United States had recognized it by suggesting that there had been no legal Polish authority for several years. His comments flatly contradicted the long-held American position that the Polish government-in-exile had *de jure* existence even though it was not resident in Poland. Roosevelt had already told Stalin in a letter on the previous day that the United States could not recognize the Warsaw regime "as now composed," confirming his reservations about the claims of the Lublin Committee to political legitimacy. Roosevelt had suggested that Bierut and Osóbka-Morawski from Warsaw, along with two or three Poles who were not part of the existing regime, come to Yalta and form "a new temporary government" which the Big Three would recognize. Roosevelt suggested that the new government, which should include Mikołajczyk, Romer, and Grabski, would function until free elections were held for a permanent government. Taken off guard by the president's initiative, Stalin unconvincingly claimed that he tried to get in touch with Bierut and the other leaders suggested by the president but could not reach them. Even a historian sympathetic with the Soviet position at Yalta commented that Stalin "was fully capable of making a dramatic act or obviously fraudulent statement to demonstrate a co-operative spirit, while in reality entirely rejecting a proposal."[22]

Stalin suggested that another matter be taken up until the Soviets had time to submit their proposals on the Polish question. Molotov later presented the Kremlin's view which, at first, seemed to go far toward accommodating the Western position. The Soviets wanted the Curzon Line but were prepared to make minor changes, in some places five to eight kilometers, in Poland's favor; they wanted the western frontier of Poland to run to the Oder and western Neisse rivers; and they wanted only some Poles from "émigré" circles to be included in the current Warsaw regime, which would call for elections as soon as possible for a permanent government. Meanwhile, the Soviet foreign minister suggested that he along with Harriman and Clark Kerr work out the details of enlarging the existing provisional government. Roosevelt had doubts about the Soviet use of the word émigré, which he did not like, and asked for time to study their proposals. Although Churchill believed that some progress had been made that day in solving the Polish problem, he strongly argued against the Soviet intention to push postwar Poland too far to the West, making his oft-quoted comment: "It would be a pity to stuff the Polish goose so full of German food that it got indigestion."[23]

Before the fifth plenary meeting on February 8, the United States had circulated its proposals which revealed agreement with the Soviets on the Curzon Line but concurred with the British in seeing no justification in drawing the Polish boundary with Germany on the western Neisse. As for the thorny problem of the government, Roosevelt offered a revised version of his proposal submitted to Stalin two days earlier. In his new version, the president proposed that a presidential committee of three men, consisting of Bierut, Grabski, and Cardinal Adam Sapieha, form a Polish government from three major sources—Warsaw Poles, representatives from Poland, and Polish leaders abroad.[24]

The meeting on February 8 was lively and revealed how far apart the two sides were on the question of the Polish government. Roosevelt and Churchill wanted to establish a new government. But Stalin was willing only to enlarge the existing Warsaw regime. Molotov, who played an important role in these discussions, tried to puff up the importance of the Lublin group. "We cannot ignore that fact—that the present government exists at Warsaw," Molotov declared. "It is now at the head of the Polish people and has great authority." And in an effort to discredit the Polish government in London, he said: "Those now in the provisional government are closely connected with great national events taking place in Poland. This is not true of Mikołajczyk, Grabski, Romer and Witos. These names are not linked with decisive events in Poland." After trying to give the impression that Roosevelt's idea of a presidential committee would create confusion because of the existence of a similar body in Poland, Molotov then came up with what was the key to Soviet negotiating strategy. Since the Big Three had agreed on the need to hold free elections for a permanent government, Molotov argued that the real issue boiled down to the establishment of a provisional government. That could be accomplished, he said, not by establishing a presidential committee but by enlarging the Polish National Council.[25]

Churchill took the floor next and eloquently argued, not without contradicting some of his earlier statements, that Britain could not simply transfer recognition from the London Poles, "the lawful government of Poland which we have recognized during five years of the war." Molotov's proposals did not go far enough, argued Churchill. "If we give up the Poles in London it should be for a new start on both sides, more or less on equal terms." But Roosevelt, anxious to emphasize the areas of agreement among the Big Three, accepted Molotov's argument. "From another hemisphere," the president intoned, "I should like to say that we are agreed on free elections. The only problem is how to govern in the meantime for a relatively few months."[26]

Stalin entered the discussion and ignored centuries of history with the claim that the war had changed Polish attitudes toward the Soviet Union. "Now there is good will toward Russia," he exaggerated. Picking up where Molotov had left off, Stalin pointed out that leaders like Bierut, Osóbka-Morawski, and Rola-Żymierski, who had collaborated with the Soviet Union and endured the hardships of war, were very popular with the Polish people. "Members of the provisional government they see there, but where are the London Poles?" Stalin asked rhetorically, resenting that the West demanded changes in Bierut's regime while de Gaulle's was no more popular. Making it clear that what they were talking about were spheres of influence and *quid pro quo,* Stalin pointedly asked Churchill for information about Greece. Making sure Churchill got the message, Stalin claimed all he wanted was information. "We have no intention of intervening there in any way," he assured.[27]

The three wartime leaders had agreed to free elections in Poland, and Stalin assured Roosevelt that the elections could be held as early as in one month. To Roosevelt, agreement appeared so close that he suggested that the foreign ministers work out the details of a solution to the Polish problem. After the exhausting session, the Allied leaders adjourned to Koreis Villa where the Soviets hosted a formal dinner, consisting of twenty courses. They proposed generous toasts to each other—Stettinius counted forty-five of them—in an atmosphere that was friendly and high-spirited. Stalin, always the realist, admonished in a toast that the real test of the unity of the Allies would be when the war ended and the interests of the Big Three tended to divide them.[28]

When the foreign ministers met on February 9, the United States backed down from insisting on the presidential committee, which the Soviets had found so objectionable, in an effort to draw the three governments closer to a general agreement on Poland. Stettinius proposed that the existing Warsaw regime "be reorganized into a fully representative government based on all democratic forces in Poland and including democratic leaders from Poland abroad, to be termed 'The Provisional Government of National Unity.'" The reorganized government, said Stettinius, would be obliged to hold free elections which would be monitored by the ambassadors of the Big Three in Warsaw.[29] The Soviets accepted the American proposal with major qualifications. Molotov did not want the words "fully representative" to apply to the reorganization of the Warsaw regime. Instead, he wanted a reorganization simply "on a wider democratic basis." Nor did he want the ambassadors to monitor the future elections in Poland. He also preferred the name "National Provisional Government of Poland" to refer to the reorganized government because it came closer to the current name of the Warsaw regime, "Provisional Government of Poland."

In the discussion during the plenary meeting on February 9, Roosevelt indicated that he believed the crux of the issue was the free election to be held in Poland, not the complexion of the interim government in Warsaw. "I want this election in Poland to be the first beyond question," the president declared. "It should be like Caesar's wife. I did not know her but they said she was pure." Stalin ominously replied: "They said that about her but in fact she had her sins." Roosevelt again invoked his Polish American citizens who, he said, wanted to be assured that the elections would be free. That was why he wanted them monitored. Churchill, who carried the burden of the debate with Stalin on the issue, strongly endorsed the president's position. The prime minister suggested that having unmonitored elections would be like Egypt where the government that held them always won. Stalin, irritated with Churchill's analogy, was adamantly opposed to the monitored elections. Roosevelt gave the impression that only semantic differences separated the leaders from an agreement. But the British did not think it was so simple. Churchill and Eden fought for the creation of an entirely "new" government, not merely an expanded Lublin-dominated regime, with guarantees for free elections.[30]

The British approach went too far for the Soviets who wanted to keep as tight a grip as they could on Poland without breaking with their allies. It also went too far for Roosevelt who, though he wanted to see an independent Poland, was unprepared to insist on specific guarantees that would alienate the Soviets and destroy a general agreement on the Polish question. After much discussion, the final text that the foreign ministers hammered out suggested ostensible agreement but in reality papered over profound differences of interpretation that each side had concerning the government of Poland. The text also revealed that the West had no solid guarantees for the free elections that were to take place in Poland, because the president was prepared to drop the reference to the observation and reporting of the Polish elections by the ambassadors. The only assurance the United States and Britain had that the elections would be "free and unfettered" was Stalin's word for it. And that was a weak reed upon which to hang the future of an independent Poland.

The text of the statement on Poland, presented to the Big Three at the plenary meeting on February 10, read:

> A new situation has been created in Poland as a result of her complete liberation by the Red Army. This calls for the establishment of a Polish Provisional Government which can be more broadly based than was possible before the recent liberation of Western Poland. The Provisional Government which is now functioning in Poland should therefore be reorganized on a broader democratic basis with the inclusion of democratic leaders from Poland itself and from Poles abroad. This new Government should then be called the Polish Provisional Government of National Unity.
>
> Mr. Molotov, Mr. Harriman and Sir A. Clark Kerr are authorized to consult in the first instance in Moscow with members of the present Provisional Government and with other Polish democratic leaders from within Poland and from abroad, with a view to the reorganisation of the present Government along the above lines. This Polish Provisional Government of National Unity shall be pledged to the holding of free and unfettered elections as soon as possible on the basis of universal suffrage and secret ballot. In these elections all democratic and anti-Nazi parties shall have the right to take part and to put forward candidates.
>
> When a Polish Provisional Government of National Unity has been properly formed in conformity with the above, the Government of the U.S.S.R., which now maintains diplomatic relations with the present Provisional Government of Poland, and the Government of the United Kingdom and the Government of the U.S.A. will establish diplomatic relations with the new Polish Provisional Government of National Unity, and will exchange Ambassadors by whose

reports the respective Government will be kept informed about the situation in Poland.[31]

Noting that there was no mention of boundaries in the text, Churchill wanted something included about them. The Big Three had agreed on Poland's eastern frontier but not on its western boundary. Churchill and Stalin agreed that some statement concerning Poland's frontiers should be included in the communiqué, but Roosevelt disagreed. A compromise was reached: The Curzon Line was mentioned but no specific reference to the Polish boundary in the west was made. The addendum to the declaration on Poland read:

> The three Heads of Government consider that the Eastern frontier of Poland should follow the Curzon Line with digressions from it in some regions of five to eight kilometers in favour of Poland. It is recognized that Poland must receive substantial accessions of territory in the North and West. They feel that the opinion of the new Polish Provisional Government of National Unity should be sought in due course on the extent of these accessions and that the final delimitation of the Western frontier of Poland should thereafter await the Peace Conference.[32]

The American delegation left Yalta convinced that the conference had resolved the Polish-Soviet imbroglio and that Allied unity had been preserved. When the president returned to the United States he told Congress that the Polish problem had been solved. He informed the legislators that free elections would be held in Poland at war's end and that the United States remained committed to a free and independent Polish nation. He contributed to the fuzzy interpretation of the Yalta agreement by referring at one and the same time to the Big Three decision to create a "new government" and "to reorganize the existing Provisional Government in Poland on a broader democratic basis."[33] Stettinius, too, reflected this lack of precision concerning what was agreed about Poland at Yalta. Shortly after his return from the Soviet Union, he told Ciechanowski that a "new" government for Poland would be created with only "elements" of the Lublin group represented in it. The secretary of state considered the Yalta conference a victory for the West because Stalin made concessions in an area that he already occupied.[34]

Other American officials echoed the sense of achievement. Hopkins stated: "We really believed in our hearts that this was the dawn of the new day we had all been praying for and talking about for so many years." James Byrnes believed that the Big Three had reached the "high tide" of unity.[35] Leahy was one of the few high-ranking officials at Yalta who pessimistically observed that the compromise on

Poland was "so vague and indefinite as to promise little toward the establishment of a government in which all the major parties will be represented." Bohlen, too, bemoaned the "hasty drafting" of the agreement on Poland which left loopholes for the Soviets to exploit.[36]

The English, on the other hand, did not exude the optimism that the Americans did. Eden thought Roosevelt had deluded himself about the Soviet Union's honoring the Yalta agreement. Writing after the event, Eden said: "Only if a genuinely representative new government had been formed in Poland quickly, would the pledge of free and unfettered elections have any meaning." Lord Charles M. Moran, Churchill's physician who accompanied the prime minister to Yalta, commenting on American enthusiasm, said wryly: "I do not know what decisions they have in mind. It was plain at Moscow, last October, that Stalin means to make Poland a Cossack outpost of Russia, and I am sure he has not altered his intention here." Moran believed that Roosevelt had invented a Soviet Union "which does not exist." Churchill, in contrast to the president, was unusually restrained when he talked about the Yalta agreement on Poland. He told the House of Commons without hyperbole that whether Poland was to be free or "a mere projection of the Soviet State," depended on the Soviet Union's good faith. But, he wrote later, "Our hopeful assumptions were soon to be falsified. Still they were the only ones possible at the time."[37] Bohlen summed it up well when he said, "Stalin held all the cards and played them well. Eventually, we had to throw in our hand."[38]

Judged by the Gallup Poll conducted after the Crimea conference, 56 percent of those polled believed that the agreement on Poland was about the best that could be worked out under the circumstances. From the standpoint of the United States, a majority thought the conference had been a success. But when asked if the agreement was fair to the Poles, only 33 percent of those polled thought so.[39]

The vast majority of Polish Americans, however, considered the Yalta agreement on Poland a mockery of the Atlantic Charter. The revelations of what had been agreed upon at the Yalta Conference broke the remaining restraints that heretofore had kept the Polish American Congress and its affiliates from frankly and directly criticizing Roosevelt's foreign policy. Charles Rozmarek called the Yalta agreement "a staggering blow to the cause of freedom" and deplored American alignment "with forces seeking the destruction of democracies." He warned that "we will reap the backwash of our spiritual and political weakness as the world did after the shame of Munich."[40] On March 9, 1945, the Polish American Congress sent a resolution to all congressmen and senators urging them not to confirm the Yalta decisions. Affiliated organizations of the Congress, like KNAPP, did the same thing. KNAPP told the legislators that another partition of Poland had been "arranged by Mr. Stalin and Mr. Churchill with the concurrence and approval of the Chief Executive of the U.S." In an open letter to the newsmen of the United States, the presidents of the three Polish American press organizations condemned the Yalta agreement as "the fifth partition." Once the Polish American Congress saw that the Yalta agreement would not be blocked by the Senate, Rozmarek, anticipating the tougher line the administration followed later toward the Kremlin, suggested that Washington cut off lend-lease aid and credits to the Soviet Union until the Soviets fulfilled their obligations as an ally. An illustration in *Dziennik Związkowy* epitomized the reactions of most Polish Americans to the Yalta decisions on Poland. It depicted a tearful woman who represented Polonia sitting opposite a picture of President Roosevelt. The caption simply read: "Bitter Disappointment."[41]

Not all Polish Americans were critics of Soviet and American policies toward Poland. In addition to the Kościuszko League, the American Polish Labor Council was a strong supporter of Washington's policy of friendship with the Soviet Union and endorsed the Big Three's decisions regarding Poland. The American Polish Labor Council was the largest Polish American group that consistently supported the White House. Organized in June 1944, the council was a bitter critic of the Polish government-in-exile and the Polish American Congress. Claiming 600,000 members, the organization propagandized its political views through a Detroit newspaper, the *Głos Ludowy (People's Voice)*.[42]

The organization was led by Leo Krzycki, vice-president of the Amalgamated Clothing Workers of America, who also headed the American Slav Congress, which had been heavily infiltrated by Communists. One historian described the American Slav Congress as Moscow's political arm in the United States. The American Slav Congress, like the American Polish Labor Council, was an ardent critic of the London Poles and espoused a postwar Poland that was friendly to Moscow. When the Kremlin established the Lublin Committee, Krzycki went so far as to describe himself as the first representative in the United States of the Lublin Committee. None of the major Polish American fraternals joined the American Slav Congress, and as a consequence, they were dubbed fascists by it.[43]

Unlike Rozmarek, who had delayed his endorsement of Roosevelt for a fourth term, Krzycki had endorsed the president's continuation in office early in 1944.[44] Assuring the president that the Polish

American Congress represented only a minority of Polish opinion in
the United States, Krzycki's association strongly endorsed the Yalta
decisions on Poland. The American Polish Labor Council in a pamphlet entitled *What is Happening in Poland?* saw a promising future
in store for Poland because of the Yalta agreement: "Poland, now
more than ever will through its Provisional Government of National
Unity, contribute greatly to the closer unity of the three major
powers: The United States, the Soviet Union and Great Britain."[45]

Unlike previous years when congressmen and senators went through
the ritual of commemorating Polish Constitution Day (May 3) or the
invasion of Poland by the Germans (September 1), the Yalta decisions
on Poland sparked the sharpest criticism of the administration in
Congress on any foreign policy issue in years and resulted
in the introduction of several motions against the Crimea decisions.[46]
Polish American congressmen were among the most vociferous in
venting their criticism and disappointment with the president over
Yalta. But congressmen and senators of other ethnic backgrounds
also supported the Polish cause against the Soviet Union. Some congressmen, like Thomas Lane of Massachusetts, adapted their remarks
to the audience they addressed. In February, Lane endorsed the Yalta
agreement but in March 1945, speaking before the Polish Relief Committee in Lawrence, Massachusetts, he said: "Many Americans are
disturbed by this turn of events. They believe that the Yalta decisions
are a repudiation of the high sentiments expressed in the Atlantic
Charter."[47]

Congressman John Lesinski, one of the staunchest critics of Roosevelt's foreign policy, told the president in a letter on February 24,
1945, that "we Americans of Polish descent feel that you, and you
alone, are responsible for yielding to Stalin's demands." Lesinski
asked Roosevelt for his observations before the congressman made a
statement in Congress on Poland. In a draft reply to the congressman,
Roosevelt took issue with Lesinski's characterization of the Yalta
agreement, concluding with a statement that the objective of an independent Poland "can be frustrated only by the members of the
Polish race themselves." When Byrnes read Roosevelt's letter he
dashed off a memorandum to the president: "These Polish friends
are so sensitive that I suggest leaving out the last sentence of your
letter to Congressman Lesinski." Roosevelt accepted the advice, and
the offensive reference to the Poles was removed from his reply to
Lesinski. But the congressman was not appeased. He told Roosevelt
on March 10, 1945, that he did not see how the president could reconcile the Yalta agreement on Poland with the ideals of the Atlantic
Charter. This was not merely "a Polish issue," he reminded Roosevelt,

but an American one because United States soldiers had fought and died for the ideals contained in the Atlantic Charter. He told the president that only two out of eighty-four Polish American newspapers supported the Yalta decisions on Poland. A few days later, nine congressmen, most of whom were Polish Americans, asked Roosevelt for an interview "to discuss in detail the agreements reached at Yalta with reference to the Republic of Poland." Roosevelt demurred.[48]

One of the most eloquent critics of Roosevelt's role in making the Yalta decisions on Poland was Congressman Philip A. Traynor of Delaware, who bitterly intoned: "On the shores of the Black Sea at Yalta, willy-nilly, whether we like it or not, as Americans we were represented by President Roosevelt in the fifth partition of Poland. If we remain silent and the decisions made on the Crimean Peninsula are confirmed at the conference to be convened shortly at San Francisco, we are as culpable as Pilate. No more than he can we wash our hands of the consequences."[49] One senator, Arthur Vandenberg, stood out as the major critic in the Senate of the way Poland had been treated at Yalta. But even he saw that it was impossible to alter decisions that Roosevelt and Churchill had approved. Writing to his friend, Franciszek Januszewski, Polish American publisher of Detroit's *Dziennik Polski,* Vandenberg said: "I could get no greater personal satisfaction out of anything more than from joining—aye, in leading—a public denunciation of Yalta and all its works as respects Poland." But, in view of Big Three agreement, Vandenberg believed that the best way to improve the situation for Poland was to ensure that an acceptable provisional government be installed in Warsaw. Another way, he said, was to cooperate with the United Nations to correct some of the inequities of the wartime decisions on Poland.[50]

To be sure, the Polish government angrily denounced the Yalta agreement on Poland, calling it the "fifth partition of Poland." When General Anders, who had been appointed acting commander-in-chief of Polish armed forces at the end of February 1945, heard of the Yalta arrangements, he asked that his troops be withdrawn from the line in Italy, which caused serious concern in Allied military circles about the success of the offensive plans of the Fifteenth Army Group. Polish soldiers were so bewildered by the Crimea conference that Anders claimed "only a sense of discipline and confidence in their officers prevented the men taking precipitate and uncontrolled action." When he learned that there were no troops readily available to replace the Poles, Anders agreed to carry on.[51]

When the Yalta conference concluded, the Allied nations appeared to have the same goals in Poland. They had agreed on an interim regime which would give way to a permanent government, elected freely by Polish citizens. United States and Soviet aims appeared to be the same when the Kremlin accepted the Declaration on Liberated Europe. But as subsequent events soon revealed, the goals of the West and of the Soviet Union were not the same at all. The bridge between the ideals of the Atlantic Charter and the Soviet desire for a sphere of influence in Poland had not been found.

VIII

YALTA'S AFTERMATH

The high hopes and expectations accompanying the Yalta Conference did not last very long. The differences in the interpretation of the agreement on Poland reflected the deep chasm between the perception of the Soviet Union on the one hand and the United States and Britain on the other concerning the future of the Polish state.

The first stumbling block in executing the Yalta agreement on Poland was the difficulty of the Polish Commission, consisting of Molotov, Clark Kerr, and Harriman, in reaching an understanding on which Polish leaders were to be invited to Moscow for the discussions that were to result in the establishment of a government which all of the members of the Big Three would recognize. When the three ministers began their talks late in February 1945, there was general understanding that Poles would be invited from the current government in Warsaw and from other leaders in Poland and in London. From the outset, however, Molotov made it clear that Mikołajczyk would not be an acceptable nominee from abroad because of his opposition to the decisions made in the Crimea. Instead, Molotov suggested the name of General Lucjan Zeligowski, the hero of the seizure of Wilno in 1920. Although no one in Washington and London seriously considered that the eighty-year-old Żeligowski should replace Mikołajczyk in any list of Polish leaders from abroad, some State Department officials saw wisdom in including a respected military officer in a newly constituted Polish government in order to mitigate the anxiety and restlessness among the officers and men of Anders' command.[1]

To the surprise of Harriman and Clark Kerr, it was Molotov who reiterated Stalin's offer, made at Yalta, that the United States and Britain send representatives to Poland to acquire firsthand information on the situation there. In view of the reports that Roosevelt and Churchill had received concerning the establishment of Communist control in Poland, Molotov's offer was all the more striking. Harriman and Clark Kerr were in agreement on the need to send representatives to Poland as soon as the details could be worked out. Harriman intended to send Francis B. Stevens, secretary of the American Embassy, and an officer attached to the Naval Mission in Moscow. But this lower level mission was not what the British had in mind. They wanted a high level one the functions of which would also include preparations for the free elections in Poland. The Soviets never alluded to their offer again, and when Harriman and Clark Kerr brought up the observers, Molotov became testy about the matter. Harriman correctly predicted on March 4 that the Soviets would not allow any Western representatives to go to Warsaw as observers.[2]

Neither the United States nor Britain favored the idea of inviting leaders from Warsaw to Moscow for consultations before the other Polish leaders because it would create the impression that the Lublinites enjoyed a preferential position with the Polish Commission. But the Soviets claimed that their copy of the Yalta agreement stipulated that the commission would "consult in Moscow *in the first instance* with members of the present Provisional Government." This meant, argued Molotov, that no Polish leaders from Poland or London should be invited to Moscow for talks unless the Lublinites agreed to the list of names. But Charles Bohlen and E. Freeman Matthews, who had kept the minutes of the meetings at Yalta, agreed that the phrase "in the first instance" had been inserted for the purpose of enabling the commission, if it wished to do so, to move on to Warsaw to continue its work. "There was never any question," wrote Joseph Grew, "of the words being interpreted to mean that the Lublin Poles should be consulted first." Moreover, the Soviet version of the Yalta text was a translation from the English one, not the other way around.[3]

During a meeting on March 6, Molotov rejected four out of the five Polish leaders from Poland that Roosevelt had suggested at Yalta. Harriman pointed out that even Stalin himself had agreed to the names suggested by the president at that time and expressed dismay when Molotov had gone back on the dictator's position. By this time Harriman had grown pessimistic about the progress of the discussions of the commission and concluded that the Soviets deliberately stalled while the Warsaw regime entrenched itself in power. Therefore, Harriman advised, and the State Department supported his recommendation, that Mikołajczyk make a public statement endorsing the Crimea decisions which would undermine Molotov's argument that only the Poles who supported what the Big Three did at Yalta should be invited for consultations in Moscow.[4]

Mikołajczyk was reluctant to issue such a statement for fear of prejudicing his influence among the Polish people. Moreover, if he were invited for the Moscow talks, he wanted several conditions met: the list of conferees to be published before they left for Moscow, the assurance that the representatives from Poland and London would have free communications among themselves and with their colleagues in Poland before and during the conference, the freedom to leave the conference when they chose to do so, and finally, the right to know American and British attitudes toward the recognition of the new Polish government to be established.[5]

By the second week of March, Churchill, who had lost two ministers from his cabinet because of their opposition to the prime minister's handling of the Polish question, wanted to take a stronger and a more direct approach with the Soviets to move the stalled Commission in Moscow. On March 8, the prime minister told the president that "if we do not get things right now, it will soon be seen by the world that you and I by putting our signatures to the Crimea settlement have under-written a fraudulent prospectus." More than Poland was at stake, he said, but a test case between the West and the Soviet Union on the meaning of "such terms as Democracy, Sovereignty, Independence, Representative Government and free and unfettered elections." Churchill suggested that Stalin should be informed that all Poles nominated by any of the three governments should be accepted for consultations in Moscow and that the members of the Polish Commission should act as arbiters, not advocates for a particular side. Churchill wanted the Soviets to restrain the Warsaw regime from entrenching itself further and to make arrangements for Western observers to get to Poland.[6]

Roosevelt agreed with Churchill on the central aim of being "firm on the right interpretation of the Crimea decision." But he admitted that he differed from his wartime friend and colleague in the tactical implementation of the objective. Roosevelt wanted a representative group of Poles in Moscow for the talks. Though reluctant to pressure the Soviets to get the observers into Poland, he went along with Churchill on the proposal but he preferred a low-level group. As for the Soviets' restraining the Warsaw regime from establishing a dictatorship in Poland, the president modestly suggested that a "political truce" be called among all Polish factions. Roosevelt preferred Harriman and Clark Kerr to work out the problems rather than he and Churchill to take direct initiative.[7]

Churchill thought the president's approach was too timid. The prime minister assumed that Roosevelt simply did not understand the impact the stalemate of the Polish Commission had on his position in Parliament, which grew increasingly critical of the government's policy toward the Soviet Union over Poland. On March 13, Churchill impatiently told the president: "At Yalta also we agreed to take the Soviet view of the frontier line. Poland has lost her frontier. Is she now to lose her freedom? That is the question which will undoubtedly have to be fought out in Parliament and in public here." Surprised by Churchill's implication that the Yalta agreement had already broken down, the president assured Churchill that there was no basic divergence of view between the United States and Britain in dealing with the Kremlin. He made it clear that he agreed with Churchill that the Warsaw Poles did not have an absolute right of prior consultation before other Polish goups, as Molotov continually claimed.[8]

The Soviets remained obdurate. They refused to consult with any Polish leaders before the Lublinites, opposed Mikołajczyk being summoned to Moscow, declined the Western proposal of observers to be sent to Poland on the grounds it injured "the national pride of the Poles," and were evasive about the list of fifteen to twenty names of Polish leaders that the United States and Britain had submitted for consultations in Moscow. Tired of the deadlock, Harriman advised the secretary of state on March 26 that the United States not insist on the observers, and he even seriously considered giving in to the Soviets on consulting the Lublinites before the other Poles.[9]

Churchill believed that the stalemate had gone far enough and that it was time for him and the president to deal directly with Stalin. He told the president on March 27: "I am extremely concerned at the deterioration of the Russian attitude since Yalta." Commenting upon negative Soviet actions concerning the German offer to surrender their forces in Italy, and the operation of the Declaration on Liberated Europe and the European Advisory Commission, Churchill told Roosevelt that there was only one alternative to "confessing our total failure" on the Polish question. And that was to tell Stalin that the West expected the Soviet Union to honor the Yalta declaration on Poland. Roosevelt reminded Churchill that at Yalta more emphasis had been placed on the Lublinites than other Polish groups from which a new Polish government would be established, but he agreed that it was time to take up some of the broader aspects of Soviet policy concerning Poland directly with Stalin. Accordingly, both men sent messages to Stalin, contesting the Soviet claim that the current Warsaw regime had the right to veto the names of Polish leaders proposed by the United States and Great Britain for the Moscow talks. They urged that the name of any candidate suggested by one power should be accepted in good faith by the others. They also repeated that they wanted to send observers to Poland. And Roosevelt suggested that the Big Three use their influence to bring about a political truce in Poland.[10]

After these messages arrived in Moscow, Harriman anticipated that
the Soviets might now make some concessions and end the stalemate.
But the meeting of the Polish Commission on April 3 brought no
major change in the Soviet position, except an indication that the
Kremlin would not oppose Mikołajczyk's coming to Moscow if the
Lublin Poles agreed to invite him. Convinced that a breaking point
had been reached with the Soviets, Harriman in despair advised that
he return home for consultations. He speculated that when the
Kremlin found out he was leaving the Soviet Union, it "might have a
salutory [*sic*] effect."[11]

No sooner had Harriman wired his recommendation home than
Stalin astonished Roosevelt and Churchill by accusing the United
States of collusion with the Germans. He charged that the Germans,
in return for the United States' easing the armistice terms, allowed
the Americans to advance on the western front. Roosevelt, outraged
by Stalin's charges, shot back angrily: "Frankly I cannot avoid a
feeling of bitter resentment toward your informers whoever they are,
for such vile misrepresentations of my actions or those of my trusted
subordinates." Agreeing with Churchill's advice that they should not
be intimidated by Stalin, the president told the prime minister, "We
must not permit anybody to entertain a false impression that we are
afraid." He added confidently, "Our armies will in a very few days be
in a position that will permit us to become 'tougher' than has heretofore appeared advantageous to the war effort." Although Roosevelt
was still hopeful that problems with the Soviets could be worked out,
it was also clear that shortly before he died the president advocated
a firmer approach in dealing with Stalin. On April 11 he told Churchill in a message that he probably drafted himself: "We must be firm,
however, and our course thus far is correct." Samuel Rosenman, a
close confidant of Roosevelt's, commented later that the president
specifically referred to "the firm, even tough, position that he and
Churchill had taken with Stalin on Poland."[12]

By the time Roosevelt died, the deadlock over Poland was complete.
Stalin rejected the West's interpretation of the Yalta agreement, but
he conceded that if Mikołajczyk made a statement recognizing the
Yalta decisions, he would persuade the Warsaw Poles to agree to the
inclusion of the former premier in the group of Polish leaders who
would be invited for the Moscow talks. Harriman thought the Soviets
had opened "the door a crack from the impasse" and urged Mikołajczyk
to make the statement the Kremlin insisted upon.[13] Churchill met
with Mikołajczyk at Chequers on April 15 and pressured him to make
the endorsement. "We have complete confidence in you," said Churchill. "Roosevelt had the same feeling about you, and that is why you

must be there. If you will be there Great Britain and the United States will support the Polish problem. Otherwise we shall not be involved at all." Uncertain whether the Polish question would be solved to Poland's satisfaction, Mikołajczyk realized that if he endorsed the Yalta decisions he would provide the basis for Anglo-American support of Poland. He was keenly aware, too, that after such an endorsement he would be attacked as a "traitor" in some Polish circles. He was especially concerned about the reaction of the Polish American Congress, which strongly opposed the Yalta decisions. No doubt Mikołajczyk was encouraged, however, by the fact that nearly half the members of the Polish National Council in London, dissolved on March 25, had signed a declaration opposing Arciszewski's policy and urging acceptance of the Yalta agreement on Poland.[14]

In a paradoxical way, the extreme policies of Arciszewski's government and of the Warsaw regime created the same results desired by the Kremlin—namely, delaying the implementation of the Yalta agreement. Delay also drove moderate groups such as the Polish American Congress toward a more uncompromising position. To Mikołajczyk, the issue came down to this: if the Soviets honored the Yalta decisions, the Poles would benefit; if the Soviets did not, then the onus would be on them instead of the Poles, who could not be accused of allowing the subjugation of their own country by failing to collaborate with the Soviets. Mikołajczyk concluded that he had no alternative but to declare that he accepted the Yalta decision on Poland and that he was available, if invited, to go to the Moscow talks. Stalin considered Mikołajczyk's first declaration unacceptable because he did not publicly declare his endorsement of the Curzon Line. That was remedied when Mikołajczyk published a signed article in the Peasant party newspaper, *Jutro Polski (Future of Poland),* on April 19, 1945, accepting the line as the Polish-Soviet boundary. Churchill promptly forwarded Mikołajczyk's second statement to Stalin, who did not reply. "As I got no answer to this it may be assumed that the Dictator was for the moment content," Churchill mused.[15]

By the end of April 1945 the Kremlin gave every indication that it intended to force the current Warsaw regime on Poland and the West. The Kremlin had handed over to the Warsaw Poles the administration of German lands, ignoring the European Advisory Commission agreement which stipulated that no part of Germany could be handed over to the administration of a nation not represented on that body. Despite Western opposition, the Kremlin signed a treaty of friendship and mutual assistance with the Warsaw regime on April 21, 1945.[16] The Soviets also requested that if a new Polish government of national unity was not agreed upon by the time of the San Francisco

Conference on the United Nations, the Warsaw Poles should be invited. The United States, which had opposed sending an invitation to the London Poles to come to San Francisco, was equally opposed to inviting the Warsaw Poles. The Soviet Union, displeased with the West, originally named Andrei Gromyko head of a low-ranking delegation to attend the San Francisco Conference. But later, after Roosevelt died and as a gesture to the new administration, Stalin appointed Molotov instead.[17] The most dramatic and obvious evidence that Stalin intended to have his interpretation of Yalta prevail was the arrest of sixteen prominent pro-West Poles, flushed out of hiding in Poland by guarantees of personal safety, who were flown to Moscow to stand trial for alleged anti-Soviet activities. The London Poles appealed to the United States and Britain to intervene in the matter early in April; but it was not until May 3, 1945, that the Soviet government finally admitted that the Polish leaders were, indeed, in Soviet confinement. By that time the Warsaw regime required Polish citizens to declare allegiance to it "as the only legal Government" of Poland.[18]

Soviet opposition to Western observers in Poland was closely tied with the problems the United States experienced at the same time in evacuating downed American air crews and prisoners of war from eastern Europe. Late in February 1945, in accordance with a Soviet-American repatriation agreement signed at Yalta, Major General Edmund W. Hill came to an understanding with Marshal S.A. Khudyakov regarding the salvage of American aircraft and the evacuation of airmen from Soviet-occupied territory. Eastern Command, AAF headquarters located at Poltava, USSR, would handle salvage and evacuation matters north of the Carpathian Mountains, and the American mission in Bucharest would deal with the same matters south of the mountain chain. No sooner had the agreement been made than the Soviets had second thoughts about it. They delayed and in many cases did not inform American military officials at Poltava or Moscow about the downed American planes and their crews. Despite Soviet behavior, AAF personnel, usually accompanied by Soviet airmen, flew several missions into Poland in the fall and winter of 1944 to evacuate airmen who had been forced to land there as well as former American prisoners of war.[19]

By March 1945 it was apparent that the Soviets did not want American contact teams in Poland or in other parts of eastern Europe. They wanted all evacuation operations concentrated in Odessa, even if it meant a special hardship for seriously sick or wounded men. When Harriman complained on March 14 about restrictions on American entry into Poland, Molotov claimed that Soviet army officers and

Polish authorities objected to the presence of AAF officers in Poland
because the United States did not have an agreement with the Warsaw
regime. Harriman told Washington: "I feel that the Soviet Government is trying to use our liberated prisoners of war as a club to induce
us to give increased prestige to the Provisional Polish Government by
dealing with it in this connection as the Soviets are doing in other
cases." Harriman wanted Washington to make a strong protest, even
to take retaliatory measures.[20] Initially, Stimson agreed with Harriman and suggested that the United States cut lend-lease supplies to
the Soviet Union to force Stalin to cooperate. But after talking with
General Marshall, Stimson changed his mind and agreed with the
general that the best approach would be for the president to send a
sharp letter to Stalin. "Only this time," Stimson said, it should be
"red hot." Stimson believed that Stalin only understood "rough talk."
Marshall prepared a draft message from Roosevelt to Stalin, later
amended by Stimson, which was approved by the President and sent
to the Soviet chief on March 17. In what was one of the sternest notes
he sent to Stalin during the war, Roosevelt complained: "Frankly I
cannot understand your reluctance to permit American officers and
means [*sic*] to assist their own people in this matter. This Government
has done everything to meet each of your requests. I now request you
to meet mine in this particular matter."[21]

Stalin was unmoved: he claimed that there were only seventeen
sick Americans in Poland and they would be moved soon to Odessa.
Moreover, he alleged that the presence of American officers in Poland
at a time when the Soviets were still fighting presented problems of
security. Besides, he asserted, former American prisoners of war who
were in Soviet camps were treated better than former Soviet prisoners of war in American camps. Harriman challenged Stalin's claims
about the number of Americans in Poland and the alleged suitability
of Soviet facilities for Americans. "Soviet facilities in Odessa," Harriman complained to Roosevelt, "meet the barest minimum needs."
Elsewhere, he added, the hardships the Americans had to endure
"have been inexcusable." Harriman said that reports from liberated
American prisoners when they arrived home revealed "gratitude for
the Polish people and the Polish Red Cross but nothing but resentment for the treatment received from the Russians." Harriman warned
Roosevelt that when the American public learned about the situation,
"there will be great and lasting resentment." Accordingly, he recommended as a *quid pro quo* that General Eisenhower limit the freedom
of Soviet contact officers in the West. Roosevelt, although disturbed
by Soviet behavior, did not go along with Harriman's advice. He was
unwilling to add more fuel to an already explosive situation in East-

West relations. Washington instructed Harriman to relate American grievances concerning access to its citizens in Poland and to express Washington's expectations that conditions would improve in the future. That was as far as he was willing to go.[22]

Meanwhile, several incidents occurred involving American military personnel in Poland. There was one involving an American Liberator bomber, commanded by Lieutenant Donald Bridge, which took off without Soviet clearance after refueling at Mielec. The Soviet base commander, probably aware of the fate that awaited him for the breach of rules, committed suicide. But the most serious incident was the attempt of Lieutenant Myron King who, after a forced landing in Warsaw, tried to smuggle out a Polish stowaway with the un-Polish name of "Jack Smith." Moscow responded by grounding all AAF aircraft, except those of the Air Transport Command, in Soviet-held territory. The Soviets detained the pilot and later turned him over to American authorities who court-martialed him. A subsequent unauthorized attempt by Eastern Command to operate a fourteen-man contact team in Lódz, Poland, for the purpose of rescue and repair work resulted in all of the men being placed under guard and evacuated by train out of the country. Harriman saw Stalin on April 15, 1945, and after the dictator accused the AAF of conspiring with the Polish underground against the Soviets, Harriman angrily replied: "You're impugning the loyalty of General Marshall." Stalin tried to mollify Harriman by saying that he would trust Marshall with his life, and that he had in mind a junior American officer.[23]

In view of Western pressures to get observers into Poland, Stalin appears to have concluded that the incidents involving American air force personnel in Poland were connected with the purpose of contacting the Polish underground as a first step in the establishment of an official observer mission on Polish soil. Air crews and former prisoners evacuated from Poland had a rare opportunity to acquire firsthand reports from Polish citizens of their treatment by the Soviets. From the Kremlin's point of view, Stalin had every reason to end these contacts, which ran the risk of seriously compromising the image of the Soviets as benevolent liberators of Poland. The Soviet embargo on United States air flights in the Soviet Union finally ended in the latter part of April 1945.[24]

Shortly after Truman assumed office he admitted to Churchill that there was little room for "optimism" in solving the Polish problem. But he assured the prime minister that he knew "in general what President Roosevelt had in mind as the next step." A few days later, on Truman's suggestion, the two leaders sent a joint message to Stalin, assuring the Soviet dictator that they never intended to deny the current Warsaw leadership a prominent role in the Provisional Government of National Unity. On the other hand, they would not accept the right of the Warsaw Poles to veto the names of other candidates nominated for consultations in Moscow. "No such interpretation in our considered opinion can be found in the Crimea decision." They also rejected Stalin's suggestion that the new Polish government be reorganized along lines similar to Yugoslavia's, a proposal the Soviets continued to urge even though it was not mentioned at Yalta. Showing Stalin that the West did not intend to invite an unlimited number of individuals for consultations, as the Soviets had charged earlier, Truman and Churchill suggested that nine Polish leaders in Warsaw and abroad be invited for the Moscow talks.[25]

While awaiting Stalin's response, Truman held a series of meetings with high-ranking State Department officials and members of his cabinet in an effort to determine what future course American policy should follow toward the Kremlin. His own instincts were to continue the firmer line that Washington began to follow toward the Kremlin in Roosevelt's last weeks in office. Key State Department and cabinet members echoed the same view. Prior to a meeting with Molotov on April 23, the president met with several high-ranking officials of the government, including Stettinius, Stimson, Leahy, Marshall, Harriman, Bohlen, and Forrestal, and asked for their views on the Polish problem and how to solve it. Most of the officials endorsed a firm policy toward the Kremlin and assumed that the Soviets would eventually compromise, except Stimson and Marshall who urged a more cautious line. Stimson, who criticized the State Department for getting the United States into a "mess" on Poland, did not share the opinion that the Soviet Union would yield to Washington because of the area's importance to Soviet security. The secretary of war believed that Poland was simply "too big an issue to take chances on," and he blamed Stettinius and the "young men" in the State Department for insisting that the United States adopt a hard line toward the Soviet Union. He recognized that the public, in his words, was "all churned up" over Poland, and he blamed the Yalta meeting because it "dealt a good deal in altruism and idealism instead of stark realities on which Russia is strong." Although the Soviets had agreed to free elections in Poland, Stimson did not put much faith in their ever being held, noting in his diary that there were few nations who had any idea "what an independent ballot is." Marshall joined Stimson in urging a restrained policy toward Moscow. The chief of staff despaired of a showdown with the Soviet Union over Poland at a time when American military experts believed Soviet help would hasten the end of the Pacific war.[26]

Confident that a firm policy toward the Soviet Union was the correct one, Truman met later the same day with Molotov and pointedly told him that an agreement had been reached on Poland at Yalta and that the Soviet Union was the chief obstacle in fulfilling it. Molotov, according to one observer, got ashen-faced when he heard the blunt remarks from Truman. The president later wrote that Molotov told him: "I have never been talked to like that in my life." And the president shot back: "Carry out your agreements and you won't get talked to like that."[27]

Neither Trumanesque language nor the earlier joint message that the president and the prime minister had sent to Stalin brought any immediate change in Soviet policy: when Stettinius, Eden, and Molotov held an evening meeting on April 23, Molotov grimly declared that the West had only two alternatives—accept the Yugoslav formula or allow the Warsaw Poles to be consulted first by the Polish Commission. What seemed to be the last word from Stalin came the next day, April 24: The Western leaders should not interfere in Poland, which was vital to Soviet security, just as the Soviet Union had not interfered in the formation of the Belgian and Greek governments. Stalin repeated what Molotov had told Stettinius and Eden the previous day that they should accept the Yugoslav formula. Truman commented later that this was "one of the most revealing and disquieting messages he had received during his early days in the White House." Eden was so upset by the situation that he saw little point in convening the San Francisco Conference until the Big Three made some progress on the Polish issue.[28]

In a long emotional message, Churchill tried again to persuade Stalin to bend on Poland by forecasting disaster in East-West relations if he did not. The prime minister declared that it was not much "comfort" to look ahead to a world divided into Communist and non-Communist sides and appealed to history's verdict: "It is quite obvious that their quarrel would tear the world to pieces and that all of us leading men on either side who had anything to do with that would be shamed before history." Churchill confided to Truman that the only way out of the impasse was another meeting of the Big Three. But, meanwhile, he urged that Western armies should hold their existing positions and not retire behind agreed upon occupation lines until the West was satisfied about the Polish situation. On his part, the newly appointed ambassador to the Polish government-in-exile, Arthur Bliss Lane, who was still in Washington, recommended that the American public be told about the deterioration of Soviet-American relations over Poland and be informed that the Kremlin was to blame. He even suggested that the breakdown could be

dramatized by his own resignation and the assignment of his staff to
other duties. Lane wrote later: "I maintained that the suggested action, if taken immediately, would indicate that the United States
Government had no intention of appeasing the Soviet Government
further, and that we definitely refused to whitewash the Soviet-controlled regime in Warsaw as a democratic government."[29]

American policymakers were not oblivious to the use of economic
measures to pressure the Soviets to bend on political issues. Harriman
espoused the use of economic measures to break the deadlock over
Poland with the zeal of a missionary. On April 4, he told Washington:
"Our policy toward the Soviet Union should, of course, continue to
be based on our earnest desire for the development of friendly relations and cooperation both political and economic, but always on a
quid pro quo basis. This means tying our economic assistance directly
into our political problems with the Soviet Union." Truman, who
quickly familiarized himself with the details of Soviet-American relations over Poland, agreed with Harriman's assessment. On May 9,
Stettinius joined Harriman in proposing that the United States cut
back on lend-lease shipments to the Soviet Union, ostensibly because
of Germany's surrender. The policy, said Stettinius, should be "firm
while avoiding any implication of a threat or any indication of political bargaining."[30] Grew, undersecretary of state, and Leo T. Crowley,
who headed the Federal Economic Administration, recommended to
Truman on May 11 that he approve cutting off lend-lease shipments
to the Soviet Union as soon as possible, except aid intended for use
against the Japanese and material needed to complete industrial projects still under construction. In addition, no new aid protocol was to
be negotiated with the Soviet Union. Truman approved the proposal
the same day. According to John Gaddis, "Crowley interpreted the
lend-lease curtailment directive far more literally than Truman or
Harriman had intended." Even ships at sea containing goods for the
Soviet Union were ordered to return to port. Truman countermanded
his order, but the damage had been done. Stalin was furious with the
bungled attempt to blackmail the Kremlin.[31]

Something had to be done to improve Soviet-American relations,
which had reached their lowest point of the war. Bohlen suggested
that Hopkins, who enjoyed Stalin's confidence, might be able to improve the situation between the two countries. Bohlen and Harriman
went to Hopkins' Georgetown home to broach the idea. Hopkins,
though extremely ill, was amenable to the urging of another mission
to Moscow. A few days later, Truman appointed Hopkins his envoy
to Stalin, instructing him "to use diplomatic language or a baseball
bat if he thought that was the proper approach," in order to

emphasize that the United States wanted a fair understanding with Stalin over Poland. Ironically, Truman sent Hopkins to Moscow to solve a problem that the United States had consistently indicated during the war was essentially a British matter without even consulting Churchill beforehand. Although angry with Truman, Churchill supported the Hopkins mission to the Soviet Union.[32]

Hopkins arrived in Moscow on May 25 and had six conversations with Stalin before he left the Soviet Union on June 7, 1945. The two men met in Stalin's Kremlin office, facing each other behind a green baize-covered table in an atmosphere that was relaxed and agreeable. Stalin, apparently impressed by Truman's initiative in sending Hopkins, seemed to want to make some gesture toward conciliation. But he did not yield anything to Hopkins.[33]

During his first meeting on May 26, Hopkins impressed Stalin by his emphasis on the deterioration of confidence of the American public in Soviet-American relations because of the Polish stalemate. Stalin, blaming the British for allegedly wanting to create a *cordon sanitaire* around the Soviet Union, revealed that he thought the Polish question could be settled. But the next day, Stalin launched into an angry tirade over the American cutback in lend-lease and lectured Hopkins that it had been a mistake.[34]

The meeting on May 30 was crucial: after Stalin agreed to the democratic principles which were to govern the establishment of a Polish government, Hopkins assured Stalin that Truman and Churchill were agreeable to the Warsaw Poles constituting a majority in a new Polish government and opposed inviting leaders from the Polish government-in-exile or their agents in Poland for consultations in Moscow.[35] These assurances completely undermined the position of the Polish government in London and abandoned the arrested Polish leaders to the Kremlin. Now Stalin had a free hand to try the sixteen Poles. Hopkins' revelations to Stalin were consistent with Washington's wartime policy toward the Kremlin over Poland—affirmation of American interest in the establishment and independence of the Polish nation but unwillingness to make too much of an issue over the details to implement the objective for fear of wrecking a general agreement on the Polish question with the Soviets.

From that point on, the discussions between the two men on the names of the non-Lublin Poles to be invited to Moscow moved quickly. During the meeting on May 30, Stalin suggested that eight Poles, exclusive of the representatives of the Warsaw government, should come to Moscow and agreed to Stanisław Mikołajczyk, Stanisław Grabski or Jan Stańczyk (Western nominees), and Antoni Kolodziej (Soviet nominee), from London. Wincenty Witos or Cardinal Adam Sapieha,

Zygmunt Żuławski, Stanisław Kutrzeba (Western nominees), Henryk
Kołodziejski and Adam Krzyżanowski (Soviet nominees) from Poland
were suggested. Hopkins urged Truman to approve the list because "it
carries out the Yalta agreement in all its essential respects." Truman
gave his "whole-hearted" approval to the names, though later Stalin
indicated that he would not insist on Kolodziej and suggested Juliusz
Zakowski as an alternative. In the meantime, Hopkins, on Truman's
instructions, appealed several times to Stalin to release the sixteen
arrested Polish leaders and warned about the implications of their
confinement on the forthcoming Big Three meeting at Potsdam.
Stalin told Hopkins that the men would be treated leniently. The
United States accepted the assurance and promptly dropped the matter.[36]

The assessments of the Hopkins mission to Moscow were mixed.
Harriman enthusiastically observed to Truman: "Harry did a first
rate job in presenting your views and in explaining the most important matters, particularly Poland, which were causing concern."
Stettinius was happy, too, noting that Hopkins' success coincided
with his at the San Francisco Conference.[37] Mikołajczyk was skeptical: he noted that half the men who were invited to Moscow had no
party backing and therefore would find it difficult to resist pressure.
Moreover, he considered the list of outside Poles too lopsided in favor
of pro-Communists, such as Zakowski, Krzyżanowski, and Kołodziejski.[38] Churchill offered the most perceptive analysis: he told Truman
that what was done by Hopkins was "no advance on Yalta," only "an
advance upon the deadlock." He admonished the president that there
should be no newspaper publicity claiming a solution to the Polish
problem. "Renewed hope and not rejoicing is all we can indulge in
at the moment," the prime minister cautioned.[39]

On June 11, 1945, invitations were sent to the list of Poles agreed
upon by Hopkins and Stalin to come to Moscow to establish a Polish
government as provided by the Yalta agreement. Witos, in ill health,
declined. Zakowski, a prominent Warsaw architect before the war,
was puzzled why he had been chosen. He declined on the grounds he
was not a politician.[40] Even Mikołajczyk was uncertain at first about
going to Moscow, but after several members of his former cabinet
appealed to him, Mikołajczyk began to think differently. Even
Arciszewski told him: "In your hands lies the future of Poland. You
are the only person who can still save it." Churchill strongly admonished Mikołajczyk not to lose what he considered was the last chance
for the Polish leader "to get not only your foot but your leg in the
door." Before Mikołajczyk left for the Soviet Union, Churchill tear-
fully vowed: "We are responsible for your journey. If something

should happen to you we shall start fighting." Meanwhile, the Soviet Union agreed to accept Władysław Kiernik to replace Witos in return for the West's agreement to Kołodziej, the replacement for Zakowski.[41]

The Soviets made it unmistakably clear to the world which nation controlled events in Poland. The Kremlin staged the trial of the sixteen leaders in Moscow precisely at the same time Polish leaders tried to reach agreement on the composition of a new government for Poland. The trial ended on June 21, 1945, the same day the Polish leaders reached agreement on a cabinet. Commenting on the Kremlin's timing of the trial, Truman said: "The deliberate timing of events by the U.S.S.R. in order to confront the negotiators with a *fait accompli* at the very outset of discussions was fast becoming part of the habitual pattern of Russian tactics." Of the sixteen arrested men, one was not tried because of illness and three were acquitted. The remainder received sentences from four months to ten years. The State Department conjectured that Western intervention had been a significant factor in the relatively mild sentences. Of those tried, only one of the Poles did not break down and sign a prefabricated confession. As it turned out, several of the men died in prison and many of those later released were arrested again in Poland. A few subsequently managed to flee to the West.[42]

Polish leaders who participated in the Moscow talks included: Bolesław Bierut, Władysław Kowalski, Edward Osóbka-Morawski, and Władysław Gomulka from the Warsaw regime; Władysław Kiernik, Henryk Kołodziejski, Adam Krzyżanowski, Stanisław Kutrzeba, and Zygmunt Żuławski from Poland; and Stanisław Mikołajczyk, Antoni Kołodziej, and Jan Stańczyk from London. After several days of difficult negotiations, the Poles reached an agreement on a new Polish government. Although the arrangement was unsatisfactory to him, Mikołajczyk went along with it. He and other non-Communist Poles were so disturbed about the situation in Poland that they were willing to accept almost anything that offered some hope for Polish independence.[43] The composition of the Polish Provisional Government of National Unity included sixteen Lublinites and five non-Communists. They included: Edward B. Osóbka-Morawski, premier; Władysław Gomulka, vice-premier; Stanisław Mikołajczyk, vice-premier and minister of agriculture and agrarian reform; Wincenty Rzymowski, minister of foreign affairs; Marshal Michał Rola-Żymierski, minister of national defense; Władysław Kiernik, minister of public administration; Stanisław Radkiewicz, minister of public security; Konstanty Dąbrowski, minister of finance; Hilary Minc, minister of industry; Jan Rabanowski, minister of communications; Michał Kaczorowski, minister of reconstruction; Jan Stańczyk, minister of labor and social welfare; Czesław Wycech, minister of education; Henryk Światkowski, minister of justice; Władysław Kowalski, minister of culture and art; Stefan Matuszewski, minister of public information; Franciszek Litwin, minister of public health; Mieczysław Thugutt, minister of posts and telegraph; Jerzy Sztachelski, minister of supplies and trade; Stefan Jędrychowski, minister of foreign trade; and Stanisław Tkaczów, minister of forestry. The non-Communist member of the cabinet included: Mikołajczyk, Stańczyk, Kiernik, Thugutt, and Wycech. Thugutt reportedly declined his portfolio. Grabski and Witos, though ill, were to serve on the Communist-dominated Presidium of the National Council of Poland.[44]

Although disappointed that the non-Communist Poles had not gotten more seats in the new government, Harriman was guardedly optimistic that if the United States continued its interest in Poland and was reasonably generous with economic aid that there was "a fair chance" of things working out in Poland from the American point of view. When the Polish government accepted the Crimea decisions, thus affirming that free elections would be held in Poland, the United States and England extended diplomatic recognition to it on July 5, 1945.[45] The United States had intended to recognize the Polish government two days earlier but Churchill balked, pointing out with irritation to Truman that at least twenty-four hours notice to the London Poles was necessary. "Our position is different from yours," he reminded the president. The Polish government had a large staff and administered a huge army, he added.[46] On his part, Ambassador Ciechanowski tried to stave off the inevitable by trying to persuade the American government not to extend *de jure* recognition to the new Warsaw regime until free elections were held in Poland. But the effort failed. In a final defiant gesture, Ciechanowski tried to deed the property of the Polish Embassy in Washington to the Polish American Congress rather than see it occupied by representatives of the new Communist-dominated government of Poland. But American officials frustrated his effort by declaring his action illegal.[47]

The American public welcomed the Yalta decision to establish a Polish government on a broader democratic basis, though the impasse that had been reached in the Polish Commission created consternation in people's minds. Even American observers who were usually sympathetic to the Soviet Union criticized the Kremlin's uncooperative tactics. The trial of the sixteen Polish leaders brought a large number of American commentators to draw unfavorable analogies with the Stalin purge trials of the 1930s, although the lenient sentences tended to offset earlier criticisms of the Kremlin. By the end of June, however, there was widespread American support for withdrawing recognition from the London Poles and recognizing the new Polish government in Warsaw. According to one survey of public opinion,

> The tenor of recent press and radio comment suggests that American opinion accepts the present solution as a necessary condition for preserving Allied unity. It thinks the solution to be "less than perfect" justice; and sympathy for the London Poles is stronger than support for them. But there is considerable acceptance of the necessity for establishing a Polish government able to get along with the Soviet Union, even one at least partially subservient to the latter.

Joseph C. Harsch, a CBS commentator, summed up this point of view when he said: "We're moving into a new world in which we as a nation are committed officially to finding a way to live at peace with Russia. The Polish group in London never succeeded in adjusting itself to that concept."[48]

When Truman assumed office, Polish Americans hoped that he would take a stronger stand on behalf of Poland against the Soviets. But they were soon to be bitterly disappointed. Rozmarek urged the new president to insist on guarantees that would enable Allied supervision of the free elections that were supposed to be held in Poland. No such guarantees had been provided for at Yalta, and Truman did not press the matter. The PRCU and the Coordinating Committee of American-Polish Associations in the East appealed to Truman to prevent the trial of the sixteen underground leaders arrested by the Soviets, to send a delegation to Poland to investigate conditions there, and to invite the London Poles to the San Francisco Conference of the United Nations. When Truman went on to recognize the Lublin-dominated provisional government in July 1945, Rozmarek labeled it "a tragic historical blunder" and "a moral defeat for the democracies."[49] The *Bulletin* of the Polish American Congress, which once had blamed Poland's troubles entirely on the Soviet Union, now declared in its August-September 1945 issue: "It was not Russia but *America* that broke Poland!"[50]

After the recognition of the Polish government, the United States continued to identify strongly with the holding of free elections in Poland. The State Department, which in March had opposed sending observers to supervise elections in Poland, reversed itself in June 1945 and recommended that the United States do so. The State Department felt that with American support of the democratic members of the Warsaw regime the Polish people would have a better chance of selecting a permanent government of their own choice. In a Briefing Book Paper prepared before the Potsdam meeting, the State Department pointed out that through credits and other means aimed at the reconstruction of Poland's industrial and agricultural apparatus, it might be possible to establish "a truly independent democratic Polish state." The State Department therefore urged that aid to Poland should be on a national basis, as opposed to an international agency, and recommended that the United States get a promise from the Warsaw regime to follow an open-door policy regarding American interests in trade, investments, and access to information. Sensitive to the impact of Polish American opinion on relations between Warsaw and Washington, the State Department declared: "The large population of Polish extraction in the United States will undoubtedly seek to make an internal American political issue of Polish affairs if free relations between the two countries are seriously impeded." Harriman, a staunch advocate of the efficacy of economic means to achieve political ends, believed that an immediate credit for Polish reconstruction would help to implement the free elections in Poland, "the final step" of the Yalta agreement.[51]

Washington moved rapidly in its economic and relief efforts to assist Poland, clearly aware that beyond humanitarian and economic considerations the aid would influence the political future of Poland. In addition to aid from the Red Cross and the United Nations Relief and Rehabilitation Administration (UNRRA), the United States intended to help Poland by giving it loans, sending vehicles to help in its transportation crisis, improving the 1931 Polish-American Treaty of Friendship, Commerce, and Consular Rights, and dispatching American technical specialists.[52] UNRRA aid began to arrive in Warsaw early in June 1945, but the Soviets conspicuously refused to issue transit visas for an UNRRA delegation to enter Poland in order to negotiate an agreement with the Polish government until July 6, 1945, one day after Anglo-American recognition of the Warsaw government.[53]

By the summer of 1945 American policy toward Poland was clear: it would not oppose preponderant Soviet influence there, but it would not tolerate Soviet subjugation of the country. Economic measures and insistence that free elections be held in Poland were the means Washington expected to prevent Soviet domination of the country. Yet mounting evidence of Soviet repression in Poland revealed the limitations of American power to influence political events in the country. The Office of Strategic Services concluded that it was "unlikely" the United States could save eastern Europe from Soviet domination. After Ambassador Lane arrived in Poland in July 1945, his reports to Washington made it evident that there would never be free elections in the country as long as the Soviet army was there. After only a few weeks in the Polish capital, Lane predicted that

when the elections were finally held—delayed until January 1947—
they would be nothing more than a one-party ballot. In October 1945
Lane said that if free elections were held, the Lublin Poles would receive only 5 to 10 percent of the vote. Harriman had come to the
same conclusion: he wrote later that Bierut probably had told Stalin
shortly after the Yalta meeting that a free election in Poland would
result in a Mikołajczyk victory. "They must have decided that the
risk was too great," Harriman observed.[54]

Faced with an agonizing dilemma, Truman believed that the United
States could do no more than reiterate the principles of the Yalta
agreement and withhold credits from Warsaw until free elections were
held. The sad fact was that the American commitment to safeguard
an independent Poland had clearly outpaced its capacity to do so.
But the United States continued to call for free elections in Poland,
a policy that collided with Soviet intentions to dominate the country
and led to the rupture in the Allied alliance.

IX

CONCLUSION

There was always more sympathy than support for Poland in the United States during World War II. After the Soviet Union's involvement in the war, the United States revealed that Poland did not have the same priority as the Soviet Union in American policy. The United States made this clear from the outset when the Beaverbrook-Harriman mission to Moscow did not specifically earmark war supplies from the United States and Great Britain for the Polish army in the Soviet Union. The United States, before the Yalta Conference in February 1945, preferred to maintain a low profile concerning the Polish question in East-West relations. To be sure, there were occasions when the United States took diplomatic initiatives in trying to resolve one or more of the disturbing problems in Polish-Soviet relations. In the summer of 1943, Hull departed from the role of honest broker in the Polish-Soviet dispute and attempted to deal with the relief and citizenship problems involving Poles in the Soviet Union. But the United States preferred Great Britain to assume the activist role in trying to resolve the outstanding issues in Polish-Soviet relations. Neither the president nor the State Department suggested at any time to the Kremlin prior to the Yalta meeting that Poland was an issue of vital concern to the United States. If anything, American diplomacy suggested the opposite to Stalin. It was only at Yalta that President Roosevelt took a decisive initiative on the Polish question and belatedly asserted America's serious interest in Poland's future.

Throughout the war American officials continually repeated that Washington's policy was based on the Atlantic Charter, and that territorial settlements should be deferred until after the war. The official position of the American government, violated by Roosevelt himself first at Tehran and later at Yalta, suggested to the Polish government-in-exile that it had more support in the United States than it really had. The London Poles had every reason to be gratified by the enunciation of a public policy that came close to their own—the re-creation of Poland as an independent state and refusal to negotiate Poland's eastern frontier with the Soviets during the war.

As long as Soviet armies were not in Poland, the United States could afford the luxury of repeating the principles and ideals of the Atlantic Charter without running political risks at home and abroad. The London Poles, too, could bathe in the deceptive glow of alleged American support for the Polish government. But all this changed when the Soviets entered Poland and were able to secure by force what they had sought by diplomacy—namely, the Curzon Line as the Polish-Soviet boundary and a government that would be friendly to the Kremlin.

Stalin's aims in Poland have long been the subject of debate. It does not appear that he wanted a break with his allies over Poland any more than the United States and Britain did. Yet his policy of includ-ing Poland within a Soviet sphere of influence was made clear enough as early as 1941. He left no doubt about the fact that he did not ac-cept the restoration of the Riga Line as the postwar Polish-Soviet frontier. He continually reiterated that he wanted the Curzon Line and a friendly government before he resumed relations with the Pol-ish government-in-exile after the Katyn affair. His creation of the Union of Polish Patriots and later, more importantly, the Lublin Com-mittee, which he made a government on the eve of the Yalta Confer-ence, revealed how far he would go to get his way in Poland. His behavior at the time of the Warsaw Uprising graphically revealed that he wanted to humiliate the Polish government-in-exile and to destroy the pro-West Polish underground, important obstacles that had to be eliminated before he extended diplomatic recognition to his Lublin protégés as the provisional government of Poland. Curiously, despite Stalin's public record on the subject, the United States somehow never completely understood how important it was for the Soviet Union to dominate Poland.

Although American interests never were considered vitally involved in Poland, Washington did not reassess its policy toward the Polish government in London. It was content to repeat idealistic phrases about a free and independent Poland being recreated after the war, even when it became increasingly apparent to policymakers that to accomplish such an objective would be difficult, if not impossible. On the rare occasions that serious thought was given to viewing Wash-ington's policy in terms of American interests, the State Department did not recommend substantive changes in policy to the White House, which glibly repeated a line that grew more and more unrealistic with the passage of time. If policymaking toward Poland had been anything

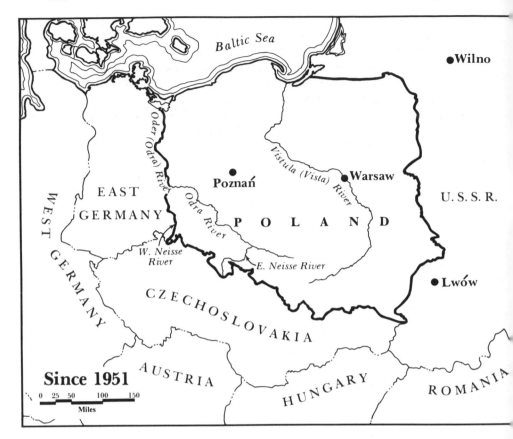

more than the casual, idiosyncratic phenomenon it was during the war years, a change consistent with American interests and the limitations of its power at the time had a good chance of receiving public endorsement, considering the Russophilia that gripped American public opinion.

The basic American interest in the war was to keep the Soviet Union fighting Germany and to try to get the Soviet Union into the Pacific conflict. The United States never allowed any Polish issue—the refugees, the Polish army, the boundary problem, the complexion of the Polish government—seriously to threaten Soviet-American rapprochement. When Washington took the initiative on Poland's behalf and the Kremlin expressed its displeasure, the United States usually backed off in order not to jeopardize the alliance. This was especially true in the early years of the war, when the Soviets carried the main burden of the struggle against the Germans. Even when a serious crisis arose over locating and evacuating American servicemen from

Poland in 1945, Roosevelt did not push the matter to the breaking point with the Soviets, though he was as upset over Soviet behavior as over anything that had occurred in Soviet-American relations during World War II. Even at the Yalta Conference, when Roosevelt departed from previous American policy and took the initiative in trying to resolve the Polish question, he never insisted upon measures that would have ensured free elections in Poland. And Truman was no different: although he interceded on behalf of the sixteen arrested Polish leaders he promptly dropped the matter when Stalin insisted he was going to try them anyway.

Roosevelt and Truman sought in their own ways to preserve the wartime relationship with the Kremlin and to solve the Polish question without simply capitulating to Stalin's terms. The essential difference between the two men was stylistic, not substantive: the difference between the urbane landlord of the Hudson and the blunt shopkeeper of the Midwest. After all, it was Roosevelt who insisted that Mikołajczyk have an important place in the postwar Polish government and refused to abandon the London Poles for the Lublinites until a reconstructed government of some kind had been created. Stalin simply did not understand the emotional and political capital, stemming from American idealism, that the United States had invested in Poland, which had made it impossible for Washington to write the Soviet dictator a blank check.

Roosevelt's inconsistency concerning Poland may not have been intentional, but it was no less dangerous. On the one hand, Roosevelt had agreed to the Curzon Line at Tehran and his agreement was kept secret for domestic political reasons until Molotov blurted it out to Mikołajczyk one year later. While Roosevelt never categorically insisted to Polish leaders that they recognize the Curzon Line and reorganize their government with pro-Soviet personnel to make it more acceptable to the Soviets, the president endorsed such changes both privately and in his dealings with the Kremlin. Roosevelt's handling of the Polish problem undermined the work of Churchill, who had assumed the major burden until the Yalta Conference of trying to end the Polish-Soviet schism. The prime minister could not convince the Polish government in London of the necessity of compromising with the Kremlin on the boundary matter and of changing the complexion of its cabinet to be more acceptable to Stalin because the United States had left Polish leaders with the impression that later in the war, when the balance of power in Europe improved in the West's favor, Washington could and would do more for Poland.

Roosevelt's reluctance to be more candid about Poland's frontiers and the future complexion of Poland's government stemmed at least partially from fears of American Polonia, which had completely mobilized behind a literal fulfillment of the Atlantic Charter concerning Poland by the spring of 1944. After all, the architect of the design for the postwar world could hardly tinker with a plan to construct a mansion and convert it into a barn at a time when the end of the war was imminent and the presidential election was just around the corner. To the end, the buoyant Roosevelt clung optimistically to the belief that a solution would be found to the stubborn Polish problem that would be satisfactory to all parties concerned.

It was obvious by the time of the Warsaw Uprising that the United States had serious limitations in being able to influence events in eastern Europe. Without Soviet airfields, even American air force aid to the Varsovians could not be given. American insistence on helping the Poles collided with Soviet determination to see them crushed. At no time had the aims of the two nations come so directly into a collision course. Anglo-American pressures on the Kremlin finally brought a reluctant Stalin to help the Poles and to give the United States the military bases, but it was too late for the beleaguered Poles who were only a few weeks away from defeat. Stalin had given a candid preview of what he wanted in Poland to Roosevelt and Churchill at Warsaw during the summer of 1944. For Roosevelt and Churchill to have assumed that Stalin was prepared for anything other than a Soviet-controlled Poland at the Yalta Conference six months later was one of the biggest misjudgments in modern diplomatic history. After the Yalta meeting, the stalemate provoked by the Kremlin's interpretation of the agreement had dragged on so long that when it finally ended, it appeared that a genuine breakthrough had been made in East-West relations over Poland. But as Churchill said, the Hopkins mission to the Soviet Union in 1945 was nothing more than an advance on the deadlock over the implementation of the Yalta agreement.

Stalin, too, had made a grave miscalculation. The United States and Britain had shown the Kremlin during the Warsaw Uprising how far they were willing to go to help the Poles, even if it risked a confrontation with the Soviet Union. Yet Stalin for months after the Yalta meeting insisted that the Lublin Poles have veto power over the names of Polish leaders suggested by the West who were to be invited to Moscow for the conversations that would ostensibly result in a Polish provisional government agreeable to all members of the Big Three. When he belatedly realized the depth of American and British commitment to salvage something for the pro-West Poles, Stalin relented and Polish leaders were invited for the talks that resulted in the formation of the Lublin-dominated government which the Big Three recognized. Stalin's mistake was to create and aggravate a crisis over Poland at a time when mutual suspicions and doubts on both sides of the Allied camp began to undermine the alliance seriously.

At first glance, American Polonia appears not to have had direct political influence on Washington's policy toward the Soviet Union over Poland. But in their insistent and united demand that the Atlantic Charter and the Four Freedoms not be abandoned, American Poles, organized in the Polish American Congress, were the largest anti-Soviet bloc of American citizens who played a moral role in reminding the administration that American foreign policy since the beginning of the war had been tied to ideals which they saw as synonymous with United States interests. Ironically, the Polish American Congress had adopted a position concerning Poland's frontiers and its relations with the Soviet Union that was even more extreme than that of the Mikołajczyk government. But if Polish Americans had exaggerated the role of the ideals of the Atlantic Charter in American foreign policy, Washington officials exaggerated the impact that economic measures would have in preventing Poland from falling completely into the Soviet orbit.

By the time of the Potsdam Conference in mid-July 1945, when the Polish Provisional Government of National Unity won Big Three recognition of its occupation of German lands between the western and eastern Neisse rivers, the Communist Poles had begun to tighten their control over Poland. At Potsdam, the Big Three had taken "note" of the agreement of the Polish government to hold "free and unfettered elections as soon as possible." The elections were delayed until January 1947—and they were neither free nor unfettered.

In retrospect, American policy toward Poland during World War II was based more on sentiment than on a clear perception of what was meant by an American commitment to the re-creation of an independent Polish state. There were no conspiracies—political or economic—in United States policy toward the Soviet Union over Poland. Increasingly, Washington officials became aware that the best the United States could do for Poland was to get Stalin to endorse publicly free elections in the country after the war. Roosevelt believed that a postwar détente between the United States and the Soviet Union, the crushing of Germany, and the creation of the United Nations would give Stalin the assurances he needed about Soviet security and thereby allow the Poles to have a reasonable amount of political freedom within a Soviet sphere of influence. Roosevelt's expectations were dashed, however, by the Soviet dictator who combined the realpolitik of a Bismarck and the guile of a Machiavelli.

ABBREVIATIONS USED IN THE NOTES

DPSR	*Documents on Polish-Soviet Relations*
DS/NA	Department of State Files, National Archives
FDR/L	Franklin D. Roosevelt Library
FR	*Foreign Relations of the United States*
HST/L	Harry S. Truman Library
IMT/NA	International Military Tribunal Documents, National Archives
Ltr.	Letter
MD/LC	Manuscript Division, Library of Congress
Memo	Memorandum
Msg.	Message
OF	Office File
OSS	Office of Strategic Services
PDR	*Polish Documents Report*
PPF	President's Personal File
PSF	President's Secretary's File
PSZ	*Polskie Siły Zbrojne w Drugiej Wojnie Światowej*
SP/PI	Sosnkowski Papers, Piłsudski Institute
UV/L	University of Virginia Library
WUP/PI	Warsaw Uprising Papers, Piłsudski Institute
YU/L	Yale University Library

NOTES

Chapter I

1. See Peter Filene, *Americans and the Soviet Experiment* (Cambridge, Mass.: Harvard Univ. Press, 1967), and Meno Lovenstein, *American Opinion of Soviet Russia* (Washington, D.C.: American Council on Public Affairs, 1941).

2. See the news stories and editorials in the *New York Times* in Sept., 1939. A Gallup poll showed that almost 90 percent of the American public supported Poland when Hitler invaded it. *New York Times,* Sept. 1, 1939.

3. Msg., Roosevelt to governments of Great Britain, France, Italy, Germany, and Poland, Sept. 1, 1939, in OF, 463C, Box 5, FDR/L; Anthony D. Biddle, Jr., "Report on the Polish-German Conflict," in PSF, Poland, Box 66, FDR/L; Msg., Gunther to Hull, Oct. 4, 1939; Memo, Roosevelt to Hull, Oct. 19, 1939; Msg., Hull to Gunther, Oct. 25, 1939; Msg., Gunther to Hull, Oct. 25, 1939; Msg., Gunther to Hull, Oct. 26, 1939; Memo, Roosevelt to Hull, Oct. 28, 1939; Msg., Gunther to Hull, Dec. 1, 1939; Msg., Gunther to Hull, Dec. 25, 1939, in U.S., Department of State, *Foreign Relations of the United States: Diplomatic Papers, 1939.* Vol. II: *General, The British Commonwealth and Europe* (Washington, D.C.: United States Government Printing Office, 1956), pp. 696–706 (hereafter cited as *FR, 1939,* II).

4. Msg., Biddle to Hull, Apr. 6, 1940; Ltr., Welles to Roosevelt, Apr. 8, 1940, in OF, 463, Box 1, FDR/L; Ltr., Paderewski to Roosevelt, Nov. 30, 1940, in PPF 881, FDR/L; Ltr., Joseph Winnicki to Roosevelt, July 18, 1941, in OF, 463A, Box 3, FDR/L. There are other examples of efforts to help individual Poles. For example, Adolf Berle tried and eventually succeeded in securing a permanent visa for a Polish professor, isolated by the war in the United States. See Beatrice B. Berle and Travis B. Jacobs, eds., *Navigating the Rapids, 1918–1971: From the Papers of Adolf A. Berle* (New York: Harcourt, 1973), p. 256.

5. Ltr., Biddle to Roosevelt, Oct. 22, 1940; Ltr., Biddle to Roosevelt, Nov. 13, 1940, in PSF, Poland, Box 65, FDR/L.

6. Msg., Polish Union of America to Roosevelt Sept. 11, 1939; Msg., Group 205, Polish National Alliance, to Roosevelt, Sept. 11, 1939; Resolution, Polish National Alliance, Civil League, District 13, Jan. 31, 1941; Ltr., F. Wos to Roosevelt, Mar. 20, 1941; Ltr., Polish Veterans' Club, Hamtramck, Michigan, to Roosevelt, Mar. 2, 1941, in OF, 463A, Box 3, FDR/L.

7.   Note, Sikorski to Churchill, Sept. 17, 1941, in General Sikorski Historical
Institute, *Documents on Polish-Soviet Relations. 1939-1945.* Vol. I: *1939-1943*
(London: Heinemann, 1961), pp. 167–68 (hereafter cited as *DPSR,* I); Ltr.,
Francis Świetlik to Roosevelt, May 13, 1941, in OF, 463A, Box 3, FDR/L.
Paderewski appealed to Roosevelt to have the American representative to Vichy,
Admiral William Leahy, exert a protective attitude toward Polish Red Cross com-
mittees who were looking after an estimated 450,000 Poles there. Roosevelt
promised Paderewski he would try to do all he could. See Ltr., Paderewski to
Roosevelt, Nov. 30, 1940; Ltr., Roosevelt to Paderewski, Dec. 17, 1940, in PPF
881, FDR/L. Several months later, Ciechanowski told Hull there were 700 Polish
engineers marooned in Vichy, France, who could help the American war industry
if they could be evacuated. Memo of conversation by Hull, Aug. 20, 1941, in
Hull Papers, LXI, MD/LC.
8.   Memo of conversation by Long, Feb. 29, 1940; Msg., Hull to Biddle, June
11, 1940; Msg., Schoenfeld to Zaleski, Nov. 6, 1940; Msg., Schoenfeld to Hull,
Nov. 11, 1940; Msg., Welles to Schoenfeld, Nov. 13, 1940; Msg., Achilles to Hull,
Jan. 7, 1941, in U.S., Department of State, *Foreign Relations of the United States:
Diplomatic Papers, 1941.* Vol. I: *General, The Soviet Union* (Washington, D.C.:
United States Government Printing Office, 1958), pp. 213–15, 216–17, 222–25,
227–30 (hereafter cited as *FR*, 1941, I). Ltr., Wacław Jędrzejewicz to writer,
Dec. 15, 1974. Hull's strong reaction was partially owing to the fact that Rajch-
man also engaged in activities unrelated to Polish relief. He was an adviser to
T. V. Soong, the Chinese emissary to the United States. As late as Dec., 1941, the
Department of State told the Chinese Embassy that it was "unable to recognize
Dr. Rajchman as having the status of a foreign government official in the United
States, since it would be contrary to the policy of the Department to recognize
a national of one foreign country as having the status of an official of another
country." See *FR*, 1941, I, fn. 60, 228–29. Before Potocki left Washington, he
told Hull he planned to go to Latin America, where he hoped to get permission
from various governments to allow Polish refugees to live there. Memo of conversation by Hull, Dec. 10, 1940, in Cordell Hull Papers, LXI, MD/LC.
9.   Memo of conversation by Henderson, Feb. 29, 1940; Msg., Hull to Johnson,
Feb. 22, 1940; Aide-memoire, British Embassy to Department of State, July 17,
1940, in U.S., Department of State, *Foreign Relations of the United States:
Diplomatic Papers, 1940.* Vol. II: *General and Europe* (Washington, D.C.: United
States Government Printing Office, 1957), pp. 755–58, 762–63 (hereafter cited as
FR, 1940, II); "War Relief Summary," Feb. 17, 1941, in OF, 124, Box 4, FDR/L.
10.   Republic of Poland, *Polish-Soviet Relations, 1918-1943: Official Docu-
ments* (Washington, D.C., n.d.), pp. 102–105; *DPSR*, I, 93.
11.   Memo of conversation by James Dunn, Dec. 20, 1939; Memo by Henderson,
Dec. 8, 1940; Memo of conversation by Welles, Apr. 9, 1941, in *FR*, 1941, I,
210–11, 225–26, 233–34; Ltr., Lesinski to Roosevelt, Feb. 19, 1941; Ltr., Henry
Cabot Lodge, Jr., to Roosevelt, Feb. 21, 1941, in OF, 463A, Box 3, FDR/L;
U.S., *Congressional Record,* 77 Cong., 1 sess., 1941, LXXXVII, Pts. 10–12, App.,
A1931–32, A2531.
12.   Memo, Atherton to Long, Apr. 16, 1941, in *FR*, 1941, I, 234–35.
13.   Edward Raczyński, *In Allied London* (London: Weidenfeld and Nicolson,

1962), pp. 76, 85; *New York Times,* Apr. 7, 1941. Sikorski told Polish Americans that they constituted a large "reserve" which could be used in the Polish war effort. *Dziennik Związkowy,* May 20, 1941, p. 2.

14. Ltr., Welles to Roosevelt, Apr. 7, 1941, *FR, 1941,* I, 232–33; Msg., Hopkins to Biddle, June 19, 1941, in *FR, 1941,* I, 232–33, 236; Jan Ciechanowski, *Defeat in Victory* (Garden City, NY: Doubleday, 1947), p. 55; Ltr., Sikorski to Hopkins, Aug. 5, 1941; Memo, McCabe to Roosevelt, Mar. 28, 1942, in Hopkins Papers, Boxes 209, 313, FDR/L. As of the end of Mar. 1942, only $1,584 worth of military items had been exported under lend-lease for the Poles. See Memo, McCabe to Roosevelt, Mar. 28, 1942, in Hopkins Papers, Boxes 209, 313, FDR/L.

15. Memo of conversation by Hull, Aug. 20, 1941, in Hull Papers, LXI, MD/LC; U.S., Department of State, *Foreign Relations of the United States: Diplomatic Papers, 1942.* Vol. III: *Europe* (Washington, D.C.: United States Government Printing Office, 1961), fn. 13, p. 216 (hereafter cited as *FR, 1942,* III); *Naród Polski,* July 24, 1941, Aug. 14, 1941, Aug. 21, 1941, Mar. 24, 1942.

16. Ltr., Department of State to Ciechanowski, Mar. 30, 1942; Ltr., Ciechanowski to Hull, July 6, 1942; Ltr., Welles to Ciechanowski, Sept. 1, 1942, in DS/NA.

17. Richard C. Lukas, *Eagles East: The Army Air Forces and the Soviet Union, 1941–1945* (Tallahassee: Florida State Univ. Press, 1970), pp. 15, 37–55.

18. Broadcast by Sikorski, "Poland and the German-Soviet War," June 23, 1941, in General Sikorski Historical Institute, *DPSR,* I, 108–12; Msg., Biddle to Hull, June 23, 1941, *FR,* I, 236.

19. Ivan Maisky, *Memoirs of a Soviet Ambassador* (New York: Scribners, 1968), p. 169.

20. Record of conversation between Sikorski and Eden, July 4, 1941, *DPSR,* I, 116. A Tass correspondent in London told a Polish official a few days earlier that Poland "must forfeit her former Great Power policy and accept the principle of a national, ethnographic Poland, . . . " See Note No. 91, *DPSR,* I, 574–75.

21. Record of conversation between Sikorski and Maisky, July 5, 1941, *DPSR,* I, 117–19; Memo of conversation by Welles, July 8, 1941, *FR, 1941,* I, 241–42.

22. Msg., Biddle to Hull, July 16, 1941, *FR,* I, 242–43; Record of conversation among Sikorski, Zaleski, Eden, and Maisky, July 11, 1941, *DPSR,* I, 128–32.

23. Draft agreement between Poland and the Soviet Union proposed by Poland, July 13, 1941; Draft agreement between Poland and the Soviet Union proposed by Poland, July 17, 1941; Ltr., Sikorski to Eden with Polish amendments to Soviet proposal, July 17, 1941; Note No. 100, *DPSR,* I, 134–38, 576.

24. Note No. 100, *DPSR,* I, 576.

25. Record of conversation among Sikorski, Zaleski, Eden, and Maisky, July 11, 1941; Note, British Foreign Office, July 30, 1941; Statement by Eden to House of Commons, July 30, 1941; Draft Note, Zaleski to Eden, July 17, 1941; Draft Note, Eden to Zaleski, July 18, 1941; Ltr., Sikorski to Zaleski, July 19, 1941; Ltr., Sikorski to Eden, July 21, 1941, *DPSR,* I, 128–32, 142–44, 138–40, 580.

26. Msg., Biddle to Hull, July 17, 1941, in DS/NA; Memo, Zaleski to Eden, July 8, 1941, *DPSR,* I, 123–24.

27. Note No. 94; Note No. 105, *DPSR,* I, 575, 578–79.

28. Note No. 166; Broadcast by Sikorski, July 31, 1941, *DPSR,* I, 592–93, 144.

29. Note No. 105; Final Draft, Polish-Soviet Treaty, July 30, 1941; Note No. 106, *DPSR,* I, 578–79, 141–42, 581. According to Stanisław Mikołajczyk, the man who succeeded Sikorski as premier in 1943, an amnesty under Soviet law did not relieve a person of guilt. Thus he could still be detained. See *FR,* I, fn. 93, p. 244.

30. Broadcast by Sikorski, July 31, 1941, *DPSR,* I, 144; *FR,* 1941, I, 246.

31. Msg., Biddle to Hull, Aug. 2, 1941, *FR,* 1941, I, 245–46; Memo, Atherton to Welles, Aug. 5, 1941, in DS/NA; Draft msg., Hull to Biddle, Aug. 5, 1941, *FR,* 1941, I, 247–48.

32. Ciechanowski, *Defeat in Victory,* pp. 35–41.

33. Raczyński, *In Allied London,* p. 96; John Pomian (ed.), *Joseph Retinger: Memoirs of an Eminence Grise* (Sussex: At the Univ. Press, 1972), p. 111.

34. Msg., Biddle to Secretary of State, Feb. 20, 1942, in DS/NA; Ltr., Jędrzejewicz to writer, Dec. 15, 1974.

Chapter II

1. Protocol No. 2, Polish-Soviet Military Conference, Aug. 19, 1941; General Instructions to Kot, Aug. 28, 1941; Record of conversation between Kot and Stalin, Nov. 14, 1941; Minutes of conversation between Sikorski and Stalin, Dec. 3, 1941, in General Sikorski Historical Institute, *DPSR,* I, 151–53, 158, 205–13, 231–43; Władysław Anders, *An Army in Exile* (London: Macmillan, 1949), pp. 63–64.

2. Msg., Steinhardt to Secretary of State, Aug. 25, 1941; Msg., Steinhardt to Secretary of State, Sept. 6, 1941; Msg., Harriman to Roosevelt and Hopkins, Sept. 20, 1941, in U.S., Department of State, *FR,* 1941, I, 250–51, 253–54.

3. Notes, conversation between Sikorski and Harriman, Sept. 19, 1941; Note No. 124, in General Sikorski Historical Institute, *DPSR,* I, 169–70, 583; Msg., Roosevelt to Harriman, Sept. 22, 1941, in U.S., Department of State, *FR,* 1941, I, 254.

4. Ciechanowski, *Defeat in Victory,* pp. 62–63; Stanisław Kot, *Conversations with the Kremlin and Dispatches from Russia.* Trans. H.C. Stevens (London: Oxford Univ. Press, 1963), pp. xvi–xvii, 43–44; Ltr., Sikorski to Churchill, Oct. 8, 1941, in General Sikorski Historical Institute, *DPSR,* I, 174–75.

5. Note, conversation between Sikorski and Churchill, Aug. 23, 1941; General Instructions to Kot, Aug. 28, 1941; General Instructions to Anders, Sept. 1, 1941, Msg., Sikorski to Ismay, Sept. 26, 1941; Note of conversation between Sikorski and Churchill, Oct. 24, 1941; Ltr., Eden to Sikorski, Oct. 28, 1941, in General Sikorski Historical Institute, *DPSR,* I, 156–57, 159, 163–64, 170–71, 183–85.

6. Note, Sikorski to Churchill, Sept. 17, 1941; Msg., Sikorski to Kot, Oct. 28, 1941; Minutes of conversation between Sikorski and Stalin, Dec. 3, 1941, *ibid.,* pp. 167–68; 185–86; 231–43. Kot reported that it took five days by train from Moscow to Buzuluk, the Polish military headquarters in the Soviet Union. Telephone connections were very bad, too: it took days to complete a telephone call from the Polish Embassy to Buzuluk. Under these circumstances, Kot asked:

"Out of this chaotic mass who will be able to arrange for the transport of soldiers to Great Britain in any brief space of time?" He also related that Anders was "fretting and fuming" with Sikorski for making the suggestion because it might undermine his position in the Soviet Union. Kot, *Conversations with the Kremlin,* pp. 55-56.

7. Msg., Steinhardt to Secretary of State, Oct. 25, 1941; Msg., Hull to Steinhardt, Nov. 7, 1941, in U.S., Department of State, *FR,* 1941, I, 257-58; Note No. 134; Note with memo, Ciechanowski to Roosevelt, Oct. 31, 1941; Msg., Panfilov to Anders, Nov. 6, 1941, in General Sikorski Historical Institute, *DPSR,* I, 584-86, 187-89, 197-98.

8. Note No. 136; Note No. 148, in General Sikorski Historical Institute, *DPSR,* I, 586-87, 588-89; Ciechanowski, *Defeat in Victory,* pp. 60-61. For difficulties in getting supplies through Iran to the Soviet Union, see T.H. Vail Motter, *The Persian Corridor and Aid to Russia* (Washington, D.C.: Department of the Army, 1952).

9. Note, Polish Embassy to People's Commissariat for Foreign Affairs, Nov. 10, 1941, in General Sikorski Historical Institute, *DPSR,* I, 200-201; Kot, *Conversations with the Kremlin,* pp. 1, 61-62, 182-86; Anders, *An Army in Exile,* pp. 77-78. The Soviets were so zealous to prevent Jews from joining the Polish Army they even examined men for circumcision. See Kot, *Conversations with the Kremlin,* pp. 229-30. When the Polish army evacuated the Soviet Union, several thousand Jews left with it. See Anders, *An Army in Exile,* p. 113; Msg., Standley to Secretary of State, Sept. 30, 1942, in U.S., Department of State, *FR,* 1942, III, 191-92. Soviet discrimination against Polish Jews ironically led to Jews abroad blaming Polish authorities for anti-Semitism.

10. Kot, *Conversations with the Kremlin,* pp. 79-80, 93-96. Kot told Vyshinsky that Sikorski was "Poland's man of Providence." Kot, *ibid.,* p. 162.

11. Record of conversation between Kot and Stalin, Nov. 14, 1941, in General Sikorski Historical Institute, *DPSR,* I, 205-13; Kot, *Conversations with the Kremlin,* pp. 104-16, 123, 163-64, 139-40, xxvi-xxvii.

12. Minutes of conversation between Sikorski and Stalin, Dec. 3, 1941, in General Sikorski Historical Institute, *DPSR,* I, 231-43.

13. Kot, *Conversations with the Kremlin,* p. xiv; Ciechanowski, *Defeat in Victory,* p. 56.

14. Note of conversation between Sikorski and Stalin, Dec. 4, 1941, in General Sikorski Historical Institute, *DPSR,* I, 244-46.

15. Msg., Thurston to Secretary of State, Dec. 8, 1941; Msg., Thurston to Secretary of State, Dec. 9, 1941; Msg., Thurston to Secretary of State, Dec. 11, 1941, in U.S., Department of State, *FR,* 1941, I, 267, 195-96, 267-68; Minutes of conversation between Sikorski and Stalin, Dec. 3, 1941, in General Sikorski Historical Institute, *DPSR,* I, 231-43.

16. Kot, *Conversations with the Kremlin,* pp. xxvii, 156, 173, 180-81, 169, 171. When Kot later asked Vyshinski to release Polish Christians from labor for the Easter holidays, he also asked that the same privilege be granted to Polish Jews. Vyshinsky said that the question was complicated by the question of citizenship: since Nov. 1941, the Russians considered Jews living in the Western Ukraine and Belorussia as Soviet citizens. Kot replied: "I'm sorry, but here I represent all Polish citizens." Kot, *Conversations with the Kremlin,* pp. 225-26.

17. Ltr., Sikorski to Churchill, Dec. 17, 1941, in General Sikorski Historical Institute, *DPSR,* I, 254–57.

18. Anders, *An Army in Exile,* pp. 61–76, 81, 83, 93.

19. Anders, *ibid.,* pp. 96–97; Msg., Anders to Sikorski, Feb. 4, 1942; Msg., Sikorski to Anders, Feb. 7, 1942, in General Sikorski Historical Institute, *DPSR,* I, 277, 279–80.

20. Record of conversation between Anders and Stalin, Mar. 18, 1942; Memo of conversation between Sikorski and Harriman, Apr. 15, 1942, in General Sikorski Historical Institute, *DPSR,* I, 301–10, 328. Clemens exaggerates that the Polish army rose to a high of 96,000 men. See Diane Shaver Clemens, *Yalta* (London: Oxford Univ. Press, 1970), p. 13. The 25,000 soldiers, airmen, and sailors that Stalin had agreed to evacuate to the West months earlier were still in the Soviet Union. See Record of conversation between Anders and Stalin, Mar. 18, 1942, in General Sikorski Historical Institute, *DPSR,* I, 301–10.

21. Anders, *An Army in Exile,* p. 100. According to Polish military reports, as of mid-Apr. 1942, the following had been evacuated from the Soviet Union: 30,030 soldiers, 1,150 women of the Women's Auxiliary Formation, 12,619 civilians and 100 Boy Scouts. Memo, Ciechanowski to Welles, Apr. 13, 1942, in PSF, Poland, Box 65, FDR/L. Anders, despite the opposition of Kot and Sikorski's chief of staff, insisted on evacuating the civilians also, because he believed that it was their only chance of getting out of the Soviet Union. See Anders, *An Army in Exile,* pp. 101–103.

22. Note No. 198; Msg., Sikorski to Churchill, Apr. 1, 1942; Note, Molotov to Kot, May 14, 1942, in General Sikorski Historical Institute, *DPSR,* I, 595–96, 319–20, 351–52.

23. Msg., Hull to Standley, May 19, 1942; Msg., Standley to Hull, May 28, 1942; Ltr., Biddle to Hull, June 2, 1942 (Polish Series 157); Ltr., Biddle to Hull, June 2, 1942 (Polish Series 158), in U.S., Department of State, *FR,* 1942, III, 146–51; Ltr., Sikorski to Roosevelt, June 17, 1942, in General Sikorski Historical Institute, *DPSR,* I, 372–73.

24. Ciechanowski, *Defeat in Victory,* pp. 98–99, 111–13.

25. Anders, *An Army in Exile,* pp. 102, 105–106, 108–109; Note No. 213; Instructions, Sikorski to Anders, May 1, 1942; Note No. 235, in General Sikorski Historical Institute, *DPSR,* I, 597–98, 344–48, 600–601; Raczyński, *In Allied London,* p. 114.

26. Ltr., Biddle to Secretary of State, Feb. 2, 1942, in U.S., Department of State, *FR,* 1942, III, 102–103. Anders, *An Army in Exile*, p. 81.

27. Anders, *An Army in Exile,* pp. 108–109, 113, 115.

28. *Ibid.,* p. 116; Raczyński, *In Allied London,* p. 117. Ciechanowski erroneously claims that it was Stalin who ordered all Poles out of the Soviet Union. Ciechanowski, *Defeat in Victory,* p. 109.

29. Anders, *An Army in Exile,* p. 98.

30. Stanisław Mikołajczyk, *The Rape of Poland* (New York: McGraw-Hill, 1948), p. 18; Ciechanowski, *Defeat in Victory,* pp. 43–48. Kot cabled Ciechanowski at the end of Oct. 1941, that Polish refugees especially needed clothing and footwear. He urged Ciechanowski: "Please stir up Polonia and the Red Cross." Kot, *Conversations with the Kremlin,* pp. 79–80.

31. Kot, *Conversations with the Kremlin,* pp. 11, 14, 26–37, 39–40; Memo of conversation by Hull, Oct. 14, 1941, in Hull Papers, LXI, MD/LC.

32. Kot, *Conversations with the Kremlin,* pp. 81–86; Note of conversation between Cripps and Vyshinsky, Nov. 5, 1941; Note of conversation between Kot and Vyshinsky, Nov. 5, 1941, in General Sikorski Historical Institute, *DPSR,* I, 191–94, 195–96.

33. Note No. 586, in General Sikorski Historical Institute, *DPSR,* I, 586; Kot, *Conversations with the Kremlin,* pp. 130–33, 163; Memo, by Ciechanowski, Nov. 17, 1941, in U.S., Department of State, *FR,* 1941, I, 263–64.

34. Note No. 136; Pro-memoria Commissariat for Foreign Affairs, Nov. 1941; Note No. 166, in General Sikorski Historical Institute, *DPSR,* I, 586–87, 220–21, 592–93; Msg., Steinhardt to Secretary of State, Nov. 14, 1941; Memo, by Ciechanowski, Nov. 17, 1941, in U.S., Department of State, *FR,* 1941, I, 262–64; Kot, *Conversations with the Kremlin,* pp. 128, 157, 178.

35. Kot, *Conversations with the Kremlin,* pp. 230, 232, 259, 164, 208–209.

36. Record of conversation between Kot and Vyshinsky, July 8, 1942; Note, People's Commissariat for Foreign Affairs to Embassy of the Polish Republic, July 10, 1942; Aide-memoire, Novikov to Sokolnicki, Oct. 16, 1942; Aide-memoire, Soviet Embassy to Raczyński, Oct. 28, 1942, in General Sikorski Historical Institute, *DPSR,* I, 381–86, 391, 440, 444.

37. Note, Sokolnicki to Vyshinsky, July 19, 1942, *ibid.*

38. Aide-memoire, Raczyński to Eden, July 26, 1942; Note No. 271, in General Sikorski Historical Institute, *DPSR,* I, 413–17, 604; Memo, Ciechanowski to Welles, Oct. 26, 1942, in PSF, Poland, Box 65, FDR/L; Raczyński, *In Allied London,* pp. 114–15.

39. Record of conversation between Kot and Vyshinsky, June 2, 1942; Record of conversation between Kot and Vyshinsky, July 8, 1942; Memo, Polish Ministry for Foreign Affairs to Biddle, May 29, 1942; Ltr., Sikorski to Roosevelt, June 17, 1942, in General Sikorski Historical Institute, *DPSR,* I, 357–63, 381–86, 355–57, 372–73; Memo, "Location of Polish Refugees," Apr. 8, 1944, No. M-66, in Henry Field Papers, FDR/L; Ltr., Crowley to Roosevelt, June 3, 1944, in OF, 463, Box 1, FDR/L; Memo, Tellier to Johnson, Jan. 5, 1944, in War Refugee Board Papers, Box 18, FDR/L. The United States Navy assisted in transporting 706 refugees from Bombay, India, to San Pedro, California, from where the men, women, and children were sent to Mexico. For Polish refugees in Africa, see Memo, "Polish Refugees in Iran, Africa, and India," Sept. 2, 1943, No. M-24, in Henry Field Papers, FDR/L. For lend-lease to Poland, see Report to the President on Operations of the Lend-Lease Administration, Sept. 16, 1941, to Sept. 23, 1943, in Hopkins Papers, Box 167, FDR/L.

40. Ltr., Ciechanowski to Welles, Feb. 8, 1943, in PSF, Poland, Box 65, FDR/L.

41. Note of conversation between Sikorski and Stalin, Dec. 4, 1941, in General Sikorski Historical Institute, *DPSR,* I, 244–46. Ciechanowski was critical of Sikorski for not discussing the frontier question with Stalin when he flew to Moscow in Dec. 1941.

42. Note, People's Commissariat of Foreign Affairs to Polish Embassy, Jan. 16, 1943, in General Sikorski Historical Institute, *DPSR,* I, 473–74.

43. Memo of conversation by Henderson, Dec. 29, 1941, in U.S., Department

of State, *FR,* I, 270–71; Memo of conversation by Berle, Feb. 24, 1942; Memo of conversation by Standley, Mar. 4, 1942, in U.S., Department of State, *FR, 1942,* III, 111–13; Msg., Matthews to Secretary of State, Feb. 17, 1943, in U.S., Department of State, *Foreign Relations of the United States: Diplomatic Papers, 1943.* Vol. III: *The British Commonwealth, Eastern Europe, The Far East* (Washington, D.C.: United States Government Printing Office, 1963), pp. 334–35 (hereafter cited as *FR, 1943,* III); Note on conversation between Morawski and Bogomolov, Mar. 2, 1942, in General Sikorski Historical Institute, *DPSR,* I, 285–86; Ltr., Biddle to Roosevelt, Feb. 15, 1943, in PSF, Poland, Box 65, FDR/L; Sikorski speech before Overseas Press Club, Dec. 16, 1942, in Henry Morgenthau Diary, DLXXXXIX, FDR/L.

44. Note of conversation between Sikorski and Cripps, Jan. 26, 1942; Ltr., Sikorski to Eden, Mar. 9, 1942; Extract of conversation between Sikorski, Churchill *et al.,* Mar. 11, 1942, in General Sikorski Historical Institute, *DPSR,* I, 270, 289–99.

45. Msg., Biddle to Secretary of State, Feb. 20, 1942, in DS/NA; Raczyński, *In Allied London,* pp. 119, 124, 125. Raczyński was critical of some of his compatriots for being too suspicious of the sincerity of Edward Beneš, president of the Czechoslovak government. See Raczyński, *In Allied London.*

46. Memo, Hopkins to Roosevelt, Mar. 6, 1942, in Hopkins Papers, Box 313, FDR/L; Memo by Roosevelt, Mar. 7, 1942; Msg., Biddle to Secretary of State, *FR, 1942,* III, fn. 34, 111, 117.

47. Msg., Biddle to Secretary of State, Feb. 2, 1942, in U.S., Department of State, *FR, 1942,* III, 102.

48. Note of conversation between Sikorski and Roosevelt, Mar. 24, 1942, in General Sikorski Historical Institute, *DPSR,* I, 310–11, fn. 1, p. 311; Berle and Jacobs, eds., *Navigating the Rapids,* p. 406. Yet, on Apr. 30, 1942, anticipating an early end to the war, Roosevelt told Berle he would not mind if the Soviets took the Baltic States and eastern Poland. Berle and Jacobs, eds., *ibid.,* p. 412.

49. Memo of conversation by Berle, Feb. 24, 1942, in U.S., Department of State, *FR, 1942,* III, 111; Ciechanowski, *Defeat in Victory,* pp. 93–94.

50. U.S., Department of State, *FR, 1942,* III, fn. 8, p. 155.

51. Memo of conversation by Hull, June 13, 1942, in Hull Papers, LXI, MD/LC; Raczyński, *In Allied London,* pp. 112–13; Notes of conversation between Sikorski and Eden, June 8, 1942, in General Sikorski Historical Institute, *DPSR,* I, 364–66.

52. Lukas, *Eagles East,* p. 139; Record of conversation between Sikorski and Churchill, Aug. 30, 1942, in General Sikorski Historical Institute, *DPSR,* I, 427–29.

53. Instruction, Sikorski to Rowecki, Nov. 28, 1942, in General Sikorski Historical Institute, *DPSR,* I, 457–58; Ciechanowski, *Defeat in Victory,* pp. 122–23.

54. Ciechanowski, *Defeat in Victory,* pp. 125–35.

55. Memo of conversation by Welles, Dec. 4, 1942, with draft letter from Sikorski; Memo, Atherton to Secretary of State, Dec. 9, 1942, with annex, in U.S., Department of State, *FR, 1942,* III, 199–203, 204–208.

56. Memo of conversation by Welles, Jan. 4, 1943; Ltr., Welles to Roosevelt with draft letter from Roosevelt to Sikorski, Jan. 5, 1943; Memo of conversation

by Welles, Jan. 6, 1943, in U.S., Department of State, *FR*, 1943, III, 314–18, 319–20, 320–21. For Soviet claims that the Poles were reluctant to fight while they were in the Soviet Union, see note, Bogomolov to Raczyński, Oct. 31, 1942, in General Sikorski Historical Institute, *DPSR*, I, 447–52.

57. Ltr., Ciechanowski to Welles, May 20, 1942, in Hopkins Papers, Box 331, FDR/L; Ltr., Leahy to Onacewicz, Dec. 6, 1942; Memo, Arnold to JCS, Dec. 8, 1942; Ltr., Sikorski to Arnold, Dec. 10, 1942; Ltr., Sikorski to Roosevelt, Dec. 22, 1942; Ltr., Roosevelt to Sikorski, Jan. 9, 1942; Ltr., Roosevelt to Churchill, Jan. 9, 1942, in Arnold Papers, Box 38, MD/LC.

58. Mikołajczyk, *Rape of Poland*, pp. 25–26.

59. Memo, Visson to Davies, May 5, 1943, in Davies Papers, Box 64, MD/LC.

60. Msg., Biddle to Secretary of State, Jan. 28, 1943; Memo of conversation by Welles with annex, Jan. 30, 1943, in U.S., Department of State, *FR*, 1943, III, 323–25, 325–27; Excerpts, minutes of meeting between Romer and Molotov, Feb. 20, 1943, in General Sikorski Historical Institute, *DPSR*, I, 484.

61. Ciechanowski, *Defeat in Victory*, pp. 142–43; Memo of conversation by Welles, Feb. 17, 1943, in U.S., Department of State, *FR*, 1943, III, 333–34. Congress was poorly informed about Polish-Soviet relations at this time. Senator Elbert D. Thomas of Utah observed that the Kremlin acted in a humanitarian way by granting Soviet citizenship to Polish refugees. See memo of conversation by Henderson, Mar. 26, 1943, in U.S., Department of State, *FR*, 1943, III, 363.

62. Memo of conversation by Welles, Feb. 5, 1943; Ltr., Ciechanowski to Welles, enclosing message from Sikorski to Ciechanowski, Feb. 8, 1943, in U.S. Department of State, *FR*, III, 1943, 328–30.

63. Msg., Ciechanowski to Roosevelt, conveying text of letter, Sikorski to Churchill, Feb. 13, 1943, *ibid.*, 331–32.

64. Minutes of meeting among Romer, Stalin, and Molotov, Feb. 26/27, 1943, in General Sikorski Historical Institute, *DPSR*, I, 489–500.

65. Excerpts of minutes of conversation between Romer and Molotov, Mar. 9, 1943, Mar. 18, 1943, in General Sikorski Historical Institute, *DPSR*, I, 504–11, 511–19; Ltr., Hull to Roosevelt, Apr. 6, 1943, with three enclosed memoranda, in PSF, Poland, Box 65, FDR/L.

66. Ciechanowski, *Defeat in Victory*, pp. 146–47, 152–53; Msg., Matthews to Secretary of State, Mar. 3, 1943, in U.S., Department of State, *FR*, 1943, III, 337–38. One of the few periodicals in the United States to react to the ban on press coverage of the Polish-Soviet crisis was *Christian Century*. See editorial, "Polish-Russian Tension Growing Dangerous," *Christian Century* (Mar. 17, 1943), p. 317.

67. Newsclip, *Ottawa Canada Citizen*, Apr. 27, 1943, in Davies Papers, Box 64, MD/LC; Msg., Matthews to Secretary of State, Feb. 17, 1943; Ltr., Biddle to Secretary of State, Mar. 3, 1943; Msg., Biddle to Secretary of State, Mar. 6, 1943, Memo by Durbrow, Apr. 9, 1943, in U.S., Department of State, *FR*, 1943, III, 334–35, 338–43, 372–73; Ltr., Biddle to Roosevelt, Mar. 17, 1943, with enclosure, in PSF, Poland, Box 65, FDR/L; Stanisław Kot, *Listy z Rosji do Generala Sikorskiego* (London: St. Martin's, 1956), p. 130. Sikorski won many enemies, too, in the Polish Army for retiring over 1,000 older officers by mid-1942.

68. Msg., Standley to Secretary of State, Mar. 9, 1943; Msg., Standley to

Secretary of State, Mar. 10, 1943; Msg., Welles to Thompson, Mar. 11, 1943, in U.S., Department of State, *FR*, 1943, III, 344-48.

69. Anthony Eden, *The Memoirs of Anthony Eden, Earl of Avon: The Reckoning* (Boston: Houghton, 1965), p. 432; Robert E. Sherwood, *Roosevelt and Hopkins: An Intimate History* (New York: Harper, 1948), p. 710; Joseph E. Davies Diary, May 20, 1943, in Davies Papers, MD/LC.

70. Memo on Polish-Soviet relations, Mar. 22, 1943; Msg., Standley to Secretary of State, Mar. 22, 1943; Memo of conversation by Henderson, Mar. 26, 1943, in U.S., Department of State, *FR*, 1943, III, 354-58, 361, 362; Ltr., Hull to Roosevelt with enclosures, Apr. 6, 1943, in PSF, Poland, Box 65, FDR/L.

71. Kot, *Conversations with the Kremlin,* pp. 159-60, 227; Ltr., Thomas to Hopkins, Sept. 4, 1942; Ltr., Berle to Thomas, Sept. 16, 1942, in Harry L. Hopkins Papers, Box 331, FDR/L; General Sikorski Historical Institute, *DPSR,* I, 357-63, 503; Ciechanowski, *Defeat in Victory,* p. 121. The *Nation* even criticized the Soviet Union for executing the leaders: "Not only was the incident bad justice, but it was also bad propaganda." See "The Shape of Things," *Nation,* CLVI (Mar. 13, 1943), 362.

72. Msg., Standley to Secretary of State, Apr. 3, 1943; Ltr., Ciechanowski to Roosevelt, Apr. 4, 1943; Memo of conversation by Welles, Apr. 8, 1943, in U.S., Department of State, *FR,* 1943, III, 363-64, 365-67, 370-71; Davies Diary, May, 1943, in Davies Papers, MD/LC.

Chapter III

1. Communiqué by Kukiel, Apr. 17, 1943; Msg., Biddle to Hull, Apr. 17, 1943; Msg., Biddle to Hull, Apr. 23, 1943, in U.S., Department of State, *FR,* 1943, III, 376-79, 386-88; Kot, *Conversations with the Kremlin,* p. xvi; Record of conversation between Sikorski and Eden, July 16, 1942, in General Sikorski Historical Institute, *DPSR,* I, 401; Clemens, *Yalta,* p. 14.

2. Communiqué by Berlin Broadcasting Station, Apr. 13, 1943, in General Sikorski Historical Institute, *DPSR,* I, 523-24. For an account of the atrocity, see J.K. Zawodny, *Death in the Forest* (Notre Dame: Univ. of Notre Dame Press, 1962). Mikołajczyk put the figure of murdered officers as high as 15,000. See Mikołajczyk, *Rape of Poland,* p. 34. Woodward says there were 4,510 bodies in the graves at Katyn. See Sir Llewellyn Woodward, *British Foreign Policy in the Second World War* (London: Her Majesty's Stationery Office, 1971), II, 626.

3. Communiqué by Soviet Information Bureau, Apr. 15, 1943; Communiqué by Polish Minister of National Defense, Apr. 16, 1943; Official Statement by Polish Government, Apr. 17, 1943; Msg., Stalin to Churchill, Apr. 21, 1943; Msg., Churchill to Stalin, Apr. 24, 1943, in General Sikorski Historical Institute, *DPSR,* I, 524-25, 525-28, 530-33; Msg., Churchill to Roosevelt, Apr. 25, 1943, in U.S., Department of State, *FR,* 1943, III, 393-95.

4. Msg., Roosevelt to Stalin, Apr. 26, 1943; Msg., Standley to Hull, Apr. 26, 1943, in U.S., Department of State, *FR,* 1943, III, 395-96, 396-98; Lynn Etheridge Davis, *The Cold War Begins: Soviet-American Conflict over Eastern Europe* (Princeton: Princeton Univ. Press, 1974), fn. 19, pp. 45-46.

5. Msg., Biddle to Hull, Apr. 27, 1943; Msg., Biddle to Hull, May 1, 1943;

Msg., Standley to Hull, Apr. 28, 1943; in U.S., Department of State, *FR*, 1943, III, 398–400, 403–404, 400–402. Rumors persisted that Polish troops in the Middle East, angry over Soviet refusals to allow their civilian friends and relatives out of the Soviet Union, wanted to throw out Sikorski. Other Poles had lost confidence in Sikorski's leadership for failing to reveal the truth about Polish-Soviet relations. See Raczyński, *In Allied London*, pp. 133–34.

6. Msg., Standley to Hull, Apr. 28, 1943; Msg., Biddle to Hull, May 2, 1943, in U.S., Department of State, *FR*, 1943, III, 402, 404–405.

7. Davies Diary, Apr. 28, 1943, in Davies Papers, Box 64, MD/LC.

8. *New York Times*, May 5, 1943; May 6, 1943.

9. Statement by Vyshinsky on Polish-Soviet relations, May 6, 1943; Note No. 8, in General Sikorski Historical Institute, *Documents on Polish-Soviet Relations, 1939–1945*. Volume II: *1943–1945* (London: Heinemann, 1967), pp. 7–10, 706. Even the pro-Soviet *Nation* was critical of Vyshinsky's statement. See "The Shape of Things," *Nation* CLVI (May 15, 1943), 686.

10. Msg., Biddle to Hull, May 10, 1943; Msg., Hull to Biddle, May 14, 1943; Msg., Biddle to Hull, May 15, 1943, in U.S., Department of State, *FR*, 1943, III, 418–20.

11. Ltr., Davies to Mrs. Davies, May 23, 1943; Davies Diary, May, 1943, in Davies Papers, Box 13, MD/LC.

12. Ltr., Sikorski to Roosevelt, May 4, 1943; Ltr., Biddle to Hull, June 2, 1943, in U.S., Department of State, *FR*, 1943, III, 410–12, 424–26; Raczyński, *In Allied London*, pp. 139, 150.

13. Msg., Hull to Standley, June 12, 1943; Msg., Hull to Standley, June 29, 1943, in U.S., Department of State, *FR*, 1943, III, 428–30, 432–34.

14. Msg., Standley to Hull, June 18, 1943; Msg., Hull to Standley, June 29, 1943; Msg., Hull to Standley, July 10, 1943, in U.S., Department of State, *FR*, 1943, III, 432–43; fn. 94, p. 437; fn. 99, p. 443. Commenting on Sikorski's death, Berle concluded "there is no replacement for him." See Berle and Jacobs, eds., *Navigating the Rapids*, p. 439. There has been much interest in the circumstances surrounding Sikorski's death. Stalin accused the British of shooting down the premier's plane. Rolf Hochuth in his play, *Soldiers*, put the blame on Churchill. But David Irving in his book, *Accident: The Death of General Sikorski*, suggests that it was a freak accident that took the life of the Polish premier and his entourage. See Clemens, *Yalta*, pp. 16–17.

15. Memo by Clark Kerr, presented Aug. 11, 1943; Msg., Standley to Hull, Aug. 12, 1943; Aide-memoire, People's Commissariat for Foreign Affairs, Sept. 27, 1943, in U.S., Department of State, *FR*, 1943, III, 451–53, 461–67; Note No. 25, in General Sikorski Historical Institute, *DPSR*, II, 713.

16. Ciechanowski, *Defeat in Victory*, pp. 179–86.

17. Mikołajczyk, *Rape of Poland*, p. 41; Władysław R. Malinowski, "Toward Polish-Soviet Understanding," *New Europe and World Reconstruction, Supplement* (Nov. 1943), p. 9; Max Laserson, *The Curzon Line: A Historical and Critical Analysis* (New York: Carnegie Endowment for International Peace, 1944), pp. 21–22; *FR*, 1943, III, fn. 8, p. 447.

18. Statement by Mikołajczyk, July 16, 1943, in General Sikorski Historical Institute, *DPSR*, II, 24–25; Address by Mikołajczyk to the Polish National

Council, July 27, 1943, in Hull Papers, LXI, MD/LC; Memo by Ciechanowski, July 7, 1943, in U.S., Department of State, *FR,* 1943, III, 440; U.S., Department of State, *The Department of State Bulletin,* July 10, 1943, p. 20.

19. Memo of conversation with Roosevelt, Oct. 5, 1943, in U.S., Department of State, *Foreign Relations of the United States: Diplomatic Papers, 1943.* Vol. I: *General* (Washington, D.C.: United States Government Printing Office, 1963), pp. 541–42 (hereafter cited as *FR,* 1943, I).

20. Leahy Diary, Sept. 22, 1943, in MD/LC.

21. Memo of conversation by Harriman, Oct. 24, 1943, in U.S., Department of State, *FR,* 1943, I, 622–23.

22. Summary of Proceedings of the Eleventh Session of the Tripartite Conference, Oct. 29, 1943, *ibid.,* 667–68; Msg., Hull to Roosevelt, Oct. 29, 1943, in U.S., Department of State, *FR,* 1943, III, 476–77; Herbert Feis, *Churchill, Roosevelt, Stalin: The War They Waged and the Peace They Sought* (Princeton: Princeton Univ. Press, 1967), pp. 196–97.

23. General Sikorski Historical Institute, *DPSR,* II, Note No. 49, p. 721; Ciechanowski, *Defeat in Victory,* pp. 234–36; Msg., Ciechanowski to Minister of Foreign Affairs, Nov. 20, 1943, in Ciechanowski Papers, Hoover Institution.

24. Ltr., Ciechanowski to Dunn, Nov. 17, 1943, in U.S., Department of State, *FR,* 1943, III, 478–81. Ciechanowski said much the same thing to Hull. See Msg., Ciechanowski to Minister of Foreign Affairs, Nov. 20, 1943.

25. Msg., Mikołajczyk to Biddle, General Sikorski Historical Institute, *DPSR,* II, 101–102.

26. Memo of conversation by Hull, Nov. 19, 1943; Msg., Hull to Biddle, Nov. 25, 1943, in U.S., Department of State, *FR,* 1943, III, 484–85, 486–87; Msg., Ciechanowski to Minister of Foreign Affairs, Nov. 20, 1943. Ciechanowski urged the United States to do two things to deter a political *fait accompli* by the Soviet government when its armies occupied Poland—namely, to inform the Soviets that Washington would not recognize any government other than that of the London Poles and to remind the Soviets that the United States had recognized the Riga Line as the Polish-Soviet boundary in 1923.

27. *Ibid.,* fn. 47, p. 478.

28. Mikołajczyk, *Rape of Poland,* pp. 46–47; Msg., Biddle to Hull, Nov. 20, 1943, in U.S., Department of State, *FR,* 1943, III, 485; Dispatch, Sosnkowski to Kukiel, Nov. 25, 1943, in General Sikorski Historical Institute, *DPSR,* II, 95–96.

29. Msg., Hull to Biddle, Nov. 25, 1943; Ltr., Biddle to Hull, Oct. 14, 1943, in U.S., Department of State, *FR,* 1943, III, 486–87, 472–75; Msg., Hull to Roosevelt, Nov. 23, 1943, in U.S., Department of State, *Foreign Relations of the United States, Diplomatic Papers: The Conferences at Cairo and Tehran, 1943* (Washington, D.C.: United States Government Printing Office, 1961), pp. 381–85 (hereafter cited as *FR,* 1943, *Cairo and Tehran*); Order, Home Army commander to Home Army units, Nov. 20, 1943, in General Sikorski Historical Institute, *DPSR,* II, 88–89. Ciechanowski described the attitude of the CCS toward supplying the AK as "ominous." See Ciechanowski, *Defeat in Victory,* p. 233.

30. Feis, *Churchill, Roosevelt, Stalin,* p. 196; Msg., Harriman to Roosevelt, Nov. 4, 1943, in U.S., Department of State, *FR,* 1943, *Cairo and Tehran,* pp. 152–55.

31. John Lewis Gaddis, *The United States and the Origins of the Cold War, 1941–1947* (New York: Columbia Univ. Press, 1972), pp. 137–38.

32. Bohlen Minutes, Tripartite Dinner Meeting, Nov. 28, 1943, in U.S., Department of State, *FR, 1943, Cairo and Tehran,* pp. 509–12; Winston S. Churchill, *Closing the Ring* (Boston: Houghton, 1951), pp. 361–62.

33. Bohlen Minutes, Tripartite Meeting, Dec. 1, 1943, in *ibid.,* pp. 596–604; Churchill, *Closing the Ring,* pp. 394–97.

34. Churchill, *Closing the Ring,* pp. 394–97.

35. Bohlen Minutes, Roosevelt-Stalin Meeting, Dec. 1, 1943, in *ibid.,* p. 594; Charles Bohlen, *Witness to History, 1929–1969* (New York: Norton, 1973), p. 152. The so-called Curzon Line, named after the British Secretary for Foreign Affairs, was contained in a note of July 1920 to the Soviet government and constituted the basis of a settlement to end the Polish-Soviet War. Curzon's proposed line was in part a restatement of an earlier one, the boundary of Dec. 8, 1919, which the Supreme Council of the Allied Powers approved for the northern part of the eastern frontier of postwar Poland. This line was not drawn to the south because the Supreme Council intended to establish eastern Galicia, including the city of Lwów, as a separate state under a Polish mandate. Curzon's note to the Soviets, however, extended the original line of Dec. 8 to the south but left eastern Galicia out of Poland. The Soviet government rejected Curzon's proposal and, as it turned out, later agreed to the Polish-Soviet Treaty of Riga, signed in Mar. 1921, which established the Polish frontier east of the Curzon Line. There is still disagreement concerning what the British really meant in their note to the Soviets in July 1920. Some historians convincingly argue that the extension of the Dec. 8 line into eastern Galicia was, in fact, an unintentional mistake of the British Foreign Office. The question became more than an academic one during World War II when Stalin argued for the Curzon Line, based on the note of July 1920, to be the Soviet-Polish frontier. See Herbert Feis, *Churchill, Roosevelt, Stalin,* pp. 657–60; and Titus Komarnicki, *Rebirth of the Polish Republic: A Study in the Diplomatic History of Europe, 1914–1920* (London: Heinemann, 1957), pp. 611–13.

36. Eden, *Reckoning,* pp. 482 ff.; Memo of conversation by Matthews, Dec. 14, 1943; Msg., Schoenfeld to Hull, Dec. 24, 1943, in U.S., Department of State, *FR, 1943,* III, 489–94.

37. *Complete Presidential Press Conferences of Franklin D. Roosevelt.* Volume XXI: *1943* (New York: Da Capo Press, 1972), pp. 212–28.

38. Msg., Schoenfeld to Hull, Jan. 5, 1944; Msg., Harriman to Hull, Jan. 11, 1944; Msg., Schoenfeld to Hull, Jan. 14, 1944; Memo of conversation by Hull with annex, Jan. 26, 1944, in U.S., Department of State, *Foreign Relations of the United States: Diplomatic Papers, 1944.* Vol. III: *The British Commonwealth and Europe* (Washington, D.C.: United States Government Printing Office, 1965), pp. 1216–17, 1218–20, 1226, 1236–37 (hereafter cited as *FR, 1944,* III); Eden, *Reckoning,* pp. 504–506; Mikołajczyk, *Rape of Poland,* p. 51.

39. Stimson, Diary, XXXXVI, p. 14, YU/L.

40. Msg., Harriman to Hull, Jan. 11, 1944; Memo by Durbrow, Jan. 11, 1944, in U.S., Department of State, *FR, 1944,* III, 1221–24; Berle and Jacobs, eds., *Navigating the Rapids,* p. 450.

41. Msg., Harriman to Hull, Jan. 21, 1944, in U.S., Department of State, *FR,* 1944, III, 1232–34; Msg., Molotov to Hull, Jan. 23, 1944, in General Sikorski Historical Institute, *DPSR,* II, 152. Hull complained to Harriman that the Soviet Union's insistence on a reconstruction of the Polish government with people of the Kremlin's choosing gave credence to those who said "you can't do business with Russia." See Msg., Hull to Harriman, Jan. 25, 1944, in U.S., Department of State, *FR,* 1944, III, 1234–35. For a discussion of Matuszewski and his writing, see ch. 6.

42. Msg., Stettinius to Harriman, Feb. 10, 1944, in U.S., Department of State, *FR,* 1944, III, 1248–49.

43. Eduard Beneš, *Memoirs of Dr. Eduard Beneš: From Munich to New War and New Victory* (London: Allen and Unwin, 1954), pp. 147–49, 180–86, 193, 195, 254–58; Msg., Churchill to Roosevelt, Jan. 28, 1944; Msg., Winant to Hull, containing Msg., Churchill to Roosevelt, Feb. 11, 1944, in U.S., Department of State, *FR,* 1944, III, 1240–43, 1249–57.

44. Msg., Roosevelt to Stalin, Feb. 7, 1944, in U.S., Department of State, *FR,* 1944, III, 1243–45; Memo, Stettinius to Dunn, Feb. 19, 1944, in Stettinius Papers, Box 216, UV/L.

45. Msg., Stettinius to Harriman, Feb. 19, 1944, in U.S., Department of State, *FR,* 1944, III, 1258–59; Attachments to Memo, Hull to Roosevelt, Mar. 28, 1944, in PSF, Poland, Box 66, FDR/L.

46. Msg., Churchill to Roosevelt, Feb. 20, 1944; Msg., Churchill to Roosevelt, Feb. 21, 1944; Msg., Roosevelt to Stalin, undated, but delivered by Harriman, Feb. 28, 1944, in U.S., Department of State, *FR,* 1944, III, 1259–64; Mikołajczyk, *Rape of Poland,* pp. 54–55.

47. Eden, *Reckoning,* p. 509; Msg., Stalin to Roosevelt, Mar. 3, 1944; Msg., Harriman to Hull, Mar. 3, 1944, in U.S., Department of State, *FR,* 1944, III, 1264–66.

48. Msg., Stalin to Churchill, Mar. 23, 1944, in U.S., Department of State, *FR,* 1944, III, 1268–70; Memo, prepared by Division of European Affairs of the Department of State, Mar. 24, 1944, in U.S., Department of State, *Foreign Relations of the United States: Diplomatic Papers, 1944.* Vol. IV: *Europe* (Washington, D.C.: United States Government Printing Office, 1966), pp. 841–42 (hereafter cited as *FR, 1944,* IV).

49. Msg., Churchill to Roosevelt, Apr. 1, 1944, in Francis L. Loewenheim, Harold D. Langley, and Manfred Jonas, *Roosevelt and Churchill: Their Secret Wartime Correspondence* (New York: Saturday Review Press, 1975), pp. 477–78; Note of conversation between Mikołajczyk and Churchill, Apr. 9, 1944, in General Sikorski Historical Institute, *DPSR,* II, 221; Mikołajczyk, *Rape of Poland,* p. 57.

50. Msg., Wasilewska to Roosevelt, June 17, 1943, in OF, 463A, Box 4, FDR/L; Memo by Durbrow, Sept. 6, 1943, in U.S., Department of State, *FR,* 1943, III, 459–60.

51. F.F. Wasell, "Attitudes of the Various Polish-American Organizations Toward American Foreign Policy Affecting Poland: 1939–1945," Master's thesis, Columbia Univ., 1946, pp. 29–30, 35.

52. Feis, *Churchill, Roosevelt, Stalin,* p. 299; Marcin Rylski, "Poland and Russia," *Nation* CLVII (Oct. 9, 1943), 408–10.

53. Memo, Stettinius to Roosevelt, Mar. 8, 1944; Msg., Hull to Harriman, Mar. 24, 1944; Memo, Hull to Roosevelt, Mar. 24, 1944; Msg., Harriman to Hull Mar. 27, 1944, in U.S., Department of State, *FR,* 1944, III, 1402–1404; Cordell Hull, *The Memoirs of Cordell Hull,* 2 vols. (New York: Macmillan, 1948), II, 1442.

54. U.S., Department of State, *FR,* 1944, III, fn. 56, 1406; Msg., Hamilton to Hull, May 4, 1944, with enclosures, in DS/NA.

55. Memo by Durbrow, June 28, 1944, in U.S., Department of State, *FR,* 1944, III, 1418–22; Msg., Hamilton to Hull, May 13, 1944; Msg., Hamilton to Hull, May 18, 1944; Msg., Hamilton to Hull, May 20, 1944, in DS/NA; Lange Report, in Davies Papers, Box 121, MD/LC.

56. Msg., Hamilton to Hull, May 7, 1944, in U.S., Department of State, *FR,* 1944, III, 1407–1409; Memo of conversation by Dewitt C. Poole, May 27, 1944, in PSF, Poland, Box 66, FDR/L; "Polish American Priest Visits Stalin," *Catholic World,* CLIX (June, 1944), 274–76. The *Nation* was critical of Orlemanski's suspension. See "The Shape of Things," *Nation,* CLVIII (May 20, 1944), 582.

57. "Polish American Priest Visits Stalin," *Catholic World,* pp. 274–76; Wacław Jędrzejewicz, *Polonia Amerykańska w Polityce Polskiej: Historia Komitetu Narodowego Amerykanów Polskiego Pochodzenia* (New York: National Committee of Americans of Polish Descent, 1954), p. 100; *Naród Polski,* May 11, 1944.

58. Memo of conversation by Dunn, May 2, 1944, in U.S., Department of State, *FR,* 1944, III, 1406–1407; Calendar Notes and Phone Conversations, May, 1944, in Stettinius Papers, Box 240, UV/L; Hull, *Memoirs,* II, 1443–44; Memo, Roosevelt to Hull, May 31, 1944; Memo, Hull to Roosevelt, June 2, 1944, in DS/NA.

59. Ltr., Biddle to Roosevelt, Oct. 18, 1943; Ltr., Roosevelt to Biddle, Nov. 8, 1943; Msg., Churchill to Roosevelt, Dec. 27, 1943, Msg., Roosevelt to Churchill, Dec. 28, 1943, in U.S., Department of State, *FR,* 1943, III, 475, 477–78, 494–95; Memo, Hull to Roosevelt, Jan. 26, 1944; Msg., Hull to Schoenfeld, Jan. 26, 1944; Memo, Hassett to Hull, Jan. 27, 1944; Memo, with enclosure, Hull to Roosevelt, Mar. 28, 1944; Memo, Hull to Roosevelt, May 18, 1944; Ltr., Roosevelt to Mikołajczyk, May 23, 1944, in PSF, Poland, Box 66, FDR/L; Ciechanowski, *Defeat in Victory,* p. 282; Memo by Stettinius, May 23, 1944, in U.S., Department of State, *FR,* 1944, IV, 873–74.

60. Raczyński, *In Allied London,* p. 218; Memo by Dunn, May 24, 1944, in U.S., Department of State, *FR,* 1944, IV, 874.

61. Mikołajczyk, *Rape of Poland,* pp. 59–61; Ciechanowski, *Defeat in Victory,* pp. 291–95, 303–305.

62. *Ibid.,* pp. 295–300; Calendar Notes and Phone Conversations, June, 1944, in Stettinius Papers, Box 240, UV/L. "Tabor" was a *nomme de guerre.*

63. General Sikorski Historical Institute, *DPSR,* II, Note No. 144, 755–56.

64. Msg., Hull to Harriman, July 18, 1944, in U.S., Department of State, *FR,* 1944, III, 1365.

65. Calendar Notes and Phone Conversations, June, 1944, in Stettinius Papers, Box 240, UV/L; Memo, Stettinius to Matthews, June 14, 1944, in Stettinius Papers, Box 216, UV/L; Memo, Stettinius to Hull, June 12, 1944, in U.S., Department of State, *FR,* 1944, III, 1280–82. Stettinius persuaded Mikołajczyk

to see Lange before he left the United States. See Mikołajczyk, *Rape of Poland,* pp. 62–64.

66. Msg., Mikołajczyk to Delegate of the Government in Poland, June 21, 1944; Memo, Mikołajczyk to State Department, undated, in General Sikorski Historical Institute, *DPSR,* II, 269–70, 251–53. According to Ciechanowski, Stettinius indicated that when the military balance between the Soviet Union and the West had been restored, Roosevelt would be in a position to do more for the Poles. See Ciechanowski, *Defeat in Victory,* pp. 301–302.

67. Ciechanowski, *Defeat in Victory,* p. 313; Aleksander Skarżyński, *Polityczne Przyczyny Powstania Warszawskiego* (Warsaw: Państwowe Wydawnictwo Naukowe, 1964), pp. 77–78, Eden, *Reckoning,* pp. 539–40; Raczyński, *In Allied London,* p. 227; Msg., Harriman to Hull, June 7, 1944; Msg., Harriman to Hull, June 12, 1944; Msg., Roosevelt to Stalin, June 17, 1944, in U.S., Department of State, *FR,* 1944, III, 1276–77, 1282–84.

68. Memo of press and radio news conference by M.J. McDermott, June 15, 1944, in Hull Papers, CXXXXI-CXXXXII, MD/LC.

69. Msg., Schoenfeld to Hull, July 9, 1944, in U.S., Department of State, *FR,* 1944, III, 1292–96; Mikołajczyk, *Rape of Poland,* pp. 64–65.

70. Clemens, *Yalta,* p. 23.

71. Msg., Hull to Harriman, June 1, 1944; Msg., Harriman to Hull, June 12, 1944; Msg., Harriman to Hull, June 13, 1944; Msg., Harriman to Hull, July 3, 1944; Msg., Stalin to Churchill, July 23, 1944; Msg., Harriman to Hull, Aug. 6, 1944, in U.S., Department of State, *FR,* 1944, III, 1414–18, 1422, 1424–25, 1429.

Chapter IV

1. Message, Sikorski to Bór, Mar. 26, 1943, in Warsaw Uprising Papers, Piłsudski Institute (hereafter cited as WUP/PI).

2. George Bruce, *The Warsaw Uprising: 1 August–2 October 1944* (London: Rupert Hart-Davis, 1972), p. 51.

3. Skarżyński, *Polityczne Przyczyny,* pp. 146–47, 151, 201–202.

4. Duchess of Atholl, *The Tragedy of Warsaw and Its Documentation* (London: John Murray, 1945), p. 9.

5. Transcripts of both radio broadcasts appear in translation in message, Winant to Secretary of State, Sept. 6, 1944, DS/NA.

6. R. Umiastowski, *Poland, Russia and Great Britain, 1941–1945: A Study of Evidence* (London: Hollis and Carter, 1946), pp. 281–82.

7. Skarżyński, *Polityczne Przyczyny,* pp. 210–11; Komisja Historyczna Polskiego Sztabu Głównego w Londynie, *Polskie Siły Zbrojne w Drugiej Wojnie Światowej.* Vol. III: *Armia Krajowa* (London: Instytyt Historyczny Im. Gen. Sikorskiego, 1950), pp. 657–58 (hereafter cited as *PSZ*).

8. Skarżyński, *Polityczne Przyczyny,* pp. 206–207, 293–94.

9. Komisja Historyczna, *PSZ,* p. 658; Jan M. Ciechanowski, *Powstanie Warszawskie: Zarys Podloza Politycznego i Dyplomatycznego* (London: Odnowa, 1971), p. 262.

10. Jan Ostaszewski, *Powstanie Warszawskie* (Rzym, 1945), pp. 29–30, 36;

Jerzy Sawicki, *Przed Polskim Prokuratorem: Dokumenty i Komentarze* (Warsaw, Iskry, 1958), p. 113; Mikołajczyk, *Rape of Poland,* p. 68; Adam Borkiewicz, *Powstanie Warszawskie, 1944* (Warsaw, 1957), p. 35.

11. Skarżyński, *Polityczne Przyczyny,* pp. 293-98, 302-306, 320.

12. *Ibid.,* p. 217.

13. Raczyński, *In Allied London,* p. 303.

14. Komisja Historyczna, *PSZ,* p. 664; Skarżyński, *Polityczne Przyczyny,* pp. 228-37.

15. Jerzy Kirchmayer, *Powstanie Warszawskie* (Warsaw: Książka i Wiedza, 1970), pp. 42ff.

16. Sosnkowski Papers in Piłsudski Institute (hereafter cited as SP/PI). Ciechanowski, *Defeat in Victory,* p. 319; Mikołajczyk, *Rape of Poland,* pp. 70-71.

17. Mikołajczyk, *Rape of Poland,* p. 71.

18. Ciechanowski, *Powstanie Warszawskie,* pp. 287-91, 292-93, 306.

19. Bruce, *Warsaw Uprising,* p. 98.

20. Excerpts of operational plans in SP/PI.

21. Kirchmayer, *Powstanie Warszawskie,* pp. 139, 166; Borkiewicz, *Powstanie Warszawskie,* pp. 29-31, 37-41; Anton Przygoński, *Z Problematyki Powstania Warszawskiego* (Warsaw: Wydawnictwo Ministerstwa Obrony Narodowej, 1964), pp. 55-56; Hanns von Krannhals, *Der Warschauer Aufstand, 1944* (Frankfort on the Main: Bernard & Graefe Verlag fur Wehrwesen, 1962), p. 120. Krannhals' figure of 12,060 German troops seems low. He does not count assorted units of the Bahnschutz, Werkschutz, etc. Neither does he count troops at installations just as close to Warsaw as Bielany and Okęcie, which he does include in his estimates.

22. Krannhals, *Der Warschauer Aufstand,* p. 119.

23. Interrogations of Bach-Zelewski in the International Military Tribunal Documents, National Archives (hereafter cited as IMT/NA).

24. *Ibid.*

25. Szymon Datner, "Destruction of Warsaw," in *1939-1945: War Losses in Poland* (Poznań: Wydawnictwo Zachodnie, 1960), p. 121.

26. Interrogations of Bach-Zelewski, in IMT/NA.

27. Datner, "Destruction of Warsaw," p. 121.

28. Krannhals, *Der Warschauer Aufstand,* p. 124.

29. Interrogations of Bach-Zelewski, in IMT/NA.

30. *Ibid.;* Sawicki, *Przed Polskim Prokuratorem,* pp. 68, 340, 342.

31. Ciechanowski, *Powstanie Warszawskie,* pp. 287-93, 306.

32. Winston S. Churchill, *Triumph and Tragedy* (Boston: Houghton, 1953), pp. 130-31.

33. Józef Garlinski, *Poland, SOE and the Allies,* Trans. by Paul Stevenson (London: Allen and Unwin, 1969), pp. 208-209.

34. Ltr., Colonel Leon Mitkiewicz, former Polish military attaché to the United States, to writer, Aug. 9, 1972.

35. Msg., Hull to Harriman, July 18, 1944; Memo, Stettinius to Hull, Aug. 4, 1944, *FR,* 1944, III, 1365, 1370; Memo, Secretary of State for president, Aug. 19, 1944, in PSF, Box 7, FDR/L; Skarżyński, *Polityczne Przyczyny,* p. 75.

36. General Sikorski Historical Institute, *DPSR*, II, 339.

37. Lukas, *Eagels East,* pp. 192–229.

28. Msg., Schoenfeld to Secretary of State, Aug. 12, 1944, in DS/NA.

39. Msg., Harriman to president, Aug. 15, 1944 (no. 3000); Msg., Harriman to president, Aug. 15, 1944 (no. 3002), in *FR,* 1944, III, 1374–77.

40. Churchill, *Triumph and Tragedy,* p. 134.

41. Lukas, *Eagles East,* p. 204; Msg., Spaatz to Walsh, Aug. 13, 1944, in Spaatz Papers, Box 18, MD/LC.

42. Msg., Hull to Harriman, Aug. 17, 1944, in *FR,* 1944, III, 1378–79; Churchill, *Triumph and Tragedy,* p. 135.

43. Msg., Harriman to president, Aug. 17, 1944 (no. 3021); Msg., Harriman to president, Aug. 17, 1944 (no. 3028); Msg., Harriman to president, Aug. 17, 1944 (no. 3049), in DS/NA.

44. Msg., Hull to Harriman, Aug. 19, 1944, in *FR,* 1944, III, 1381–82; Msg., Harriman to Hull, Aug. 21, 1944, in DS/NA. Polish airmen in the PAF continued to make the dangerous flights to Warsaw during the uprising.

45. Msg., Churchill and Roosevelt to Stalin, Aug. 20, 1944; Msg., Stalin to Churchill and Roosevelt, Aug. 22, 1944, in Ministry of Foreign Affairs of the USSR, *Stalin's Correspondence with Churchill, Attlee, Roosevelt, and Truman: 1941–1945,* 2 vols. (London: Lawrence and Wishart, 1958), I, 255.

46. General Sikorski Historical Institute, *DPSR*, II, 309–22, 375, 378; Mikołajczyk, *Rape of Poland,* pp. 72–75.

47. Msg., Churchill to Roosevelt, July 25, 1944; Msg., Churchill to Roosevelt, July 29, 1944; in Loewenheim, *Roosevelt and Churchill,* pp. 554–57; Msg., Roosevelt to Stalin, Aug. 12, 1944, in *FR,* 1944, III, 1432; Mikołajczyk, *Rape of Poland,* pp. 82, 286–87.

48. General Sikorski Historical Institute, *DPSR,* II, 309–22; Mikołajczyk, *Rape of Poland,* pp. 72–76.

49. Mikołajczyk, *Rape of Poland,* pp. 76–77. Anders was critical of Mikolajczyk for even talking with the Lublin Poles. See Anders, *An Army in Exile,* pp. 212–13.

50. Mikołajczyk, *Rape of Poland,* p. 78.

51. Andrzej Pomian, *The Warsaw Rising: A Selection of Documents* (London, 1945), p. viii; Eden, *Reckoning,* p. 548; Msg., Harriman to Roosevelt Aug. 10, 1944, in DS/NA; Msg., Harriman to Roosevelt, Aug. 12, 1944, *FR,* 1944, III, 1313–15.

52. Edward J. Rozek, *Allied Wartime Diplomacy: A Pattern in Poland* (New York: Wiley, 1958), pp. 249–50.

53. General Sikorski Historical Institute, *DPSR,* II, 354, 386. Many Poles were bitterly disappointed with the meager aid from the West. One Warsaw diarist likened Churchill and Roosevelt to Pilate, anxious to wash their hands of the Polish people. See Aleksander W. Rudziński, *Dziennik z Powstania Warszawskiego* (London: Oficyna Poetów i Malarzy, 1974), p. 37.

54. Msg., Roosevelt to Churchill, Aug. 24, 1944, in FDR/L; General Sikorski Historical Institute, *DPSR,* II, 362–63; Churchill, *Triumph and Tragedy,* pp. 139–41.

55. Department of State Press Release, Aug. 29, 1944, in OF, Box 4, FDR/L. The United States government was sensitive to the fact that the declaration

would also strengthen the position of Mikołajczyk within his own government against his opposition. See Memo, Hull to Roosevelt, Aug. 28, 1944, *FR, 1944,* III, 1393–94.

56. Eden, *Reckoning,* pp. 549–50; Churchill, *Triumph and Tragedy,* pp. 140–43.

57. Ltr., Hopkins to Winant, Sept. 4, 1944, in Sherwood Papers, Box 324, FDR/L.

58. Ltr., Charles Rozmarek to Roosevelt, Aug. 16, 1944, in OF, Box 4, FDR/L. See ch. 6 for a full discussion of the administration and Polish Americans.

59. Ltr., Frank Nurczyk to Roosevelt, Sept. 13, 1944, in OF, Box 4, FDR/L; Ltr., Joseph Janus to Hull, Sept. 7, 1944, in DS/NA.

60. Churchill, *Triumph and Tragedy,* p. 142.

61. Msg., Roosevelt to Churchill, Sept. 5, 1944, in MRF, Box 31, FDR/L.

62. Memo for the President, Sept. 6, 1944, in DS/NA.

63. Ltr., with report, Anderson to Spaatz, Oct. 9, 1944, in Spaatz Papers, Box 182, MD/LC.

64. Msg., Harriman to Secretary of State, Sept. 10, 1944, in DS/NA.

65. Krannhals, *Der Warschauer Aufstand,* pp. 154–57.

66. Tadeusz Bór-Komorowski, *The Secret Army* (New York: Macmillan, 1951), pp. 342–43; Kirchmayer, *Powstanie Warszawskie,* pp. 504–505. Rokossovsky says the Soviet Air Force flew 4,821 sorties—2,535 of them with supplies—on behalf of the insurgents during the period Sept. 13–Oct. 1. See K. Rokossovsky, *A Soldier's Duty* (Moscow: Progress Publishers, 1970), p. 261.

67. Pomian, *Warsaw Rising,* pp. 23, 25.

68. Memo, Putnam to Secretary of State, Sept. 12, 1944; Msg., Secretary of State to Harriman, Sept. 12, 1944; Msg., Harriman to Roosevelt, Sept. 14, 1944, in MRF, Box 31, FDR/L; Eden, *Reckoning,* p. 551.

69. Ltr., with report, Anderson to Spaatz, Oct. 9, 1944; "Daily Int/Tops Summary No. 243, Allied Expeditionary Air Force" in United States Air Force Historical Archives, Maxwell Air Force Base, Alabama.

70. Memo., McDonald to Anderson, Oct. 14, 1944, in Spaatz Papers, Box 139, MD/LC.

71. Msg., Spaatz to Arnold, Sept. 21, 1944, in Spaatz Papers, Box 182, MD/LC.

72. Extract of Memo, Marshall to Brown, Sept. 21, 1944, in MRF, Box 31, FDR/L; Memo Roosevelt to Leahy, Sept. 29, 1944, in PSF, Box 37, in FDR/L.

73. Transcript of telephone conversation between Churchill and Anderson, Sept. 29, 1944, in Spaatz Papers, Box 19, MD/LC.

74. Msg., Kessler to Spaatz, Oct. 1, 1944, in Spaatz Papers, Box 182, MD/LC.

75. Zenon Kliszko, *Powstanie Warszawskie: Artykuły, Przemowienia, Wspomnienia, Dokumenty* (Warsaw: Książka i Wiedza, 1967), pp. 269–71.

76. Bór-Komorowski, *Secret Army,* pp. 362–63; Pomian, *Warsaw Rising,* p. 35.

77. The extent of the Soviet setback at the Vistula in Aug. 1944, is a highly controversial point and is beyond the scope of this book. But based on this writer's examination of the Records of German Field Command Armies, "AOK 9, Kriegstagebuch Nr. 11," Rolls 343–46, the evidence suggests that by Sept. 1944, the Soviets could have established, if they wanted to, at least beachheads of substantial strength to bring greater relief to the AK, and probably could have taken the city itself.

78. Ltr., Biddle to Roosevelt, Mar. 6, 1943; Memo, Marshall to Roosevelt, Aug. 26, 1943; Ltr., Biddle to Roosevelt, Jan. 20, 1944; Memo, Hull to Roosevelt, Jan. 20, 1944, in OF, 1667, FDR/L. Ciechanowski mistakenly interprets Biddle's resignation as a consequence of his disagreement with Roosevelt over American policy toward Poland. See Ciechanowski, *Defeat in Victory,* p. 259. Ciechanowski warned Hull that the failure of the United States to appoint immediately a new ambassador to the Polish government played into the hands of German and Soviet propaganda, which claimed Washington was no longer interested in the Poles. Msg., Ciechanowski to minister of Foreign Affairs, Jan. 27, 1944, in Ciechanowski Papers, Hoover Institution.

79. Arthur Bliss Lane, *I Saw Poland Betrayed: An American Ambassador Reports to the American People* (Indianapolis: Bobbs-Merrill, 1948), p. 28.

80. *Ibid.,* pp. 29–33; Lane Papers in YU/L; Memo, Roosevelt to Stettinius, Dec. 13, 1944, in PSF, Poland, Box 66, FDR/L. In the meantime, Rudolf Schoenfeld represented the United States as Chargé d'Affaires ad interim with the Polish and other exiled governments in London. Memo, Hull to Roosevelt, Jan. 28, 1944, in OF, 5487, FDR/L.

81. Ltr., Lane to Wiley, Jan. 9, 1945, in Lane Papers, Box 69, YU/L; Lane, *I Saw Poland Betrayed,* pp. 29–33.

Chapter V

1. There are several studies dealing with the stopgap and long-range aspects of American aid to the Soviet Union. See Lukas, *Eagles East;* Raymond H. Dawson, *The Decision to Aid Russia, 1941: Foreign Policy and Domestic Politics* (Chapel Hill: Univ. of North Carolina Press, 1959); George C. Herring, *Aid to Russia, 1941–1946: Strategy, Diplomacy, The Origins of the Cold War* (New York: Columbia Univ. Press, 1973).

2. Ciechanowski, *Defeat in Victory,* pp. 54–55; Ltr., Hull to Roosevelt, Sept. 30, 1941, transmitting ltr. from Ciechanowski, in PSF, Poland, Box 65, FDR/L; Kot, *Conversations with the Kremlin,* p. 181. Kot continued to complain about the lack of religious freedom for the Poles until he left the Soviet Union in the summer of 1942. See Kot, *Conversations with the Kremlin,* pp. 357–63.

3. *Press Conferences,* XVII–XVIII, 187–88.

4. General Sikorski Historical Institute, *DPSR,* I, Note No. 207, p. 596; Ltr., Taylor to Roosevelt, July 17, 1944, in U.S., Department of State, *FR,* 1944, IV, 1217–21.

5. Henry C. Cassidy, *Moscow Dateline, 1941–1943* (Boston: Houghton, 1943), pp. 354–56; "Break-Through on Church," *Time,* XLII (Dec. 27, 1943), 53–58. Perhaps Eugene Tarle's *Napoleon's Invasion of Russia: 1812* was at least partially intended to mitigate Western suspicions about Soviet political ambitions in Europe. Tarle, an eminent Soviet historian, made Marshal Michael Kutuzov, not Tsar Alexander I, the hero of the book. Significantly, it was Kutuzov who wanted only to liberate Russia from the French and not to pursue the enemy into Poland and Germany as the tsar had wished.

6. Jack L. Hammersmith, "The U.S. Office of War Information (OWI) and the Polish Question, 1943–1945," *Polish Review,* XIX, No. 1 (1974), pp. 67–76.

7. Mikołajczyk, *Rape of Poland,* pp. 25, 58; Memo of telephone conversation by Stettinius, June 12, 1944, in Stettinius Papers, Box 240, UV/L.

8. Ciechanowski, *Defeat in Victory,* p. 116. Also see U.S., Department of State, *FR* 1942, III, 161.

9. Melvin Small, "How We Learned to Love the Russians: American Media and the Soviet Union during World War II," *The Historian: A Journal of History,* XXXVI (May, 1974), 459-62.

10. On Polish Constitution Day, May 3, 1944, 183 members of Congress rose to pay tribute to Poland. Most saluted Polish heroism in this and previous wars in history. See U.S., *Congressional Record,* 78 Congress, 2 sess., 1944, LXXXX, Pts. 9-10, App.; U.S., *Congressional Record,* 77 Congress, 2 session, 1942, LXXXVIII, Pts. 9-10, App., A3170. Churchill says there were 180,000 Poles fighting with the British at war's end. See Churchill, *Triumph and Tragedy,* p. 652.

11. *New York Times,* Aug. 1, 1941.

12. Robert C. McClelland, "The Soviet Union in American Opinion, 1933-1942," Ph.D. diss., West Virginia Univ., 1950, pp. 86, 128.

13. James M. Gillis, "Covenant with Hell," *Catholic World* (Aug. 1941), pp. 513-19; Paul Hanly Furfey, "Glance to the Left," *Catholic World* (Nov. 1941), pp. 145-50.

14. Sister Mary Assumpta Mazza, "A Survey of Changing Attitudes Toward the Soviet Union as Reflected in American Periodicals, 1942-1949," Ph.D. diss., St. John's Univ., 1957, pp. 10, 14-15.

15. McClelland, "The Soviet Union in American Opinion," p. 88.

16. Joseph E. Davies, "Russia Will Hold This Summer," *Saturday Evening Post,* CLXIV (June 20, 1942), 16-17, 88-89; Ralph Parker, "Timoshenko, Red Army Hero," *New York Times Magazine,* Feb. 8, 1942, p. 23; "Man of the Year," *Time,* XXXV (Jan. 1, 1940), 14-17; "Man of the Year," *Time* XLI (Jan. 4, 1943), 21-24.

17. Small, "How We Learned to Love the Russians," p. 456.

18. Mazza, "A Survey of Changing Attitudes Toward the Soviet Union," pp. 66-69; "Strategic Frontiers and Collective Security," *Nation,* CLVI (Mar. 13, 1943), 364-65; Blair Bolles, "What Eden is After," *Nation,* CLVI (Mar. 27, 1943), 442-44; "The Fact of Russia," *Christian Century,* LX (Dec. 8, 1943), 1430-31; Demaree Bess, "What does Russia Want?," *Saturday Evening Post,* CCXV (Mar. 20, 1943), 19, 91, 94; Kingsbury Smith, "Our Foreign Policy Goes Realist," *American Mercury,* LVII (Dec. 1943), 665-70; "The Soviets and the Post-War," *Life,* XIV (Mar. 29, 1943), 49.

19. "The Shape of Things," *Nation,* CLVI (May 1, 1943), 613-14; *New York Times,* Apr. 27, 1943; "The Russian-Polish Lid Blows Off," *Christian Century,* LX (May 5, 1943), 532; "Victims of Which Propaganda," *Saturday Evening Post,* CCXV (May 22, 1943), 108.

20. The Poles and the Russians," *New Republic,* CVIII (May 10, 1943), 623-24; "Who Can Speak for Poland?" *New Republic,* CVIII (May 7, 1943), 651-52; Heinz Eulau, "Europe's Exiled Governments," *New Republic,* CIX (Nov. 1, 1943), 614-17.

21. For example, Mikołajczyk provided the information for Burnet Hershey's "Hang the Führers," *Saturday Evening Post,* CCXV (June 12, 1943), 16-17, 40.

A Polish refugee gave Leon Dennen the facts for his article, "Inside Poland Today," *American Mercury,* LVII (Nov. 1943), 529–36.

22. Memo, Daniels to Roosevelt, June 2, 1944, in PSF, Poland, Box 66, FDR/L.

23. Press Research, June 4, 1945, in Lubin Papers, Box 20, FDR/L; Newsclip, *PM,* May 7, 1944, in Davies Papers, Box 64, MD/LC; Memo, Daniels to Roosevelt, June 2, 1944.

24. See issues of *Poland Fights, Polish Review,* and *Polish Facts and Figures.* For example, the May 1944 issue of *Polish Review* had two articles on the Polish resistance against the Germans, one on Tatar minorities in eastern Poland, a feature on Antoni Osinski who came from southeastern Poland, and one on Jewish theater in Poland. Kot particularly urged his government to enlist the support of Jewish organizations abroad. See Kot, *Conversations with the Kremlin,* pp. 246–47.

25. See ch. 6 for more information on KNAPP.

26. Memo, Hull to Roosevelt, Apr. 8, 1944; Memo, Daniels to Roosevelt, June 2, 1944; Memo, Lubin to Roosevelt, June 5, 1944, in PSF, Poland, Box 66, FDR/L; Ltr., Ciechanowski to Hull, July 19, 1943, in Hull Papers, LX, MD/LC.

27. U.S., *Congressional Record,* 78 Cong., 2 sess., 1944, LXXXX, Pt. 4, 5315.

28. See ch. 6.

29. Ciechanowski, *Defeat in Victory,* pp. 170–71.

30. Mikołajczyk, *Rape of Poland,* pp. 25, 119–20.

31. Władysław R. Malinowski, "Toward Polish-Soviet Understanding," *New Europe and World Reconstruction: Supplement* (Nov. 1943), pp. 3–12.

32. Mikołajczyk, *Rape of Poland,* p. 25.

33. Eden, *Reckoning,* pp. 504–506.

34. Raczyński, *In Allied London,* pp. 175, 183, 209–13, 217.

35. Msg., Churchill to Stalin, May 12, 1943, in General Sikorski Historical Institute, *DPSR,* II, 13; Note No. 7, p. 706; *Wiadomośći Polskie,* a rightist Polish newspaper published in England, not only underwent prior censorship before publication but also was threatened by the Ministry of Information with the loss of its paper allocation if it did not stop attacking the Soviet Union. See Raczyński, *In Allied London,* p. 173.

36. For a discussion of this subject, see later pages in this ch.

37. Frederick L. Schuman, "The Polish Frontier: A Test for the United Nations," *New Republic,* CX (Jan. 31, 1944), 138–41; "Russia's Western Claims," *New Republic,* CX (Jan. 17, 1944), 72; Heinz Eulau, "Poland and Russia," *New Republic,* CXI (Aug. 7, 1944), 156–57; Jerome Davis, "Russia's Postwar Aims," *New Republic,* CXI (Sept. 4, 1944), 276–77; "Italy and Poland," *New Republic,* CXI (Dec. 4, 1944), 733.

38. "America Must Speak Up for a Real Peace," *Saturday Evening Post,* CCXVI (Jan. 15, 1944), 96; Forrest Davis, "What Really Happened at Teheran?" *Saturday Evening Post,* CCXVI (May 13, 1944), 12–13, 37, 39, 41; Forrest Davis, "What Really Happened at Teheran?," *Saturday Evening Post,* CCXVI (May 20, 1944), 20, 23, 44, 46, 48; Edgar Snow, "Eastern Europe Swings Left," *Saturday Evening Post,* CCXVII (Nov. 11, 1944), 9–11, 70–71.

39. "Russia's Plans for Postwar Poland," *Christian Century,* LXI (Jan. 12, 1944), 35.

40. William Henry Chamberlin, "Preview of the Postwar World: The Soviet Union," *Christian Century,* LXI (Mar. 22, 1944), 364–66; Mazza, "A Survey of Changing Attitudes Toward the Soviet Union," pp. 114–15, 124–25.

41. Eugene Lyons, "Letter to American Liberals," *American Mercury,* LVIII (May, 1944), 569–70.

42. *New York Times,* July 27, 1944; Apr. 4, 1944; Oct. 3, 1944.

43. *Boston Evening Globe,* Aug. 4, 1944.

44. *St. Louis Post Dispatch,* Aug. 5, 1944.

45. *St. Louis Post Dispatch,* Sept. 3, 1944; *Washington Post,* Aug. 13, 1944; Quentin Reynolds, *The Curtain Rises* (New York: Random, 1944), p. 144; *Nashville Tennessean,* Aug. 3, 1944; *St. Louis Post Dispatch,* Aug. 24, 1944. One historian of the subject commented bitterly: "These correspondents raised the Lublin Committee from a motley group of political bandits to protectors of Polish independence." See Darrel T. Charlton, "The United States and the Warsaw Uprising," (Master's thesis, Tennessee Technological Univ., 1971), p. 90.

46. *Chicago Daily Tribune,* Aug. 1, 1944; Sept. 1, 1944.

47. "Defeat of Patriots at Warsaw Widens Polish-Russian Breach," *Newsweek,* XXIV (Oct. 16, 1944), 48–49; Władysław R. Malinowski, "Uprising in Warsaw," *Nation,* CLIX (Sept. 23, 1944), 347–48.

48. "From Warsaw to Paris," *New Republic,* CXI (Sept. 11, 1944), 295–96; Anna Louise Strong, "Bór's Uprising," *Atlantic Monthly,* CLXXVI (Dec. 1945), 80–85.

49. *Detroit News,* Aug. 1, 1944; Charlton, "The United States and the Warsaw Uprising," pp. 84, 92–93.

50. *New York Times,* Aug. 17, 1944; Oct. 3, 1944; Oct. 4, 1944.

51. *Ibid.,* Oct. 3, 1944.

52. *Press Conferences,* XXIV, 151–52; Memo of press and radio news conference, September 5, in Hull Papers, CXXXXI, MD/LC.

53. U.S., *Congressional Record,* 78 Cong., 2 sess., 1944, LXXXX, Pts. 10–11, App. A3851, A4349. For the reactions of the Polish American Congress to the Warsaw Uprising, see ch. 6.

54. *Ibid.,* Pt. 11, A4241–A4242, A4035, A4822.

55. U.S., Department of State, Office of Public Information, "Public Attitudes on Foreign Policy," No. 46, Dec. 1, 1944, and No. 65, July 23, 1945, in Stettinius Papers, Box 229, UV/L. Wartime opinion polls were not the sophisticated tools they later became. Two polls taken about the same time revealed opposite results. One poll concluded that most Americans with opinions on the subject did not believe the Soviet Union would try to take more land after the war but would try to ensure that friendly governments were installed in neighboring countries like Poland. Another poll, on the other hand, suggested that most Americans who expressed an opinion believed that the Soviet Union would "want more territory after the war than she had before the war started." Significantly, the respondents were about evenly divided about whether the United States should try to stop the Soviets from getting it. See U.S., Department of State, "Public Attitudes on Foreign Policy," No. 46, *passim.* According to Gaddis, "only about one out of four American adults consistently demonstrated any thorough knowledge of foreign affairs." See Gaddis, *The United States and the Origins of the Cold War,* p. 46.

56. Alice Payne Hackett, *70 Years of Best Sellers, 1895-1965* (New York: Bowker, 1967), pp. 165-69.

57. Joseph Davies, *Mission to Moscow* (New York: Simon, 1941), pp. 511, 12.

58. Mazza, "A Survey of Changing Attitudes Toward the Soviet Union," pp. 4, 43.

59. Gaddis, *The United States and the Origins of the Cold War,* p. 35; Mazza, "A Survey of Changing Attitudes Toward the Soviet Union," pp. 4-5.

60. Reynolds, *The Curtain Rises,* pp. 165, 134, 139, 142-43, 145. This is the same journalsit who wrote two years earlier about the Poles: "One felt like taking off one's hat in the presence of any Pole. Such magnificence of spirit, such fortitude under adversity and such insistence upon vengeance against the Nazi spoilers of their home were inspiring. The Poles were very wonderful." Quentin Reynolds, *Only The Stars Are Neutral* (New York: Random, 1942), p. 157.

61. Small, "How We Learned to Love the Russians," pp. 463-64; Eve Curie, *Journey Among Warriors* (Garden City, NY: Doubleday, 1943), pp. 256-76, 484.

62. Wendell L. Willkie, *One World* (Urbana: Univ. of Illinois Press, 1966), pp. v, 50-54, 87.

63. Walter Lippmann, *U.S. Foreign Policy: Shield of the Republic* (Boston: Little, 1943), pp. 137-54; Sumner Welles, *The Time for Decision* (New York: Harper, 1944), pp. 330-31, 354, 405-406; Walter Lippmann, *U.S. War Aims* (Boston: Little, 1944), Chapter XI.

64. Simon Segal, *New Order in Poland* (New York: Knopf, 1942); Ministerstwo Informacji, *Black Book of Poland* (New York: Putnam's, 1942); Oskar Halecki, *History of Poland* (New York: Roy Publishers, 1943); Stanisław Strzetelski, *Where the Storm Broke* (New York: Roy Publishers, 1943); Manfred Kridl, Władysław R. Malinowski and Józef Wittlin, eds., *For Your Freedom and Ours* (New York: Ungar, 1942).

65. Jan Karski, *Story of a Secret State* (Boston: Houghton, 1944); Kazimierz Wierzyński, *Forgotten Battlefield* (New York: Roy Publishers, 1944); Ksawery Pruszyński, *Poland Fights Back: From Westerplatte to Monte Casino* (New York: Roy Publishers, 1944); Jacob Apenszlak, *Black Book of Polish Jewry: An Account of the Martyrdom of Polish Jewry under the Nazi Occupation* (New York: Roy Publishers, 1944); Dorothy Adams, *We Stood Alone* (New York: Longmans, Green and Co., 1944); Ann S. Cardwell, *Poland and Russia: The Last Quarter Century* (London: Sheed and Ward, 1944).

66. Foster Rhea Dulles, *The Road to Teheran: The Story of Russia and America, 1781-1943* (Princeton: Princeton Univ. Press, 1944), pp. 1-2, 245; Pitirim Sorokin, *Russia and the United States* (New York: Dutton, 1944), p. 209.

67. Paul V. Harper, ed., *The Russia I Believe In: The Memoirs of Samuel N. Harper, 1902-1941* (Chicago: Univ. of Chicago Press, 1945); Mazza, "A Survey of Changing Attitudes Toward the Soviet Union," pp. 26-32, 112.

68. Bernard Pares, *Russia and the Peace* (New York: Macmillan, 1944), pp. 1, 15, 32, 33, 131-32, 146, 282. Professor E. H. Carr, another eminent English scholar, believed eastern Europe should become a Soviet sphere of influence. *The Times* (London), Mar. 10, 1943.

69. David Dallin, *Russia and Postwar Europe* (New Haven: Yale University Press, 1943), pp. 206-207; David Dallin, "Russia's Aims in Europe," *American*

Mercury, LVII (Oct. 1943), 391–402; David Dallin, "Russia's Aims in Europe," *American Mercury,* LVII (Nov. 1943), 599–601; Mazza, "A Survey of Changing Attitudes Toward the Soviet Union," p. 5.

70. Small, "How We Learned to Love the Russians," pp. 460–61.

71. *New York Times,* Apr. 25, 1943; James Agee, "Mission to Moscow," *Nation,* CLVI (May 22, 1943), 745–46; Melvin Small, "Buffoons and Brave Hearts: Hollywood Portrays the Russians, 1939–1944," *California Historical Quarterly,* LII (Winter, 1973), p. 330.

72. *Macmillan Audio Brandon Films: 16 mm Collection of International Cinema, 1974–75* (NC, 1975), p. 127; Small, "Buffoons and Brave Hearts," p. 334.

73. *New York Times,* June 11, 1943, Nov. 5, 1943, March 9, 1944.

Chapter VI

1. Joseph Wytrwal, *America's Polish Heritage: A Social History of the Poles in America* (Detroit: Endurance Press, 1961), pp. 191, 203, 212–13, 224–25, 227; Louis Adamic, *A Nation of Nations* (New York: Harper, 1945), p. 295; Ltr., Świetlik to Roosevelt, July 15, 1943, in PPF, 2731, FDR/L; *Naród Polski,* Mar. 19, 1942.

2. Summary of correspondence, Oct. 1942; Ltr., Świetlik to Roosevelt, May 13, 1941, in OF, 463A, Box 3, FDR/L.

3. Jędrzejewicz, *Polonia,* pp. 57–59; Msg., Januszewski to Roosevelt, June 24, 1942, in OF, 463A, Box 3, FDR/L. There was a long discussion concerning what the organization should be called. Before the delegates agreed on KNAPP some wanted the name of Piłsudski to be part of the designation of the new organization. Jędrzejewicz, *Polonia,* pp. 27–36.

4. Jędrzejewicz, *Polonia,* pp. 37, 39; Ltr., Jedrzejewicz to writer, Dec. 15, 1974.

5. Jędrzejewicz, *Polonia,* pp. 51–55; Komitet Narodowy Amerykanów Pochodzenia Polskiego, *Biuletyn Organizacyjny,* I (January 1943), 3–5.

6. Komitet Narodowy Amerykanów Pochodzenia Polskiego, *Biuletyn Organizacyjny,* I, 5, 10.

7. Jędrzejewicz, *Polonia,* pp. 70–71.

8. Komitet Narodowy Amerykanów Pochodzenia Polskiego, *Biuletyn Organizacyjny,* I (May, 1943), 1–2; *Ibid.,* I (June–Aug. 1943), 1.

9. *Ibid.,* I (May 1943), 7–8. Most Polish American newspapers—liberal and conservative—suspected that the Soviets were responsible for the Katyn massacre.

10. *Ibid.,* I (June–Aug. 1943), 7–10.

11. Jędrzejewicz, *Polonia,* pp. 88–89; *Nowy Świat,* Mar. 12, 1944.

12. Jędrzejewicz, *Polonia,* pp. 94–99.

13. *Ibid.,* pp. 42–50.

14. *Ibid.,* p. 121. Matuszewski helped to get Polish gold out of the country. Transported first to France, the gold later was shipped to French West Africa. By mid-1943, the Polish government wanted American help to ship sixty-five tons of it from Africa to the United States. See Ignacy Matuszewski, *What Poland Wants* (New York: KNAPP, 1942), introduction; Ltr., Hull to Morgenthau, July 23, 1943; Ltr., Morgenthau to Hull, Aug. 4, 1943, in Morgenthau Diary, DLIII FDR/L.

15. Komitet Narodowy Amerykanów Pochodzenia Polskiego, *Biuletyn Organizacyjny*, I (Jan. 1943), 8–10.

16. Ignacy Matuszewski, *Hańba albo Chwała: Artykuły o Polityce Rosji* (Palestine: Związek Pracy Dla Państwa, 1944), pp. 7–8.

17. Ltr., Lubin to Acheson, Apr. 3, 1944, with enclosure, in DS/NA. Even the Roman Catholic *Naród Polski*, which was no friend of Matuszewski, despaired that Polish American money bought a substantial amount of lend-lease for the Soviet Union, a country which refused to allow aid from the United States to get to Polish refugees in the USSR. *Naród Polski*, Mar. 2, 1944.

18. Matuszewski, *Hańba albo Chwała*, pp. 28–31, 1–3. *Nowy Świat* criticized the State Department and the Office of War Information for trying to cultivate pro-Soviet sentiment in the United States. See *Nowy Świat*, Apr. 8, 1943.

19. Matuszewski, *Hańba albo Chwała*, pp. 6, 44.

20. *Dziennik Polski* (Detroit), June 15, 1945.

21. Jędrzejewicz, *Polonia*, pp. 121–23; Memo, Highlights in the Domestic Foreign Language Press, Feb. 1–15, 1943, in Nash Papers, Box 16, Harry S Truman Library, Independence, MO (hereafter cited as HST/L).

22. Newsclip, *PM*, May 17, 1945, in Davies Papers, Box 65, MD/LC.

23. Peter Davenport, "Sikorski's Opposition" *Nation*, CLVI (Jan. 30, 1943). 163–64; Eric Estorick, "Polish American Politics," *Nation*, CLVIII (May 20, 1944), 591–93.

24. Jędrzejewicz, *Polonia*, p. 121.

25. Louis Gerson, *The Hypehnate in Recent American Politics and Diplomacy* (Lawrence: Univ. of Kansas Press, 1964), pp. 134–35.

26. Hull, *Memoirs*, II, 1378.

27. Jędrzejewicz, *Polonia*, pp. 122–23.

28. Memo, Poulos to Barnes, Mar. 14, 1944; Ltr., Sadowski to Blake, Mar. 7, 1944; Memo, Lorenz to Blake, Mar. 10, 1944; Ltr., Roosevelt to Januszewski, Mar. 20, 1944, in PPF, 8727, FDR/L.

29. Memo, Foreign Nationalities Branch to Director of Strategic Services, Apr. 1, 1944, in PSF, Poland, Box 46, FDR/L.

30. *Ibid.*; Jędrzejewicz, *Polonia*, pp. 94–95.

31. Memo, Foreign Nationalities Branch to Director of Strategic Services, Apr. 1, 1944.

32. Memo, Foreign Nationalities Branch to Director of Strategic Services, June 24, 1943, in OSS Records/NA. One official in the Office of War Information argued in early 1943 that "our treatment of foreign language minorities in this country is no longer a simple administrative problem but is a matter of national policy." See memo, Nash to Kane, Feb. 15, 1943, in Nash Papers, Box 18, HST/L.

33. Memo, Cox to Hopkins, Feb. 7, 1944, in Hopkins Papers, Box 337, in FDR/L; Msg., Roosevelt to Churchill, Mar. 8, 1944, in Loewenheim, Langley, and Jonas, *Roosevelt and Churchill*, p. 466; Ltr., Lesinski to Roosevelt, with attached petition, Oct. 23, 1943; Ltr., Mruk to Roosevelt, Jan. 14, 1944, in OF, 463A, Box 4, FDR/L.

34. See correspondence on this subject in OF, 463A, Box 4, FDR/L.

35. Memo, Foreign Nationalities Branch to Director of Strategic Services, Apr. 1, 1944.

36. Printed postcards in OF, 463A, Box 4, FDR/L.

37. Polish American Congress, *Story of the Polish American Congress in Press Clippings, 1944–1948* (Chicago: Alliance Printers and Publishers, Inc., 1945), pp. 26, 13; Memo, Foreign Nationalities Branch to Director of Strategic Services, June 12, 1944, in OF, 463, Box 1, FDR/L.

38. Polish American Congress, *Polish American Congress, Inc., 1944–1948: Selected Documents* (Chicago: Polish American Congress, 1948), pp. 4–5.

39. Polish American Congress, *Story of the Polish American Congress*, p. 27, and *passim.*

40. *Ibid.*, pp. 15–16; Polish American Congress, *Selected Documents*, pp. 4–5.

41. Polish American Congress, *Story of the Polish American Congress*, p. 17; Memo, Foreign Nationalities Branch to Director of Strategic Services, June 12, 1944.

42. Memo, Foreign Nationalities Branch to Director of Strategic Services, June 12, 1944; Fred L. Israel, ed., *The War Diary of Breckinridge Long: Selections from the Years 1939–1944* (Lincoln: Univ. of Nebraska Press, 1966), p. 354; Polish American Congress, *Story of the Polish American Congress*, p. 12.

43. Polish American Congress, *Story of the Polish American Congress*, pp. 17, 24, 29.

44. Polish American Congress, *Selected Documents*, pp. 20–23.

45. Polish American Congress, *Foreign Policy of the United States: Memorandum of the Polish American Congress to Cordell Hull, Secretary of State* (Washington, D.C.: Polish American Congress, 1944). Matuszewski apparently authored the memorandum to Hull. Interview with Dr. Wacław Jędrzejewicz, July 5, 1972.

46. Memo, Foreign Nationalities Branch to Director of Strategic Services, June 12, 1944. Świetlik, who had opposed making the Polish question an issue in American Polonia, was a delegate to the Congress but had not been invited by the executive committee to sit on the dais with other notables. Many of the delegates threatened to walk out unless Świetlik was allowed to speak. Rozmarek, wisely reversing the ruling of the presiding officer, Gutowski, averted a potential crisis and allowed Świetlik to address the gathering. Polish American Congress, *Story of the Polish American Congress*, p. 35; Interview with Pelagia Łukaszewska, Delegate to the Congress, Nov. 27, 1974.

47. Memo, Foreign Nationalities Branch to Director of Strategic Services, June 12, 1944; Polish American Congress, *Story of the Polish American Congress*, preface; *Naród Polski*, Apr. 2, 1942. As early as Sept. 1941, Ambassador Ciechanowski told a Polish American audience that they should inform the American public that postwar Poland would be a democratic society. See *Naród Polski*, Sept. 25, 1941.

48. Memo, Foreign Nationalities Branch to Director of Strategic Services, June 12, 1944.

49. Memo, Niles to Tully, June 6, 1944, with report, in PSF, Poland, Box 66, FDR/L.

50. Israel, *War Diary of Breckinridge Long*, p. 354; *New York Times*, May 30, 1944; *Chicago Tribune*, June 5, 1944.

51. Ltr., Rozmarek to Roosevelt, June 7, 1944; Memo for Roosevelt, initialed "EMW," June 9, 1944; Memo, Roosevelt to Early and Rosenman, June 12, 1944, in OF, 463, Box 1, FDR/L.

52. Memo, McDermott to Early, enclosing memo from Durbrow, June 19, 1944; Memo, Daniels and Niles to Early, June 19, 1944; Memo, Early and Rosenman to Roosevelt, June 20, 1944, in OF, 463, Box 1, FDR/L.

53. Ltr., Rozmarek to Roosevelt, Sept. 6, 1944; Ltr., Rozmarek to Kelly, Sept. 9, 1944; Ltr., Kelly to Watson, Sept. 12, 1944; Memo, Niles to Rosenman, Sept. 23, 1944; Memo, "Bob" to Watson, Oct. 7, 1944; Memo, Biddle to Roosevelt, Oct. 7, 1944, in OF, 463, Box 1, FDR/L.

54. Polish American Congress, *Story of the Polish American Congress,* p. 39; U.S., *Congressional Record,* 78 Cong., 2 sess., 1944, XC, Pt. 11, App., A4045–46; Summary of Msg., Rozmarek, Olejniczak, and Wolowska, to Roosevelt, Aug. 30, 1944, in OF, 463A, Box 4, in FDR/L; *Naród Polski,* Mar. 12, 1942, Oct. 5, 1944.

55. For example, see U.S., *Congressional Record,* 78 Cong., 2 sess., 1944, XC, Pt. 11, App., A4058, A4115, A4290–91.

56. *Ibid.,* Pt. 10, App., A3230.

57. Memo, Niles to Tully, with report, June 6, 1944; Ltr., Hopkins to "Gil," Sept. 4, 1944, with attachments, in Hopkins Papers, Box 337, FDR/L.

58. Memo, Roosevelt to Hull, with summary of Mikołajczyk's messages, Sept. 19, 1944, in PPF, 8809, FDR/L.

59. Ciechanowski, *Defeat in Victory,* p. 314; Memo, Cox to Hopkins, Sept. 8, 1944, in Hopkins Papers, Box 337, FDR/L; Memo for Watson, Oct. 10, 1944; and Memo, Roosevelt to Watson, Oct. 2, 1944, in OF, 463, Box 1, FDR/L.

60. Press Release, Oct. 11, 1944, in OF, 463, Box 1, FDR/L.

61. *Ibid.;* Lane, *I Saw Poland Betrayed,* p. 60.

62. Conversation with Mrs. Wanda Rozmarek, Jan. 7, 1975. Rozek repeats Professor W.W. Kulski's claim that Rozmarek promised to support Dewey's candidacy for the presidency. See Rozek, *Allied Wartime Diplomacy,* fn. 173, p. 324. Wytrwal repeats the story in his book, too. See Wytrwal, *America's Polish Heritage,* pp. 262–66. Gaddis erroneoulsy asserts that Rozmarek was a Republican, and that the Polish leader's last-minute endorsement of Roosevelt was "an effort to save face once leaders of the Polish-American Congress realized they could not swing the Polish vote to Dewey." Gaddis, *The United States and the Origins of the Cold War,* pp. 148–49.

63. Conversation with Mrs. Wanda Rozmarek, Jan. 7, 1975; Lane, *I Saw Poland Betrayed,* pp. 60–62; Jędrzejewicz, *Polonia,* p. 130.

64. Gaddis, *The United States and the Origins of the Cold War,* p. 149.

65. *New York Times,* Oct. 9, 1944; Rozek, *Allied Wartime Diplomacy,* p. 300.

66. Press Research, June 4, 1945, in Lubin Papers, Box 20, FDR/L. Gerson claims that attempts to use the Polish American vote in the interest of Poland "may have harmed more than helped the President in the deliberations over Poland's future status." He also claims without proof that Polish artists, scholars, and scientists would have been more effective in influencing American policies than Rozmarek and other leaders who "were too closely identified with ethnic politics." Gerson, *The Hyphenate,* pp. 139–40.

67. Polish American Congress, *Story of the Polish American Congress,* pp. 46–49.

68. *Ibid.,* pp. 49, 51; Karol Rozmarek, *Stany Zjednoczone, Polska i Polonia Amerykańska* (Detroit, 1945), p. 32.

Chapter VII

1. Memo, Yost to Dunn, Oct. 14, 1944, in Stettinius Papers, Box 216, UV/L; Memo, Stettinius to Roosevelt, Oct. 31, 1944, in PSF, Poland, Box 66, FDR/L.

2. Davis, *The Cold War Begins,* pp. 118-21; Msg., Harriman to Secretary of State, Sept. 20, 1944, in U.S., Department of State, *FR,* 1944, IV, 993-97.

3. Frank P. King, "British Policy and the Warsaw Rising," *Journal of European Studies,* IV (Mar. 1974), 14; *New York Times,* Oct. 1, 1944; Anders, *Army in Exile,* p. 232.

4. Memo by Matthews, Oct. 3, 1944, in U.S., Department of State, *FR,* 1944, III, 1320-21.

5. Msg., Schoenfeld to Secretary of State, Oct. 10, 1944; Msg., Harriman to Roosevelt, Oct. 14, 1944, in U.S., Department of State, *FR,* 1944, III, 1321-23; Report on Second Journey of Mikołajczyk to Moscow, Oct. 10-22, 1944, in U.S., Congress, House, Select Committee on Communist Aggression, *Polish Documents Report: Appendix,* 83 Cong., 2 sess., 1954, pp. 110-11 (hereafter cited as *PDR*).

6. Conference of Churchill and Mikołajczyk, Oct. [14], 1944, *ibid.,* pp. 125-30; Winston S. Churchill, *Triumph and Tragedy,* p. 235.

7. Msg., Churchill to Roosevelt, Oct. 22, 1944, in U.S., Department of State, *FR,* 1944, IV, 1023; Eden, *Reckoning,* p. 563; Churchill, *Triumph and Tragedy,* pp. 240-42.

8. *New York Times,* Oct. 22, 1944; Msg., Roosevelt to Churchill, Oct. 22, 1944, in Loewenheim, *Roosevelt and Churchill,* p. 592.

9. Notes on debates of the Council of Ministers, Nov. 2, 1944, in General Sikorski Historical Institute, *DPSR,* II, 446-49; Feis, *Churchill, Roosevelt, Stalin,* pp. 518-19.

10. Ltr., Mikołajczyk to Roosevelt, Oct. 27, 1944; Memo of conversation by Bohlen, Nov. 11, 1944; Ltr., Roosevelt to Mikołajczyk, Nov. 17, 1944, in U.S., Department of State, *FR,* 1944, III, 1328-30, 1332-35.

11. Msg., Ciechanowski to Romer, Nov. 13, 1944, in General Sikorski Historical Institute, *DPSR,* II, 463-64; Memo, Stettinius to Roosevelt, Nov. 9, 1944, in PSF, Poland, Box 66, FDR/L; Hull, *Memoirs,* II, 1447-48. Ciechanowski distrusted Harriman. In a confidential report to Romer on Oct. 30, 1944, the Polish ambassador said: "However, my personal friends with whom Harriman talked confidentially about Polish-Soviet matters convinced me that we have an enemy in him and that we cannot count on his friendly attitude to the Polish problem. I am warned about this from two unconnected sources." Quoted in Rozek, *Allied Wartime Diplomacy,* p. 302.

12. Msg., Mikołajczyk to Delegate of the Polish Government, Oct. 27-28, 1944; Notes of conversations between Mikołajczyk and Harriman, Nov. 22-23, 1944; Msg., Winant to Roosevelt, Nov. 23, 1944; Note of conversation between Mikołajczyk and Eden, Nov. 27, 1944, in General Sikorski Historical Institute, *DPSR,* II, 442, 469-72, 473-74, 479; Msg., Harriman to Roosevelt, Nov. 23, 1944; Msg., Schoenfeld to Hull, Nov. 25, 1944, in U.S., Department of State, *FR,* 1944, III, 1335-36, 1337; *New York Times,* Oct. 27, 1944; Berle and Jacobs, eds., *Navigating the Rapids,* p. 432; Mikołajczyk, *Rape of Poland,* pp. 104-105.

13. Raczyński, *In Allied London,* pp. 246, 249–50, 271.

14. Memo, Stettinius to Roosevelt, Nov. 28, 1944; Memo, Stettinius to Roosevelt, Dec. 9, 1944; Msg., Winant to Secretary of State, Nov. 26, 1944, in PSF, Poland, Box 66, FDR/L; U.S., Department of State, Fortnightly Survey of American Opinion on International Affairs, No. 16, Dec. 6, 1944, in Stettinius Papers, Box 229, UV/L.

15. Msg., Winant to Hopkins, Dec. 17, 1944; U.S., Department of State, Press Release, Dec. 18, 1944, in Hopkins Papers, Box 337, FDR/L; Statement by Churchill in House of Commons, Dec. 15, 1944, in General Sikorski Historical Institute, *DPSR,* II, 493–95; U.S., Department of State, Fortnightly Survey of American Opinion on International Affairs, Jan. 6, 1945, No. 18, pp. 2–3, in Stettinius Papers, Box 229, UV/L.

16. Msg., Kennan to Secretary of State, Dec. 3, 1944; Msg., Roosevelt to Stalin, Dec. 16, 1944; Msg., Stalin to Roosevelt, Dec. 27, 1944; Msg., Roosevelt to Stalin, Dec. 30, 1944; Msg., Stalin to Roosevelt, Jan. 1, 1945, in U.S., Department of State, *FR,* 1944, III, 1345–46, 1442–43, 1438, 1444–45, 1445–46.

17. U.S., Department of State, *Foreign Relations of the United States, Diplomatic Papers, 1945.* Vol. V: *Europe* (Washington, D.C.: United States Government Printing Office, 1967), fn. 6, p. 111; fn. 16, p. 113; p. 114 (hereafter cited as *FR,* 1945, V).

18. Moran, Churchill's physician, commented that "Everyone seemed to agree that the President had gone to bits physically; . . . ." See Lord Moran, *Churchill: Taken from the Diaries of Lord Moran, The Struggle for Survival, 1940–1965* (Boston: Houghton, 1966), p. 239. James Byrnes believed that it was the president's poor health that prevented him from adequately preparing for the conference. See James F. Byrnes, *Speaking Frankly* (New York: Harper, 1947), p. 23.

19. Bohlen Minutes, Feb. 4, 1945, in U.S., Department of State, *Foreign Relations of the United States, Diplomatic Papers, 1945. The Conference at Malta and Yalta* (Washington, D.C.: United States Government Printing Office, 1955), pp. 589–91 (hereafter cited as *FR, Yalta*); Edward R. Stettinius, Jr., *Roosevelt and the Russians: The Yalta Conference* (Garden City, NY: Doubleday, 1949), p. 113.

20. Bohlen Minutes and Matthews Minutes, Feb. 6, 1945, in U.S., Department of State, *FR, Yalta,* pp. 667–69, 677–79; Bohlen, *Witness to History,* pp. 169–70; Churchill, *Triumph and Tragedy,* pp. 366–69.

21. Bohlen Minutes and Matthews Minutes, Feb. 6, 1945, in U.S., Department of State, *FR, Yalta,* pp. 669–71, 679–81; Churchill, *Triumph and Tragedy,* pp. 369–71.

22. Bohlen Minutes and Matthews Minutes, Feb. 7, 1945, in U.S., Department of State, *FR, Yalta,* pp. 709–18, 718–21, 727–28; Fred L. Israel, ed., *The War Diary of Breckinridge Long,* p. 21; Churchill, *Triumph and Tragedy,* p. 372; Clemens, *Yalta,* p. 188.

23. Bohlen Minutes and Matthews Minutes, Feb. 7, 1945, in U.S., Department of State, *FR, Yalta,* pp. 708–18, 718–21; Churchill, *Triumph and Tragedy,* pp. 373–75.

24. "United States Proposal on Poland," Feb. 8, 1945, in U.S., Department of State, *FR, Yalta,* pp. 792–93; Churchill, *Triumph and Tragedy,* pp. 376–77.

25. Matthews Minutes, Feb. 8, 1945, in U.S., Department of State, *FR, Yalta,* pp. 786-87; Churchill, *Triumph and Tragedy,* pp. 377-78.

26. Matthews Minutes, Feb. 8, 1945, in U.S., Department of State, *FR, Yalta,* pp. 787-88; Churchill, *Triumph and Tragedy,* pp. 378-80.

27. Bohlen Minutes and Matthews Minutes, Feb. 8, 1945, in U.S., Department of State, *FR, Yalta,* pp. 782, 789-91; Churchill, *Triumph and Tragedy,* pp. 380-81.

28. Matthews Minutes, Feb. 8, 1945, in U.S., Department of State, *FR, Yalta,* p. 790; Stettinius, *Roosevelt and the Russians,* pp. 219-21; Churchill, *Triumph and Tragedy,* pp. 381-82.

29. Page Minutes, Feb. 9, 1945, in U.S., Department of State, *FR, Yalta,* pp. 803-807.

30. Bohlen Minutes and Matthews Minutes, Feb. 9, 1945; "British Revised Proposal," Feb. 9, 1945, *ibid.,* pp. 842-43, 846-49, 850-54, 870-71; Stettinius, *Roosevelt and the Russians,* pp. 246-47; Churchill, *Triumph and Tragedy,* pp. pp. 382-84.

31. Bohlen Minutes, Feb. 10, 1945, in U.S., Department of State, *FR, Yalta,* p. 898.

32. Bohlen Minutes and Matthews Minutes, Feb. 10, 1945, *ibid.,* pp. 897-911; Churchill, *Triumph and Tragedy,* pp. 385-87.

33. Roosevelt's speech to Congress, Mar. 1, 1945, in Samuel Rosenman, comp., *The Public Papers and Addresses of Franklin D. Roosevelt: Victory and the Threshold of Peace, 1944-1945* (New York: Harper, 1950), pp. 570-86.

34. Stettinius, *Roosevelt and the Russians,* pp. 295, 303; Memo of conversation by Stettinius, Mar. 15, 1945, in U.S., Department of State, *FR, 1945,* V, 165-67; Ciechanowski, *Defeat in Victory,* pp. 361-63.

35. Sherwood, *Roosevelt and Hopkins,* p. 870; Byrnes, *Speaking Frankly,* p. 21.

36. Leahy Diary, Feb. 10, 1945, in Leahy Papers, MD/LC; Bohlen, *Witness to History,* pp. 191-92.

37. Eden, *Reckoning,* p. 599; Moran, *Churchill,* pp. 247, 249; Churchill, *Triumph and Tragedy,* pp. 399-400.

38. Bohlen, *Witness to History,* p. 192.

39. Gallup Poll, Reaction to Crimea Conference, Feb. 1945, in Stettinius Papers, Box 229, UV/L. According to Clemens, the *New York Times* attitude toward the Lublinites shifted to praise and it was neutral, even hostile, toward the Polish government-in-exile by the time of the Yalta Conference. See Clemens, *Yalta,* pp. 180-81. The *Wall Street Journal,* on the other hand, was skeptical about the Yalta agreement on Poland and sympathized with the London Poles. One editorial writer described Yalta as an "intolerable hypocrisy. . . in which high moral pretentions are invoked to gloss over sordid practices." *Wall Street Journal,* Feb. 16, 1945.

40. Rozmarek's statement to the Press, Feb. 12, 1945, in U.S., *Congressional Record,* 79 Cong., 1 sess., 1945, XCI, Pt. 10, App., A669-A670.

41. Polish American Congress, *Selected Documents,* p. 36; Jędrzejewicz, *Polonia,* pp. 132-33; Polish American Congress, *Bulletin,* Mar.-Apr., 1945, pp. 5-7; Polish American Congress, *The Story of the Polish American Congress,* p. 54; *Dziennik Związkowy,* Mar. 5, 1945, p. 4.

42. Wasell, "Attitudes of the Various Polish-American Organizations," pp. 26–28; Gerson, *The Hyphenate,* p. 172. A large number of the members of the American Polish Labor Council were Jewish. For a discussion of the Kościuszko League, see ch. 3.

43. Ltr., Hoover to Hassett, enclosing memo on Krzycki, Nov. 2, 1944, in OF, 463A, Box 4, FDR/L; Gerson, *The Hyphenate,* pp. 170–71; George Pirinsky, *Slavic Americans in the Fight for Victory and Peace* (NP: American Slav Congress, n.d.), pp. 17 ff.

44. Summary of msg., Krzycki to Roosevelt, Feb. 29, 1944; Ltr., Krzycki to Roosevelt, Oct. 21, 1944, in OF, 463A, Box 4, FDR/L.

45. Gerson, *The Hyphenate,* pp. 172–73; Wasell, "Attitudes of the Various Polish-American Organizations," pp. 59–60.

46. For example, House Concurrent Resolution 31 expressed disapproval of the decisions concerning Poland made at Yalta while House Joint Resolution 110 assumed responsibility for the members of the Polish Armed forces serving outside Poland because of the decisions reached in the Crimea.

47. Press Research, June 4, 1945, in Lubin Papers, Box 20, FDR/L.

48. Ltr., Lesinski to Roosevelt, Feb. 24, 1945; Memo, Byrnes to Roosevelt, Mar. 3, 1945; Ltr., Roosevelt to Lesinski, Mar. 3, 1945; Ltr., Lesinski to Roosevelt, Mar. 10, 1945; Ltr., Dingell *et al.* to Roosevelt, Mar. 15, 1945; Ltr., Roosevelt to Lesinski, Mar. 20, 1945, in OF, 463A, Box 4, FDR/L.

49. U.S., *Congressional Record,* 79 Cong., 1 sess., 1945, App., A1302.

50. Arthur H. Vandenberg, Jr., ed., *The Private Papers of Senator Vandenberg* (Boston: Houghton, 1952), pp. 155–56.

51. Ltr., Ciechanowski to Acting Secretary of State, Feb. 15, 1945, in U.S., Department of State, *FR, Yalta,* pp. 121–22; Memo, McNarney to Marshall, Mar. 5, 1945; Ltr., McNarney to Marshall, Mar. 16, 1945, in PSF, Poland, Box 66, FDR/L; Anders, *Army in Exile,* pp. 250–54. Churchill was furious with Anders' threat. Referring to the Polish troops being pulled out of Italy, the prime minister snorted: "We shall do without them." See Anders, *ibid.,* pp. 256–57. Officers and enlisted men under General Anders were so strongly opposed to the Yalta decisions concerning Poland that thirty of them committed suicide in protest. See *Dziennik Związkowy,* Feb. 21, 1945, p. 1.

Chapter VIII

1. Msg., Harriman to Secretary of State, Feb. 24, 1945; Msg., Grew to Harriman, Feb. 28, 1945, in U.S., Department of State, *FR,* 1945, V, 123–25, 130–31.

2. Memo of conversation by Bohlen, Feb. 28, 1945; Msg., Harriman to Secretary of State, Mar. 1, 1945; Msg., Grew to Harriman, Mar. 3, 1945; Msg., Harriman to Secretary of State, Mar. 4, 1945, in U.S., Department of State, *FR,* 1945, V, 132–33, 134, 138–39, 141–42. For Stalin's remarks about the West sending representatives to Poland, see U.S., Department of State, *FR, Yalta,* p. 779.

3. Msg., Harriman to Secretary of State, Mar. 2, 1945; Msg., Grew to Harriman, Mar. 3, 1945; Msg., Harriman to Secretary of State, Mar. 3, 1945; Msg., Grew to Harriman, Mar. 3, 1945, in U.S., Department of State, *FR,* 1945, V, 134–41.

4. Msg., Harriman to Secretary of State, Mar. 6, 1945; Msg., Harriman to Secretary of State, Mar. 7, 1945; Msg., Grew to Harriman, Mar. 9, 1945; Msg., Stettinius to Winant, Mar. 14, 1945, in U.S., Department of State, *FR,* 1945, V, 142-44, 145-47, 153, 163.

5. Msg., Schoenfeld to Secretary of State, Feb. 24, 1945, in U.S., Department of State, *FR,* 1945, 125-28.

6. Msg., Churchill to Roosevelt, Mar. 8, 1945; Msg., Churchill to Roosevelt, Mar. 10, 1945, in U.S., Department of State, *FR,* 1945, V, 147-50, 153-54.

7. Msg., Grew to Harriman, Mar. 8, 1945; Msg., Roosevelt to Churchill, Mar. 11, 1945; Msg., Roosevelt to Churchill, Mar. 12, 1945, in U.S., Department of State, *FR,* 1945, V, 150-52, 155-58.

8. Msg., Churchill to Roosevelt, Mar. 13, 1945; Msg., Roosevelt to Churchill, Mar. 15, 1945, in U.S., Department of State, *FR,* 1945, V, 158-60, 163-64.

9. Msg., Harriman to Secretary of State, Mar. 23, 1945; Msg., Harriman to Secretary of State, Mar. 24, 1945; Msg., Harriman to Secretary of State, Mar. 25, 1945; Msg., Harriman to Secretary of State, Mar. 26, 1945, in U.S., Department of State, *FR,* 1945, V, 176-78, 179, 180-82, 183-84: fn. 46, p. 184.

10. Msg., Churchill to Roosevelt, Mar. 27, 1945; Msg., Roosevelt to Churchill, Mar. 29, 1945; Msg., Churchill to Roosevelt, Mar. 31, 1945, enclosing draft message to Stalin; Msg., Roosevelt to Churchill, Mar. 31, 1945; Msg., Roosevelt to Stalin, Apr. 1, 1945, in U.S., Department of State, *FR,* 1945, V, 185-87, 189-90, 191-93, 194-96.

11. Msg., Harriman to Secretary of State, Apr. 3, 1945, *ibid.,* pp. 196-98.

12. Msg., Churchill to Roosevelt, Apr. 5, 1945; Msg., Roosevelt to Churchill, Apr. 6, 1945; Msg., Roosevelt to Churchill, Apr. 11, 1945, in Loewenheim, *Roosevelt and Churchill,* pp. 704-708. Also see fn. 1 on page 704, and fn. 2 on page 709. Bohlen remarked that Stalin's accusation about American collusion with the Germans provoked an anger in Roosevelt that he rarely had observed in the president. See Bohlen, *Witness to History,* pp. 208-209.

13. Msg., Churchill to Roosevelt, Apr. 11, 1945, in Loewenheim, *Roosevelt and Churchill,* p. 708. Also see fn. 2, p. 708; Msg., Harriman to Secretary of State, Apr. 14, 1945, in U.S., Department of State, *FR,* 1945, V, 213-17.

14. Rozek, *Allied Wartime Diplomacy,* pp. 368-69; Msg., Schoenfeld to Secretary of State, Apr. 16, 1945, in U.S., Department of State, *FR,* 1945, V, 222. Also see fn. 23, p. 217, in U.S., Department of State, *FR,* 1945, V.

15. Churchill, *Triumph and Tragedy,* pp. 488-90.

16. Msg., Harriman to Secretary of State, Apr. 10, 1945; Msg., Kennan to Secretary of State, Apr. 18, 1945 (no. 1251); Msg., Kennan to Secretary of State, Apr. 18, 1945 (no. 1252); Msg., Harriman to Secretary of State, Apr. 16, 1945; Msg., Secretary of State to Kennan, Apr. 17, 1945, in U.S., Department of State, *FR,* 1945, V, 208, 229-31, 225-26, 227-28.

17. Loewenheim, *Roosevelt and Churchill,* fn. 5, p. 671; fn. 5, p. 675; fn. 15, p. 686; Memo of conversation by Bohlen, Apr. 20, 1945, in U.S., Department of State, *FR,* 1945, V, 231-32.

18. Msg., Ciechanowski to Secretary of State, Apr. 4, 1945, in U.S., Department of State, *FR,* 1945, V, 198-201; Rozek, *Allied Wartime Diplomacy,* pp. 370-74, 377; Lane, *I Saw Poland Betrayed,* p. 104. The arrests of the Polish

leaders followed unsuccessful efforts by the Communists to pressure them to join the Lublin regime.

19. Lukas, *Eagles East,* pp. 211–12.

20. Msg., Harriman to Secretary of State, Mar. 14, 1945, in U.S., Department of State, *FR,* 1945, V, 1079–81.

21. Stimson Diary, Mar. 16, 1945, L, p. 192 in YU/L; Msg., Roosevelt to Stalin, Mar. 17, 1945, in U.S., Department of State, *FR,* 1945, V, 1082.

22. Msg., Stalin to Roosevelt, Mar. 22, 1945; Msg., Harriman to Roosevelt, Mar. 24, 1945; Msg., Harriman to Secretary of State, Apr. 2, 1945, in U.S., Department of State, *FR,* 1945, V, 1082–83, 1084–86.

23. Lukas, *Eagles East,* pp. 190, including fn. 26; 212–23. A British mission, sent to Poland in Dec., 1944, had the same fate as the AAF team in Lódz. *Ibid.,* fn. 70, p. 213; W. Averell Harriman and Elie Abel, *Special Envoy to Churchill and Stalin, 1941–1946* (New York: Random, 1975), p. 445.

24. Harriman and Abel, *Special Envoy,* pp. 213–14; Ltr., Halifax to Stettinius, Apr. 7, 1945, in U.S., Department of State, *FR,* 1945, V, 1088–90.

25. Msg., Truman to Churchill, Apr. 13, 1945; Draft Msg., Truman to Harriman, enclosing msg. from Truman and Churchill to Stalin, n.d., in U.S., Department of State, *FR,* 1945, V, 211–12, 220–21.

26. Memo of conversation by Bohlen, Apr. 20, 1945; Memo by Bohlen of meeting at the White House, Apr. 23, 1945, in U.S., Department of State, *FR,* 1945, V, 231–34, 252–55; Stimson Diary, Apr. 23, 1945, LI, pp. 62–64, in YU/L; Walter Millis, ed., *The Forrestal Diaries* (New York: Viking, 1951), p. 51.

27. Memo of conversation by Bohlen, Apr. 23, 1945; in U.S., Department of State, *FR,* 1945, V, 256–58; Bohlen, *Witness to History,* pp. 213–14; Harry S. Truman, *Memoirs.* Vol. I: *Year of Decisions* (Garden City, NY: Doubleday, 1955), pp. 79–82. Leahy was happy at the blunt way the President talked to Molotov. Leahy personally did not see how the United States could prevent dominant Soviet influence in Poland, but "it is possible to give to the Government of Poland an external appearance of independence." See Leahy Diary, Apr. 23, 1945, in MD/LC. Obviously pleased with Truman's toughness toward Moscow, Ciechanowski predicted a new era of "hard horse-trading" by the United States with the Soviet Union. Msg., Ciechanowski to Minister of foreign affairs, Apr. 25, 1945, in Ciechanowski Papers, Hoover Institution.

28. Minutes of third meeting regarding Polish question, Apr. 23, 1945; Msg., Stalin to Truman, Apr. 24, 1945, in U.S., Department of State, *FR,* 1945, V, 259–62, 263–64; Churchill, *Triumph and Tragedy,* pp. 491–94; Truman, *Memoirs,* I, 85.

29. Churchill, *Triumph and Tragedy,* pp. 494–97, 501–503; Memo, Lane to Grew, May 4, 1945, in U.S., Department of State, *FR,* 1945, V, 278–80; Lane, *I Saw Poland Betrayed,* pp. 86–88, 105–107, 111.

30. Msg., Harriman to Secretary of State, Apr. 4, 1945; Msg., Stettinius to Grew, May 9, 1945, in U.S., Department of State, *FR,* 1945, V, 817–20, 998.

31. Memo, Grew and Crowley to Truman, May 11, 1945; Memo, Truman to Grew and Crowley, May 11, 1945, *ibid.,* pp. 999–1000; Gaddis, *The United States and the Origins of the Cold War,* pp. 219–20. For a detailed account of the United States cutting off lend-lease to the Soviet Union, see George C. Herring, *Aid to Russia,* pp. 180–211.

32. Sherwood, *Roosevelt and Hopkins,* pp. 885–87; Truman, *Memoirs,* I, 258; Memo by Hopkins, June 13, 1945, in U.S., Department of State, *FR,* 1945, V, 337–38.

33. Memo by Hopkins, June 13, 1945, in U.S., Department of State, *FR,* 1945, V, 299; Bohlen, *Witness to History,* p. 218.

34. Memo by Bohlen of first Hopkins-Stalin Conversation, May 26, 1945; Memo by Bohlen of second Hopkins-Stalin Conversation, May 27, 1945, in U.S., Department of State, *Foreign Relations of the United States, Diplomatic Papers: The Conference of Berlin (The Potsdam Conference, 1945)* (Washington, D.C.: United States Government Printing Office, 1960), I, 24–35 (hereafter cited as *FR, Berlin,* 1945, I).

35. Memo by Bohlen of fourth Hopkins-Stalin Conversation, May 30, 1945, in U.S., Department of State, *FR,* 1945, V, 301–306.

36. Msg., Hopkins to Truman, May 31, 1945; Memo by Bohlen of fifth Hopkins-Stalin Conversation, May 31, 1945; Msg., Truman to Churchill, June 1, 1945; Msg., Hopkins to Truman, June 3, 1945; Msg., Truman to Hopkins, June 5, 1945; Memo by Bohlen of sixth Hopkins-Stalin Conversation, June 6, 1945; Msg., Hopkins to Truman, June 6, 1945, *ibid.,* pp. 307–309, 309–13, 314, 318–19, 326–27, 328–29, 330–31.

37. Msg., Harriman to Truman, June 8, 1945, in U.S., Department of State, *FR, Berlin,* pp. 61–62; Msg., Stettinius to Hopkins, June 22, 1945, in Hopkins Papers, Box 338, FDR/L.

38. Msg., Schoenfeld to Secretary of State, June 8, 1945, in U.S., Department of State, *FR,* 1945, V, 332–34; Mikołajczyk, *Rape of Poland,* p. 114.

39. Msg., Churchill to Truman, June 4, 1945, in U.S., Department of State, *FR,* 1945, V, 320–21.

40. Msg., Grew to Schoenfeld, June 13, 1945; Msg., Harriman to Secretary of State, June 14, 1945, *ibid.,* pp. 337, 339–40; fn. 96, p. 336 and fn. 1, p. 337, *ibid.;* memo, Donovan to Truman, June 16, 1945, in OSS Papers, Box 15, HST/L.

41. Rozek, *Allied Wartime Diplomacy,* pp. 387–90; Mikołajczyk, *Rape of Poland,* pp. 117–18; Msg., Harriman to Secretary of State, June 15, 1945, in U.S., Department of State, *FR,* 1945, V, 344.

42. U.S., Department of State, *FR,* 1945, V, fn. 26, 350–51; General Sikorski Historical Institute, *DPSR,* II, 612–14; Raczyński, *In Allied London,* fn. 1, p. 295; Bohlen, *Witness to History,* p. 219; Rozek, *Allied Wartime Diplomacy,* p. 390; Truman, *Memoirs,* I, 320.

43. Msg., Harriman to Grew, June 23, 1945, in U.S., Department of State, *FR, Berlin,* 1945, I, 722–23; Mikołajczyk, *Rape of Poland,* p. 127; Msg., Harriman to Secretary of State, June 21, 1945, in U.S., Department of State, *FR,* 1945, V, 352–54.

44. U.S., Department of State, *FR, Berlin,* 1945, I, 716–20. Harriman expressed apprehension over Radkiewicz, a Communist, holding the Ministry of Internal Security. Harriman believed that if the non-Warsaw Poles had fought harder they would have gotten more seats in the government. See msg., Harriman to Grew, June 28, 1945, *ibid.,* pp. 727–28. Witos died in Oct. 1945. See Lane, *I Saw Poland Betrayed,* pp. 91–92.

45. Msg., Harriman to Grew, June 28, 1945; White House Press Release, July 5,

1945, in U.S., Department of State, *FR, Berlin,* 1945, I, 727–28, 735.

46. Msg., Truman to Churchill, July 2, 1945; Msg., Churchill to Truman, July 3, 1945; Msg., Truman to Churchill, July 3, 1945, *ibid.,* pp. 733–34. Out of 112,000 men of the II Polish Army Corps, only seven officers and 14,200 men applied for repatriation to Poland after V-E Day. See Anders, *Army in Exile,* p. 287. According to the *Chicago Tribune,* there were 300,000 Poles in Germany who refused to return home, preferring to remain within the American Zone. *Chicago Tribune,* July 4, 1945.

47. Ciechanowski, *Defeat in Victory,* p. 383; Newsclip, *Washington Star,* July 8, 1945, in Davies Papers, Box 65, MD/LC.

48. U.S., Department of State, Public Attitudes on Foreign Policy, Special Report, No. 65, July 23, 1945, in Stettinius Papers, Box 229, UV/L. Pro-Soviet sympathy among some newsmen was so strong that when Harriman suggested at a news conference that Soviet-American differences militated against future cooperation, Walter Lippmann walked out. See Bohlen, *Witness to History,* p. 215. It was still difficult to publish a book critical of the Soviet Union in 1945 without stirring up a hornet's nest. See Gaddis, *The United States and the Origins of the Cold War,* p. 45. To be sure, there were critics of American recognition of the expanded Warsaw regime. The *Chicago Tribune* called Truman's action one of the most "shameful chapters in our diplomatic history." *Chicago Tribune,* July 7, 1945.

49. U.S., *Congressional Record,* 79 Cong., 1 sess., 1945, XCI, Pt. 4, 4782; *Ibid.,* App., A2359; Polish American Congress, *The Story of the Polish American Congress,* pp. 65, 67.

50. Wasell, "Attitudes of the Various Polish-American Organizations," pp. 57–58.

51. Davis, *Cold War Begins,* p. 243; Briefing Book Paper, June 29, 1945; Msg., Harriman to Acting Secretary of State, June 26, 1945, in U.S., Department of State, *FR, Berlin,* 1945, I, 714–16, 784–85, 785–87.

52. Msg., Grew to Lane, July 12, 1945, in U.S., Department of State, *FR, Berlin,* 1945, I, 788–89.

53. George Woodbridge, *UNRRA: The History of the United Nations Relief and Rehabilitation Administration,* 3 vols. (New York: Columbia Univ. Press, 1950), II, 204–206.

54. Memo, with report, Donovan to Truman, May 5, 1945, in OSS Papers, Box 15, HST/L; Ltr., Lane to Durbrow, Aug. 3, 1945; Ltr., Lane to Matthews, Aug. 28, 1945; Ltr., Lane to Matthews, Sept. 6, 1945; Ltr., Lane to Durbrow, Oct. 22, 1945, in Lane Papers, Box 69, YU/L; Harriman and Abel, *Special Envoy,* p. 445.

BIBLIOGRAPHY

Unpublished Manuscripts

Henry H. Arnold, Papers, Library of Congress, Washington, D.C.
Adolf A. Berle, Papers, Franklin D. Roosevelt Library, Hyde Park, NY.
James F. Byrnes, Minutes of the Crimean Conference, Harry S Truman Library,
    Independence, MO.
Jan Ciechanowski, Papers, Hoover Institution on War, Revolution, and Peace,
    Stanford, CA.
Joseph E. Davies, Diary and Papers, Library of Congress, Washington, D.C.
Henry Field, Papers, Franklin D. Roosevelt Library, Hyde Park, NY.
Harry L. Hopkins, Papers, Franklin D. Roosevelt Library, Hyde Park, NY.
Cordell Hull, Papers, Library of Congress, Washington, D.C.
Arthur Bliss Lane, Papers, Sterling Library, Yale University, New Haven, CT.
William D. Leahy, Diary, Library of Congress, Washington, D.C.
Breckinridge Long, Diary and Papers, Library of Congress, Washington, D.C.
Isador Lubin, Papers, Franklin D. Roosevelt Library, Hyde Park, NY.
Henry Morgenthau, Diary, Franklin D. Roosevelt Library, Hyde Park, NY.
Philleo Nash, Papers, Harry S. Truman Library, Independence, MO.
Records of the Department of State, National Archives, Washington, D.C.
Records of German Field Command Armies, National Archives, Washington, D.C.
Records of the International Military Tribunal, Interrogations of General Erich
    von dem Bach-Zelewski, National Archives, Washington, D.C.
Records of Mediterranean Allied Air Forces, United States Air Force Historical
    Archives, Air University, Maxwell Air Force Base, AL.
Records of the Office of Strategic Services, National Archives, Washington, D.C.
Records of the Reich Leader of the SS and the Chief of the German Police,
    National Archives, Washington, D.C.
Records of the War Refugee Board, Franklin D. Roosevelt Library, Hyde Park, NY.
Records of the Warsaw Uprising, Józef Piłsudski Institute of America, New York,
    NY.
Eleanor Roosevelt, Papers, Franklin D. Roosevelt Library, Hyde Park, NY.
Franklin D. Roosevelt, Papers, Franklin D. Roosevelt Library, Hyde Park, NY.
Samuel I. Rosenman, Papers, Franklin D. Roosevelt Library, Hyde Park, NY.

Kazimierz Sosnkowski, Papers, Józef Piłsudski Institute of America, New York, NY.
Carl Spaatz, Papers, Library of Congress, Washington, D.C.
Edward R. Stettinius, Papers, University of Virginia Library, Charlottesville, VA.
Henry L. Stimson, Diary and Papers, Sterling Library, Yale University, New Haven, CT.
Harry S Truman, Papers, Harry S Truman Library, Independence, MO.

Correspondence and Interviews

Interview, Wacław Jędrzejewicz, July 5, 1972.
Interview, Pelagia Łukaszewska, Nov. 24, 1974; Dec. 26, 1975.
Interview, Wanda Rozmarek, Jan. 7, 1975.
Letter, with documents, Studium Polski Podziemniej to writer, Sept. 9, 1971.
Letter, Wacław Jędrzejewicz to writer, Dec. 15, 1974.
Letter, Colonel Leon Mitkiewicz to writer, Aug. 9, 1972.

Unpublished Studies

Charlton, Darrel T. "The United States and the Warsaw Uprising." Master's thesis, Tennessee Technological Univ., 1971.
Dallin, Alexander. "The Kaminsky Brigade, 1941-1944: A Case Study of German Military Exploitation of Soviet Disaffection." Study, Human Resources Research Institute, Air Univ., 1952.
Mazza, Sister Mary Assumpta. "A Survey of Changing Attitudes Toward the Soviet Union as Reflected in American Periodicals: 1942-1949." Ph.D. diss., St. John's Univ., 1957.
McClelland, Robert C. "The Soviet Union in American Opinion, 1933-1942." Ph.D. diss., West Virginia Univ., 1950.
Wagner, Stanley Paul. "The Diplomacy of the Polish Government in Exile, September, 1939, to July, 1945." Ph.D. diss., Univ. of Pittsburgh, 1953.
Wasell, F.F. "Attitudes of the Various Polish-American Organizations Toward American Foreign Policy Affecting Poland: 1939-1945." Master's thesis. Columbia Univ., 1946.

Published Documents

Complete Presidential Press Conferences of Franklin D. Roosevelt. Vols. XVII-XXV: 1941-1945. New York: Da Capo Press, 1972.
Fuehrer Directives and Other Top Level Directives of the German Armed Forces, 1939-1945. 2 vols. Washington, D.C.: 1948.
General Sikorski Historical Institute. *Documents on Polish-Soviet Relations, 1939-1945.* 2 vols. London: Heinemann, 1961-67.
Gilbert, Felix. *Hitler Directs His War: The Secret Records of His Daily Military Conferences.* New York: Oxford Univ. Press, 1950.
Jędrzejewicz, Wacław, comp. and ed. *Poland in the British Parliament, 1939-1945.* 3 vols. New York: Józef Piłsudski Institute of America, 1946-62.
Loewenheim, Francis L.; Langley, Harold D.; and Jonas, Manfred. *Roosevelt and*

Churchill: Their Secret Wartime Correspondence. New York: Saturday Review Press, 1975.

Ministry of Foreign Affairs of the U.S.S.R. *Stalin's Correspondence with Churchill, Attlee, Roosevelt and Truman: 1941-1945.* 2 vols. London: Lawrence and Wishart, 1958.

Office of United States Chief of Counsel for Prosecution of Axis Criminality. *Nazi Conspiracy and Aggression.* 8 vols. 2 supplements. Washington, D.C.: United States Government Printing Office, 1946-48.

Polish American Congress. *Foreign Policy of the United States: Memorandum of the Polish American Congress to Cordell Hull, Secretary of State.* Washington, D.C.: Polish American Congress, 1944.

Polish American Congress. *Polish American Congress, Inc., 1944-1948: Selected Documents.* Chicago: Polish American Congress, 1948.

Polish American Congress. *Story of the Polish American Congress in Press Clippings, 1944-1948.* Chicago: Alliance Printers and Publishers, Inc., 1945.

Polska i Wielka Brytania przed i po Konferencji Krmyskiej: Dokumenty. London, 1946.

Pomian, Andrzej, ed. *The Warsaw Rising: A Selection of Documents.* London: 1945.

Public Papers of the Presidents of the United States: Harry S Truman, 1945. Washington, D.C., United States Government Printing Office, 1961.

Republic of Poland. *Polish-Soviet Relations, 1918-1943: Official Documents.* Washington, D.C., n.d.

Rosenman, Samuel, comp. *The Public Papers and Addresses of Franklin D. Roosevelt: Victory and the Threshold of Peace, 1944-1945.* New York: Harper, 1950.

Trial of the Major War Criminals Before the International Military Tribunal. 42 vols. Nuremberg, 1947-49.

Trials of War Criminals Before the Nuernberg Military Tribunals Under Control Council Law No. 10., Nuernberg: October 1946-April 1949. 15 vols. Washington, D.C.: United States Government Printing Office, 1951-53.

U.S., Congress, House, Select Committee on Communist Agression, *Polish Documents Report: Appendix,* 83 Cong., 2 sess., 1954, pp. 110-11 (hereafter cited as *PDR*).

U.S., *Congressional Record.* 1941-1945.

U.S., *The Department of State Bulletin.* 1942-1945.

U.S., Department of State. *Foreign Relations of the United States: Diplomatic Papers, 1939.* Vol. II: *General, The British Commonwealth and Europe.* Washington, D.C.: United States Government Printing Office, 1956.

U.S., Department of State. *Foreign Relations of the United States: Diplomatic Papers, 1940.* Vol. II: *General and Europe.* Washington, D.C.: United States Government Printing Office, 1957.

U.S., Department of State. *Foreign Relations of the United States: Diplomatic Papers, 1941.* Vol. I: *General, The Soviet Union.* Washington, D.C.: United States Government Printing Office, 1958.

U.S., Department of State. *Foreign Relations of the United States: Diplomatic Papers, 1942.* Vol. III: *Europe.* Washington, D.C.: United States Government Printing Office, 1961.

U.S., Department of State. *Foreign Relations of the United States: Diplomatic Papers, 1943.* Vol. I: *General.* Washington, D.C.: United States Government Printing Office, 1963.

U.S., Department of State. *Foreign Relations of the United States: Diplomatic Papers, 1943.* Vol. III: *The British Commonwealth, Eastern Europe, The Far East.* Washington, D.C.: United States Government Printing Office, 1963.

U.S., Department of State. *Foreign Relations of the United States: Diplomatic Papers, The Conferences at Cairo and Tehran, 1943.* Washington, D.C.: United States Government Printing Office, 1961.

U.S., Department of State. *Foreign Relations of the United States: Diplomatic Papers, 1944.* Vol. III: *The British Commonwealth and Europe.* Washington, D.C.: United States Government Printing Office, 1965.

U.S., Department of State. *Foreign Relations of the United States: Diplomatic Papers, 1944.* Vol. IV: *Europe.* Washington, D.C.: United States Government Printing Office, 1966.

U.S., Department of State. *Foreign Relations of the United States: Diplomatic Papers, 1945.* Vol. II: *General, Political and Economic Matters.* Washington, D.C.: United States Government Printing Office, 1967.

U.S., Department of State. *Foreign Relations of the United States: Diplomatic Papers. The Conference of Berlin (The Potsdam Conference, 1945).* Vols. I–II. Washington, D.C.: United States Government Printing Office, 1955.

U.S., Department of State. *Foreign Relations of the United States: Diplomatic Papers, 1945. The Conference at Malta and Yalta.* Washington, D.C.: United States Government Printing Office, 1955.

U.S., Department of State. *Foreign Relations of the United States: Diplomatic Papers, 1945.* Vol. V: *Europe.* Washington, D.C.: United States Government Printing Office, 1967.

U.S., Congress, House. *Polish Documents Report: Appendix.* 83 Cong., 2 sess., 1954.

Memoirs, Autobiographies and Recollections

Adams, Dorothy. *We Stood Alone.* New York: Longmans, Green and Co., 1944.

Anders, W. *An Army in Exile: The Story of the Second Polish Corps.* London: Macmillan, 1949.

Beneš, Eduard. *Memoirs of Dr. Eduard Beneš: From Munich to New War and New Victory.* London: Allen and Unwin, 1954.

Berle, Beatrice B., and Jacobs, Travis B., eds. *Navigating the Rapids, 1918–1971: From the Papers of Adolf A. Berle.* New York: Harcourt, 1973.

Bohlen, Charles E. *Witness to History, 1929–1969.* New York: Norton, 1973.

+ Bór-Komorowski, Tadeusz. *The Secret Army.* New York: Macmillan, 1951.

Bourke-White, Margaret. *Shooting the Russian War.* New York: Simon, 1942.

Byrnes, James F. *Speaking Frankly.* New York: Harper, 1947.

Caldwell, Erskine. *All-Out on the Road to Smolensk.* New York: Duell, Sloan and Pearce, 1942.

Campbell, Thomas M., and Herring, George C., eds. *The Diaries of Edward R. Stettinius, Jr., 1943–1946.* New York: New Viewpoints, 1975.

Carlson, John R. *Under Cover.* New York: Dutton, 1943.

Carroll, Wallace. *We're in This With Russia.* Boston: Houghton, 1942.

Cassidy, Henry C. *Moscow Dateline, 1941–1943.* Boston: Houghton, 1943.

Chuikov, V.I. *The End of the Third Reich.* Trans. by Ruth Kisch. London: Macgibbon and Kee, 1967.

Churchill, Winston S. *Closing the Ring.* Boston: Houghton, 1951.

———. *Triumph and Tragedy.* Boston: Houghton, 1953.

Ciechanowski, Jan. *Defeat in Victory.* Garden City, NY: Doubleday, 1947.

Curie, Eve. *Journey Among Warriors.* Garden City, NY: Doubleday, 1943.

Davies, Joseph E. *Mission to Moscow.* New York: Simon, 1941.

Deane, John R. *The Strange Alliance: The Story of American Efforts at Wartime Co-operation with Russia.* London: John Murray, 1947.

Dilks, David, ed. *The Diaries of Sir Alexander Cadogan: 1938–1945.* London: Cassell, 1971.

Duranty, Walter. *U.S.S.R.: The Story of Soviet Russia.* Philadelphia: Lippincott, 1944.

Eden, Anthony. *The Memoirs of Anthony Eden, Earl of Avon: The Reckoning.* Boston: Houghton, 1965.

Graebner, Walter. *Round Trip to Russia.* Philadelphia: Lippincott, 1943.

Grew, Joseph C. *Turbulent Era: A Diplomatic Record of Forty Years, 1904–45.* Boston: Houghton, 1952.

Guderian, Heinz. *Panzer Leader.* Trans. by Constantine Fitzgibbon. New York: Dutton, 1952.

Harriman, W. Averell, and Abel, Elie. *Special Envoy to Churchill and Stalin, 1941–1946.* New York: Random, 1975.

Harper, Paul V., ed. *The Russia I Believe In: The Memoirs of Samuel N. Harper, 1902–1941.* Chicago: Univ. of Chicago Press, 1945.

Hull, Cordell. *The Memoirs of Cordell Hull.* 2 vols. New York: Macmillan, 1948.

Ismay, General Lord. *The Memoirs of General Lord Ismay.* New York: Viking, 1960.

Israel, Fred L., ed. *The War Diary of Breckinridge Long: Selections from the Years 1939–1944.* Lincoln: Univ. of Nebraska Press, 1966.

Karski, Jan. *Story of a Secret State.* Boston: Houghton, 1944.

Kennan, George F. *Memoirs: 1925–1950.* Boston: Little, 1967.

Korboński, Stefan. *Fighting Warsaw: The Story of the Polish Underground State, 1939–1945.* Trans. by F.B. Czarnomski. N.C.: Minerva Press, 1956.

Kot, Stanisław. *Conversations with the Kremlin and Dispatches from Russia.* Trans. by H.C. Stevens. London: Oxford Univ. Press, 1963.

———. *Listy z Rosji do Generala Sikorskiego.* London: St. Martin's, 1956.

Lane, Arthur Bliss. *I Saw Poland Betrayed: An American Ambassador Reports to the American People.* Indianapolis: Bobbs-Merrill, 1948.

Maisky, Ivan. *Memoirs of a Soviet Ambassador.* New York: Scribner's, 1968.

Matuszewski, Ignacy. *Hańba albo Chwała: Artykuły Polityce Rosji.* Palestine: Związek Pracy dla Państwa, 1944.

Mikołajczyk, Stanisław. *The Rape of Poland.* New York: McGraw-Hill, 1948.

Millis, Walter, ed. *The Forrestal Diaries.* New York: Viking, 1951.

Moran, Lord. *Churchill: Taken from the Diaries of Lord Moran, The Struggle for Survival, 1940–1965.* Boston: Houghton, 1966.

Nicolson, Harold. *The War Years, 1939–1945.* Vol. II: *Diaries and Letters.* Edited by Nigel Nicolson. New York: Atheneum, 1967.

Orska, Irene. *Silent is the Vistula: The Story of the Warsaw Uprising.* Trans. by Marta Erdman. New York: Longmans, Green, and Co., 1946.

Pomian, John, ed. *Joseph Retinger: Memoirs of an Eminence Grise.* Sussex: At the University Press, 1972.

Raczyński, Edward. *In Allied London.* London: Weidenfeld and Nicolson, 1962.

Reynolds, Quentin. *Only the Stars Are Neutral.* New York: Random House, 1942.

———. *The Curtain Rises.* New York: Random House, 1944.

Rokossovsky, K. *A Soldier's Duty.* Moscow: Progress Publishers, 1970.

Rozmarek, Karol. *Stany Zjednoczone, Polska i Polonia Amerykańska.* Detroit, 1945.

Rudziński, Aleksander. *Dziennik z Powstania Warszawskiego.* London: Oficyna Poetów i Malarzy, 1974.

Sherwood, Robert E. *Roosevelt and Hopkins: An Intimate History.* New York: Harper, 1948.

Slessor, John C. *These Remain: A Personal Anthology.* London: Michael Joseph, 1969.

Sosnkowski, Kazimierz. *Materiały Historyczne.* London: Gryf Publications, 1966.

Speer, Albert. *Inside the Third Reich: Memoirs.* New York: Macmillan, 1970.

Stalin, Joseph. *The Great Patriotic War of the Soviet Union.* New York: International Publishers, 1945.

Standley, William H., and Ageton, Arthur A. *Admiral Ambassador to Russia.* Chicago: Henry Regnery Co., 1955.

Stettinius, Edward R., Jr. *Roosevelt and the Russians: The Yalta Conference.* Garden City, NY: Doubleday, 1949.

Stimson, Henry L., and Bundy, McGeorge. *On Active Service in Peace and War.* New York: Harper, 1947.

Truman, Harry S *Memoirs.* Vol. I: *Year of Decisions.* Garden City, NY: Doubleday, 1955.

Vandenberg, Arthur H., Jr., ed. *The Private Papers of Senator Vandenberg.* Boston: Houghton 1952.

Welles, Sumner. *The Time for Decision.* New York: Harper, 1944.

Werth, Alexander. *Moscow War Diary.* New York: Knopf, 1942.

Willkie, Wendell L. *One World.* Urbana: Univ. of Illinois Press, 1966.

Zagorski, W. *Seventy Days.* Trans. by John Welsh. London: Frederick Muller, Ltd., 1957.

Zaremba, Zygmunt. *Wojna i Konspiracja.* London: B. Świderski, 1957.

Secondary Works

Adamic, Louis. *A Nation of Nations.* New York: Harper, 1945.

Apenszlak, Jacob. *Black Book of Polish Jewry: An Account of the Martyrdom of Polish Jewry under the Nazi Occupation.* New York: Roy Publishers, 1944.

Arnold, Stanisław, and Marion Żychowski. *Zarys Historii Polski.* N.C.: Wydownictwo Polonia, 1962.

Atholl, Duchess. *The Tragedy of Warsaw and Its Documentation.* London: John Murray, 1945.

Bartelski, Lesław M. *Powstanie Warszawskie.* Warszawa: Iskry, 1965.

Bethel, Nicholas. *The War Hitler Won: The Fall of Poland, September, 1939.* New York: Holt, 1972.

Bialer, Seweryn, ed. *Stalin and His Generals: Soviet Military Memoirs of World War II.* New York: Pegasus, 1969.

Borkiewicz, Adam. *Powstanie Warszawskie, 1944.* Warsaw: 1957.

✝ Bruce, George. *The Warsaw Uprising: 1 August–2 October 1944.* London: Rupert Hart-Davis, 1972.

Budurowycz, Bohdan B. *Polish-Soviet Relations, 1932–1939.* New York: Columbia Univ. Press, 1963.

Cardwell, Ann S. *Poland and Russia: The Last Quarter Century.* London: Sheed and Ward, 1944.

Ciechanowski, Jan M. *Powstanie Warszawskie: Zarys Podloza Politycznego i Dyplomatycznego.* London: Odnowa, 1971.

———. *The Warsaw Rising of 1944.* Cambridge: At the Univ. Press, 1974.

Clark, Alan. *Barbarossa: The Russian-German Conflict, 1941–1945.* New York: The New American Library, 1965.

Clemens, Diane Shaver. *Yalta.* London: Oxford Univ. Press, 1970.

Collier, Basil. *The Second World War: A Military History.* New York: Morrow, 1967.

Craven, Wesley Frank, and Cate, James Lea, eds. *The Army Air Forces in World War II.* Vol. III: *Europe: Argument to V-E Day, January, 1944 to May, 1945.* Chicago: Univ. of Chicago Press, 1951.

Dallin, Alexander. *German Rule in Russia, 1941–1945: A Study of Occupation Policies.* London: Macmillan, 1957.

～ Dallin, David J. *Russia and Postwar Europe.* New Haven: Yale Univ. Press, 1943.

———. *Soviet Russia's Foreign Policy, 1939–1942.* New Haven: Yale Univ. Press, 1942.

～ Davis, Lynn Etheridge. *The Cold War Begins: Soviet-American Conflict over Eastern Europe.* Princeton: Princeton Univ. Press, 1974.

Dawson, Raymond H. *The Decision to Aid Russia, 1941: Foreign Policy and Domestic Politics.* Chapel Hill: Univ. of North Carolina Press, 1959.

Debicki, Roman. *Foreign Policy of Poland, 1919–1939: From the Rebirth of the Polish Republic to World War II.* New York: Praeger, 1962.

Deborin, G. *The Second World War: A Politico-Military Survey.* Moscow: Progress Publishers, n.d.

Divine, Robert A. *Roosevelt and World War II.* Baltimore: Penguin Books, 1970.

Dulles, Foster Rhea. *The Road to Teheran: The Story of Russia and America, 1781–1943.* Princeton: Princeton Univ. Press, 1944.

～ Feis, Herbert. *Between War and Peace: The Potsdam Conference.* Princeton: Princeton Univ. Press, 1960.

———. *Churchill, Roosevelt, Stalin: The War They Waged and the Peace They Sought.* Princeton: Princeton Univ. Press, 1967.

Filene, Peter. *Americans and the Soviet Experiment.* Cambridge, Mass.: Harvard Univ. Press, 1967.

Gaddis, John Lewis. *The United States and the Origins of the Cold War, 1941–1947.* New York: Columbia Univ. Press, 1972.

Garlinski, Józef. *Poland, SOE, and the Allies.* Trans. Paul Stevenson. London: Allen and Unwin, 1969.

Gerson, Louis L. *The Hyphenate in Recent American Politics and Diplomacy.* Lawrence: Univ. of Kansas Press, 1964.

Gumkowski, Janusz, and Leszczyński, Kazimierz, *Poland under Nazi Occupation.* Warsaw: Polonia Publishing House, 1961.

Hackett, Alice Payne. *70 Years of Best Sellers, 1895–1965.* New York: Bowker, 1967.

Halecki, Oskar. *History of Poland.* New York: Roy Publishers, 1943.

Halle, Louis. *The Cold War as History.* New York: Harper, 1967.

Herring, George C. *Aid to Russia, 1941–1946: Strategy, Diplomacy, The Origins of the Cold War.* New York: Columbia Univ. Press, 1973.

Hindus, Maurice. *Hitler Cannot Conquer Russia.* Garden City, NY: Doubleday, 1941.

————. *Mother Russia.* Garden City, NY: Doubleday, 1943.

Jastrzębowski, Wacław. *Gospodarka Niemiecka w Polsce, 1939–1944.* Warsaw: Spoldzielna Wydawnicza Czytelnik, 1945.

Jędrzejewicz, Wacław. *Polonia Amerykańska w Polityce Polskiej: Historia Komitetu Narodowego Amerykanów Polskiego Pochodzenia.* New York: National Committee of Americans of Polish Descent, 1954.

Kennedy, Robert M. *The German Campaign in Poland, 1939.* Washington, D.C.: Department of the Army, 1956.

Kerr, Walter. *The Russian Army: Its Men, Its Leaders and Its Battles.* New York: Knopf, 1944.

Kirchmayer, Jerzy. *Powstanie Warszawskie.* Warsaw: Książka i Wiedza, 1970.

Kliszko, Zenon. *Powstanie Warszawskie: Artykuły, Przemowienia, Wspomnienia, Dokumenty.* Warsaw: Książka i Wiedza, 1967.

Kolko, Gabriel. *The Politics of War: The World and United States Foreign Policy, 1943–1945.* New York: Random, 1968.

Komarnicki, Titus. *Rebirth of the Polish Republic: A Study in the Diplomatic History of Europe, 1914–1920.* London: Heinemann, 1957.

Komisja Historyczna Polskiego Sztabu Głównego w Londynie. *Polskie Siły Zbrojne w Drugiej Wojnie Swiatowej.* Vol. III: *Armia Krajowa.* London: Instytut Historyczny Im. Gen. Sikorskiego, 1950.

Komitet Narodowy Amerykanów Pochodzenia Polskiego. *Biuletyn Organizacyjny.* 1942–45.

Korbel, Józef. *Poland between East and West: Soviet and German Diplomacy toward Poland, 1919–33.* Princeton: Princeton Univ. Press, 1963.

Krannhals, Hanns von. *Der Warschauer Aufstand, 1944.* Frankfort on the Main: Bernard & Graefe Verlag fur Wehrwesen, 1962.

Kridl, Manfred; Malinowski, Władysław; and Wittlin, Józef, eds. *For Your Freedom and Ours.* New York: Ungar, 1942.

Kusnierz, Bronisław. *Stalin and the Poles: An Indictment of the Soviet Leaders.* London: Hollis and Carter, 1949.

LaFeber, Walter. *America, Russia, and the Cold War, 1945–1966.* New York: John Wiley and Sons, Inc., 1967.

Laserson, Max. *The Curzon Line: A Historical and Critical Analysis.* New York: Carnegie Endowment for International Peace, 1944.

Liddell Hart, B.H. *History of the Second World War.* New York: Putnam's, 1970.

Lippmann, Walter. *U.S. Foreign Policy: Shield of the Republic.* Boston: Little, 1943.

——. *U.S. War Aims.* Boston: Little, 1944.

Lisiewicz, M., and Baykowski, J., eds. *Destiny Can Wait: The Polish Air Force in the Second World War.* London: Heinemann, 1949.

Lovenstein, Meno. *American Opinion of Soviet Russia.* Washington, D.C.: American Council on Public Affairs, 1941.

Lukacs, John. *A New History of the Cold War.* Garden City, NY: Anchor Books, 1966.

Lukas, Richard C. *Eagels East: The Army Air Forces and the Soviet Union, 1941–1945.* Tallahassee: Florida State Univ. Press, 1970.

Matuszewski, Ignacy. *What Poland Wants.* New York: National Committee of Americans of Polish Descent, 1942.

McKee, John. *Poland, Russia and Our Honor.* New York: National Committee of Americans of Polish Descent, n.d.

McNeill, William H. *America, Britain and Russia: Their Cooperation and Conflict, 1941–1946.* London: Oxford Univ. Press, 1953.

Mellenthin, F.W. von. *Panzer Battles: A Study of the Employment of Armor in the Second World War.* Trans. by H. Betzler. Norman: Univ. of Oklahoma Press, 1956.

Ministerstwo Informacji. *Black Book of Poland.* New York: Putnam's, 1942.

Motter, T.H. Vail. *The Persian Corridor and Aid to Russia.* Washington, D.C.: Department of the Army, 1952.

National Committee of Americans of Polish Descent. *Death at Katyn.* New York: National Committee of Americans of Polish Descent, 1945.

Ostaszewski, Jan. *Powstanie Warszawskie.* Rome, 1945.

Pares, Bernard. *Russia and the Peace.* New York: Macmillan, 1944.

Parkinson, Roger. *A Day's March Nearer Home: The War History from Alamein to VE Day based on the War Cabinet Papers of 1942 to 1945.* New York: David McKay, Inc., 1974.

Pirinsky, George. *Slavic Americans in the Fight for Victory and Peace.* N.C.: American Slav Congress, n.d.

Pruszyński, Ksawery. *Poland Fights Back: From Westerplatte to Monte Casino.* New York: Roy Publishers, 1944.

Przygoński, Anton. *Z Problematyki Powstania Warszawskiego.* Warsaw: Wydawnictwo Ministerstwa Obrony Narodowej, 1964.

Rozek, Edward J. *Allied Wartime Diplomacy: A Pattern in Poland.* New York: John Wiley & Sons, Inc., 1958.

Sawicki, Jerzy. *Przed Polskim Prokuratorem: Dokumenty; Komentarze.* Warsaw: Iskry, 1958.

Seaton, Albert. *The Russo-German War, 1941–1945.* New York: Praeger, 1972.

Segal, Simon. *New Order in Poland.* New York: Knopf, 1942.

Skarżyński, Aleksander. *Polityczne Przyczyny Powstania Warszawskiego.* Warsaw: Państwowe Wydawnictwo Naukowe, 1964.

Snyder, Louis L. *The War: A Concise History, 1939-1945*. New York: Dell, 1960.

Sorokin, Pitirim. *Russia and the United States*. New York: Dutton, 1944.

Stewart-Murray, Katharine M. *The Tragedy of Warsaw and its Documentation*. London: John Murray, 1945.

Strzetelski, Stanisław. *Bitwa o Warszawe (1 Sierpnia—2 Pazdziernika 1944 r): Fakty i Dokumenty*. New York: Komitetu Narodowego Amerykanów Pochodzenia Polskiego, 1945.

——. *Where the Storm Broke*. New York: Roy Publishers, 1943.

Tippelskirch, Kurt von. *Geschichte des Zweiten Weltkriegs*. Bonn: Athenaum-Verlag, 1951.

Umiastowski, R. *Poland, Russia and Great Britain, 1941-1945: A Study of Evidence*. London: Hollis and Carter, 1946.

Voight, F.A. *Poland, Russia, and Great Britain*. New York: National Committee of Americans of Polish Descent, Inc., 1943.

Wandycz, Piotr S. *Czechoslovak-Polish Confederation and the Great Powers, 1940-43*. Bloomington: Indiana Univ. Publications, 1956.

Werth, Alexander. *Russia at War, 1941-1945*. New York: Dutton, 1964.

Wierzyński, Kazimierz. *Forgotten Battlefield*. New York: Roy Publishers, 1944.

Williams, William Appleman. *The Tragedy of American Diplomacy*. New York: Dell, 1972.

Woodbridge, George. *UNRRA: The History of the United Nations Relief and Rehabilitation Administration*. 3 vols. New York: Columbia Univ. Press, 1950.

Woodward, Sir Llewellyn. *British Foreign Policy in the Second World War*. Vol. II. London: Her Majesty's Stationery Office, 1971.

Wytrwal, Joseph. *America's Polish Heritage: A Social History of the Poles in America*. Detroit: Endurance Press, 1961.

Zachodnia Agencja Prasowa. *1939-1945: War Losses in Poland*. Poznán: Wydawnictwo Zachodnie, 1960.

Zawodny, J.K. *Death in the Forest*. Notre Dame: Univ. of Notre Dame Press, 1962.

Articles and Periodicals

Agee, James. "Mission to Moscow," *Nation*, CLVI (May 22, 1943), 745–46.

"America Must Speak Up for a Real Peace," *Saturday Evening Post*, CCXVI (Jan. 15, 1944), 96.

Bess, Demaree. "What Does Russia Want?" *Saturday Evening Post*, CCXV (Mar. 20, 1943), 19, 91–92, 94.

Bolles, Blair. "What Eden is After," *Nation*, CLVI (Mar. 27, 1943), 442–44.

Bór-Komorowski, T. "The Unconquerables," *Reader's Digest* (Feb. 1946), 127–68.

"Break-Through on Church," *Time*, XLII (Dec. 27, 1943), 53–58.

Chamberlin, William Henry. "Preview of the Postwar World: The Soviet Union," *Christian Century*, LXI (Mar. 22, 1944), 364–66.

Dallin, David. "Russia's Aims in Europe," *American Mercury*, LVII (Oct. 1943), 391–402.

———. "Russia's Aims in Europe," *American Mercury*, LVII (Nov. 1943), 599–601.

Datner, Szymon. "Destruction of Warsaw," in *1939–1945: War Losses in Poland*. Poznań: Wydawnictwo Zachodnie, 1960.

Davenport, Peter. "Sikorski's Opposition," *Nation*, CLVI (Jan. 30, 1943), 163–64.

Davies, Joseph E. "Russia Will Hold This Summer," *Saturday Evening Post*, CLXIV (June 20, 1942), 16–17, 88–89.

Davis, Forrest. "What Really Happened at Teheran?" *Saturday Evening Post*, CCXVI (May 13, 1944), 12–13, 37, 39, 41.

———. "What Really Happened at Teheran?" *Saturday Evening Post*, CCXVI (May 20, 1944), 22–23, 44, 46, 48.

Davis, Jerome. "Russia's Postwar Aims," *New Republic*, CXI (Sept. 4, 1944), 276–77.

"Defeat of Patriots at Warsaw Widens Polish-Russian Breach," *Newsweek*, XXIV (Oct. 16, 1944), 48–49.

Dennen, Leon. "Inside Poland Today," *American Mercury*, LVII (Nov. 1943), 529–36.

Estorick, Eric. "Polish American Politics," *Nation*, CLVIII (May 20, 1944), 591–93.

Eulau, Heinz. "Europe's Exiled Governments," *New Republic*, CIX (Nov. 1, 1943), 614–17.

———. "Poland and Russia," *New Republic*, CXI (Aug. 7, 1944), 156–57.

"The Fact of Russia," *Christian Century* (Dec. 8, 1943), 1430–31.

Furfey, Paul Hanly. "Glance to the Left," *Catholic World* (Nov. 1941), 145–50.

Gillis, James M. "Covenant with Hell," *Catholic World* (Aug. 1941), 513–19.

Hammersmith, Jack L. "The U.S. Office of War Information (OWI) and the Polish Question, 1943–1945," *Polish Review*, XIX, No. 1 (1974), 67–76.

Hershey, Burnet. "Hang the Führers!" *Saturday Evening Post*, CCXV (June 12, 1943), 16–17, 40–42.

"Italy and Poland," *New Republic*, CXI (Dec. 4, 1944), 733.

King, Frank P. "British Policy and the Warsaw Rising," *Journal of European Studies* (Mar. 1974), 1–18.

Lukas, Richard C. "The Big Three and the Warsaw Uprising," *Military Affairs*, XXXIX (Oct. 1975), 129–34.

———. "The RAF and the Warsaw Uprising," *Aerospace Historian*, XXII (Dec. 1975), 188–94.

Lyons, Eugene. "Letter to American Liberals," *American Mercury*, LVIII (May, 1944), 569–70.

Malinowski, Władysław R. "Toward Polish-Soviet Understanding," *New Europe and World Reconstruction: Supplement* (Nov. 1943), 3–12.

———. "Uprising in Warsaw," *Nation*, CLIX (Sept. 23, 1944), 347–48.

"Man of the Year," *Time*, XXXV (Jan. 1, 1940), 14–17.

"Man of the Year," *Time*, XLI (Jan. 4, 1943), 21–24.

"Pamięci Gen. Dyw. Tadeusza Bóra-Komorowskiego Dowódcy Armii Krajowej w Okresie Burzy i Powstania Warszawskiego," *Biuletyn Informacyjny* (Aug. 1968).

Parker, Ralph. "Timoshenko, Red Army Hero," *New York Times Magazine* (Feb. 8, 1942), 23.

Pełczyński, T. "General Bór-Komorowski," *Polish Affairs* (Oct. 1966), 2–6.
Poland Fights. 1944.
— "The Poles and the Russians," *New Republic*, CVIII (May 10, 1943), 623–24.
Polish American Congress. *Bulletin.* 1944–1945.
"Polish American Priest Visits Stalin," *Catholic World*, CLIX (June, 1944),
   274–76.
Polish Facts and Figures. 1944.
Polish Review. 1942–1944.
"Polish-Russian Tension Growing Dangerous," *Christian Century*, LX (Mar. 17,
   1943), 317.
"Russia's Plans for Postwar Poland," *Christian Century*, LXI (Jan. 12, 1944), 35.
"Russia's Western Claims," *New Republic*, CX (Jan. 17, 1944), 72.
"The Russian-Polish Lid Blows Off," *Christian Century*, LX (May 5, 1943), 532.
Rylski, Marcin. "Poland and Russia," *Nation*, CLVII (Oct. 9, 1943), 408–10.
Schuman, Frederick L. "The Polish Frontier: A Test for the United Nations,"
   New Republic, CX (Jan. 31, 1944), 138–41.
"The Shape of Things," *Nation*, CLVI (Mar. 13, 1943), 362.
"The Shape of Things," *Nation*, CLVI (May 1, 1943), 613–14.
"The Shape of Things," *Nation*, CLVI (May 15, 1943), 686.
"The Shape of Things," *Nation*, CLVIII (May 20, 1944), 582.
Small, Melvin. "Buffoons and Brave Hearts: Hollywood Portrays the Russians,
   1939–1944," *California Historical Quarterly*, LII (Winter, 1973), 326–37.
——. "How We Learned to Love the Russians: American Media and the Soviet
   Union during World War II," *The Historian: A Journal of History*, XXXVI
   (May 1974), 455–78.
Smith, Kingsbury. "Our Foreign Policy Goes Realist," *American Mercury*, LVII
   (Dec. 1943), 665–70.
Snow, Edgar. "Eastern Europe Swings Left," *Saturday Evening Post*, CCXVII
   (Nov. 11, 1944), 9–11, 70–71.
"The Soviets and the Post-War," *Life*, XIV (Mar. 29, 1943), 49.
"Strategic Frontiers and Collective Security," *Nation*, CLVI (Mar. 13, 1943),
   364–65.
Strong, Anna Louise. "Bór's Uprising," *Atlantic Monthly*, CLXXVI (Dec. 1945),
   80–85.
Taub, Walter. "Warsaw Tragedy," *Collier's* (Mar. 17, 1945), 17, 79–80.
"Tragic Warsaw," *New Statesman and Nation* (Sept. 2, 1944), 146.
"Victims of Which Propaganda?" *Saturday Evening Post*, CCXV (May 22, 1943),
   108.
"From Warsaw to Paris," *New Republic*, CXI (Sept. 11, 1944), 295–96.
"Who Can Speak for Poland?" *New Republic*, CVIII (May 7, 1943), 651–52.

Newspapers

Boston Evening Globe. 1944.
Chicago Daily Tribune. 1944–1945.
Christian Science Monitor. 1944.
Dallas Morning News. 1944.

Denver Post. 1944.
Detroit News. 1944.
Dziennik Polski (Detroit). 1941–1945.
Dziennik Związkowy. 1941–1945.
Głós Polek. 1941–1945.
Los Angeles Times. 1944.
Naród Polski. 1941–1945.
Nashville Tennessean. 1944.
New York Times. 1941–1945.
Nowy Świat. 1941–1945.
Seattle Post-Intelligencer. 1944.
St. Louis Post Dispatch. 1944.
The Times (London), 1941–1945.
Wall Street Journal. 1944–1945.
Washington Post. 1944.

INDEX